Who Was Responsible for the Troubles?

WHO WAS RESPONSIBLE FOR THE TROUBLES?

The Northern Ireland Conflict

LIAM KENNEDY

McGill-Queen's University Press

Montreal & Kingston · London · Chicago

© McGill-Queen's University Press 2020

ISBN 978-0-2280-0368-7 (cloth)
ISBN 978-0-2280-0469-1 (ePDF)
ISBN 978-0-2280-0470-7 (ePUB)

Legal deposit third quarter 2020
Bibliothèque nationale du Québec

Printed in Canada on acid-free paper that is 100% ancient forest free
(100% post-consumer recycled), processed chlorine free

Library and Archives Canada Cataloguing in Publication

Title: Who was responsible for the troubles? : the Northern Ireland
    conflict / Liam Kennedy.
Names: Kennedy, Liam, 1946- author.
Description: Includes bibliographical references and index.
Identifiers: Canadiana (print) 20200267957 | Canadiana (ebook)
    20200268139 | ISBN 9780228003687 (cloth) | ISBN 9780228004691
    (ePDF) | ISBN 9780228004707 (ePUB)
Subjects: LCSH: Political violence—Northern Ireland. | LCSH:
    Social conflict—Northern Ireland. | LCSH: Northern Ireland—
    History—1968-1998. | LCSH: Northern Ireland—Politics and
    government—1968-1998.
Classification: LCC DA990.U46 K46 2020 | DDC 941.60824—dc23

For Irene Boada Montagut who brought Mediterranean
  sunshine into my heart
Per a Irene, que va portar la Llum del Mediterrani al meu cor
Do Irene, a thug grian gheal Mheánmhuiríoch isteach im chroí

Contents

Figures and Tables

FIGURES

TABLES

Preface

Writing at the outbreak of the Northern Ireland "Troubles," the historian Owen Dudley Edwards felt compelled to level with his readers.[1] His subject after all was the fiercely contested one of the "roots of conflict" in Northern Ireland. "Naturally, my approach has been affected," he admits, "as that of all commentators must be, by my background and beliefs." He goes on to suggest that the reader "needs the courtesy of being informed what these are."[2] The author then lays out family, religious, and ideological influences on his formation as a historian. I might be inclined to add social class, gender, personality, and the times we live in.[3] These are the nets that scholars strive to fly past, no doubt with varying degrees of success.

I find myself writing some two decades after the formal end of the Troubles, which offers a different vantage point and a longer time frame. I am an outsider, which also allows some distancing: in the North but not of the North, it might be said. These frictions, even contradictions, force a kind of cognitive reflection that might not otherwise have arisen. Yet the enterprise is beset by difficulties and hesitations. I have lived here through much of the Troubles and the subsequent peace process. I have spent most of my working life in Belfast, the epicentre of the triangular conflict that for three decades engulfed republicans, loyalists, and the British security forces. This experience has surely coloured my writing, including most importantly the lines of interpretation developed in this book. Still, this embeddedness has its advantages as the experiential knowledge gained has opened up new perspectives that otherwise might not have found their way into *Who Was Responsible for the Troubles?* The lived experience has also added texture, a touch of intimacy, and hopefully a degree of empathy with those caught up in the life and death struggles of the period.

But there are other dilemmas. Having lived for many years in Belfast I am conscious that I was betimes an observer, a participant, and a participant-observer, which is a situation different from that of many historians. I recall that for many years I mentally compartmentalised community action from my academic concerns. My political formation I should say was in the Irish Labour party and then the British Labour party. In the early to mid-1970s I was living and studying in the north of England. In September 1976 I got off the Dublin train at Botanic Station in Belfast, walked over sheets of broken glass on route to Queen's University, and tried to reassure my English-born wife, and myself, that the debris on the pavements was probably not due to a bomb explosion.

It proved impossible to remain insulated from the world around us. There was an early involvement with the Peace People that included demonstrating outside Harland and Wolff in support of shipyard workers trying to get to work during the loyalist workers' strike of 1977. In the late 1980s as a member of the cross-community group New Consensus, I joined other pickets outside the UDA's headquarters on the Lower New-townards Road, Belfast. This was to protest its armed attacks on nationalists, including many sectarian killings. I can still recall the looks of shocked surprise on the faces of the UDA leaders as they came out to see what was going on in their own backyard. Then there was the Peace Train movement of the 1990s, which sought to keep open the lines of communication, in the broad as well as the narrow-gauge sense, between north and south. These "new wave" peace groups were broad churches, united only in their commitment to democratic and peaceful means to effect political change.

In what was to become a continuing commitment, along with comrades and friends I campaigned against shootings and mutilations of young people by paramilitary organisations (see chapters 3 and 4) or what is referred to colloquially as "punishment" attacks. The roles of citizen and academic began to converge as time wore on, and I sometimes puzzled over the confusion of the two. I was also aware of how one part of life was eating into the time spent on the other. Economists would recognise this as opportunity cost, the benefits foregone by not pursuing an alternative course of action. Still, the imperatives arising from distant moral foundations in

Judeo-Christianity, as well as a left-wing ideological disposition, meant I found it impossible to stand aloof from the conflict that raged round the academy and that sometimes struck within with murderous effect. I recall in the early 1980s turning into University Square on my way to collect a book from the New Library at Queen's. I took in the soldiers rushing about and, virtually in the same glance, the white sheet laid on the pavement. So slight was the victim's frame it was hard to believe that anything lay beneath. Edgar Graham, a brilliant law lecturer and potential future leader of the Ulster Unionist party, had been assassinated a few minutes earlier.

The personal and the political can be exposed terrain because as historians we are committed to dispassionate analysis, a scrupulous attention to the evidence, and finely balanced judgements. Might extracurricular engagement compromise what, at its best and at its most socially valuable, is the truth-seeking quest of the historian *qua* historian? It is apprehensions of this kind, I suspect, that explain why this book was so long in the making. It is also the case that the research and the writing took me in directions I had not anticipated and which carried their own burden of discomfort in view of my Irish Catholic and nationalist background. But in the end one has to be true to the evidence and one's own understanding of the source materials, and that is the ultimate satisfaction. The critics will have their day and that is to be welcomed. Good history is the product of many voices and the continuing refinement of existing understandings of the past.

On my bookshelves is a book on the Northern Ireland conflict that has, as its subtitle, *The Human Costs*. It is a fine study that deserves to be better known and I share a concern with the three authors: "we have anxieties about the use to which our research will be put, and the actions that it may be used to justify."[4] They conclude, and I would concur, that "no faction or political grouping in Northern Ireland has a monopoly on suffering." These authors also tell us that "our work on the data on deaths [relating to the Troubles] has changed us."[5] I too have been changed, both as a person and as a historian, and perhaps the two are indissoluble at this stage, or perhaps it was always so. We have lived in times of terrible tragedy, though ones also laced with resilience, heroism, even love.

A page of my life, one unlikely to fade, contains a remembrance of one of my students, Julie-Ann Statham from Dungannon in mid-Ulster. She

came to Queen's University, Belfast, a joyous young woman, hardly outstanding academically but eager to learn. On the 30 January 1993, in her
final undergraduate year, in the bedroom of her parent's house, she committed suicide. This was less than a month after her fiancée, Diarmuid
Shields, had been murdered by loyalist "freedom fighters." He was from
the Catholic tribe, she from the Protestant. In her suicide note she explained, "When they killed my darling, they killed me too."[6] In the aftermath of these deaths, the human rights' campaigner Fr Denis Faul spoke
of a modern-day enactment of the story of Romeo and Juliet. Each was a
victim of tribal enmity.

I was at the funeral. There were throngs of people. The graveyard sloped
downwards to where the principal mourners were gathered. I stood towards the back, high up on a ridge that overlooked the open grave. As the
coffin was being lowered into the freshly opened earth I could see Julie's
mother and father clinging desperately to each other, locked in a dance of
grief, in danger of overbalancing on the edge of the grave. They seemed
lost and alone despite the many who had been drawn to share their sorrow.
When I met the mother and father shortly afterwards I choked and could
voice no words of sympathy.

On the whole, historians do not reveal much of themselves, and I have
been more than happy most of my working life to follow this convention.
The celebrity-spurning singer-songwriter Van Morrison, Belfast born and
bred, is well placed to remind us, as he has, of the value of the "gift of ano-
nymity." But in thinking, acting, and writing amidst the Troubles, on the
very subject of the Troubles, some personal stories and reflection, as above,
seem more than usually necessary. The anthropologist Martyn Hammersley states no more than the obvious when he writes that "there is no way
that students of society can escape the social world in order to study it."[7]
In a sense we are all ethnographers of our time and place but unlike the
natural scientist we are implicated in what we study, whether we care to
recognise this dilemma or not. Hence the need both to reflect on what we
are doing and how and why we came to be doing it. The corollary is trans-
parency, so that others may know more about the author, the person, and
the personal, as well as the sources used, should they so wish.

It is salutary to remind myself that "history is an argument without
end," and so I gladly acknowledge my dependence on others.[8] It is a hope-

less task to try to mention the many, many people who have helped me, sometimes unwittingly, to develop this work. I might as well quietly intone the names of my friends, colleagues, neighbours, and critics. But I will attempt to recognise some in the knowledge that I am omitting many and may well be including some who would prefer to be less honoured. Sadly, some are no longer with us.

I suppose I should start with colleagues within the academic community. These include the incomparable historians Don Akenson and Paul Bew, as well as such outstanding colleagues and friends as George Bain, Andy Bielenberg, John Brewer, Graham Brownlow, Dominic Bryan, Catherine Clinton, John Connelly, Alun Davies, Enda Delaney, Brice Dickson, Richard English, Eamonn Hughes, Fearghal McGarry, Jack Foster, Roy Foster, Graham Gudgin, Brian Gurrin, David Johnson, Dennis Kennedy, Edna Longley, Kerby Miller, Don MacRaild, Michael Moore, Duncan Morrow, Clare Murphy, John A. Murphy, Mary O'Dowd, Cormac Ó Gráda, Margaret O'Callaghan, Brendan O'Leary, Hilary Owen, Henry Patterson, Phil Ollerenshaw, Eamon Phoenix, Joe Ruane, Jennifer Todd, Brian Walker, Graham Walker, Karin White, Stephanie White, and Bernard Worthington.

Conversations with others in the wider society have influenced my thinking, one way or another. I particularly want to mention Gerry Adams, Joe Austin, Judy Barry, Boyd Black, Mairia Cahill, Seamus Close, Tim Pat Coogan, Paddy Devlin, Paul Durcan, Linda Ervine, Damien Gough, Brian Garrett, Eamon Hanna, Tom Hartley, Bronagh Hinds, John Hume, Gerry Kelly, Michael Longley, Seamus Lynch, Lyra McKee, Aodán Mac Póilin, Catherine McCartney, Mary McMahon, Alex Maskey, Chris McGimpsey, Michael McGimpsey, Phillip McGarry, Sean O'Callaghan, Seán Ó Cearnaigh, Glenn Patterson, Trevor Ringland, Peter Robinson, David Trimble, and Margaret Walsh.

Among community and peace activists I want to pay special tribute to friends and colleagues I worked closely with: Eileen Bell, Irene Boada Montagut, Lea Cramsie, Carmel Donnelly, Anne Holliday, Chris Hudson, Patricia Mallon, Jeff Maxwell, Sam McAughtry, Michael Nugent, Bernadette O'Rawe, Helmut Riethmuller, Henry Robinson, Doris Sterzer, Frank Wright, and so many others. My friends Angela and Frankie, who suffered so much, are always with me. There is a special place in heaven for the courageous journalists who helped make sense of the Troubles. They were obliged to develop their analyses more rapidly than academic commentators. The pressure of deadlines notwithstanding, their insights sometimes went deeper. I think of Deaglán de Bréadún, Liam Clarke, Mark Devenport, Newton Emerson, Ben Lowry, Henry McDonald, Jim McDowell, Lindy McDowell, David McKittrick, Fionola Meredith, Ed Moloney, Gerry Moriarty, Allison Morris, Eilis O'Hanlon, David Sharrock, and Peter Taylor. Four outstanding commentators have informed much of the later debate on the northern Troubles: Suzanne Breen, Malachi O'Doherty, Eoghan Harris, Fintan O'Toole. *Ádh mór.*

My publishing friend Lisa Hyde gave me strength when I prevaricated or my interests strayed into other research areas. Philip J. Cercone at McGill-Queen's has been a creative and supportive voice during the countdown to publishing, and the help of George Woodman who read the text from beginning to end is also much appreciated. I quote from three of my favourite poets, Paul Durcan, Ciaran Carson, and Seamus Heaney in the main text. I am grateful to their publishers for permission to borrow from their creative endeavours. My friend and near-neighbour Patrick Speight supplied the photograph of the Martin Meehan mural in Belfast; John McGurk, with great kindness, allowed me to use a copy of the family photograph of McGurk's Bar. A colleague of retiring disposition but hugely creative worked with me on the collages that introduce the various chapters.

Above all, three friends, both historians and writers of international repute, were hugely supportive. These were Don Akenson, Ruth Dudley Edwards, and David A. Wilson. Without their friendship, good humour, and belief in the book – disagreements apart – it would never have been completed. Esther Aliaga has been both a friend and a careful reader. My daughter Lia, who defines herself as Northern Irish, and my son Liam (who is working on whether to see himself as Catalan, British, Irish, or some fusion thereof), would wish to be acknowledged, and so they should. I raise a glass to all of these, and others, in joyful appreciation.

Abbreviations

DUP	Democratic Unionist Party
INLA	Irish National Liberation Army
IRA	Irish Republican Army
IPLO	Irish People's Liberation Organisation
LVF	Loyalist Volunteer Force
MP	Member of Parliament
MEP	Member of the European Parliament
NICRA	Northern Ireland Civil Rights Association
NILP	Northern Ireland Labour Party
PUP	Progressive Unionist Party
PSNI	Police Service of Northern Ireland
RAAD	Republican Action Against Drugs
RUC	Royal Ulster Constabulary
SDLP	Social Democratic and Labour Party
UDA	Ulster Defence Association
UUP	Ulster Unionist Party
UVF	Ulster Volunteer Force

Who Was Responsible for the Troubles?

The one bias to which I will readily admit is
a loathing of war and of all who celebrate the
killing of their fellow men and women.
Fergal Keane, *Wounds: A Memoir of War and Love*

Introduction

The "Troubles" is the somewhat euphemistic title for three decades of armed conflict in Northern Ireland. This book started off in a small way in 1999, the year after the signing of the Good Friday Agreement, which set a formal end to hostilities and promised new political beginnings.[1] It was sparked by a curious incident that is explained in chapter 1, but, to cut to the chase, the central question I am posing is a deeply disturbing one, indeed one which most of us would prefer to avoid. It is this: who was responsible for the Troubles? When I gave a preview of the thesis some ten years ago a young woman in the audience, almost beside herself with agitation, burst forth, "You are a disgrace. Are you really employed by a university? I can't believe it." Her reaction, and that of some others, did not encourage me to rush to publication.

The early chapters discuss the role of the British and Irish states during the Troubles, though the major focus is on nonstate actors such as civil rights campaigners, the Official and Provisional IRAs, loyalist paramilitaries, Paisley and Paisleyites, the Democratic Unionist Party, and the churches. Which collective historical actor, if any, was primarily responsible for staging thirty years of intense conflict? The term "responsibility" is of critical importance, so it is as well to specify its meaning as employed here. The criteria invoked to establish responsibility included the following: those held to be responsible must have been committed to using violence to advance a political agenda; they must have been responsible for a significant share of the killings and wounding; they must have been prepared to use violence in the long term, irrespective of popular opinion; they must have had command of the resources – people, armaments, budgets – to engage in such protracted conflict. Both state and nonstate actors come into the frame.

Many of the themes in this volume speak to a wider world. In a very real sense the Troubles is a world-class problem in miniature. The Black North went global in the later twentieth century, attracting disproportionate international academic attention. Ironically, one of the unintended consequences of the Troubles was an efflorescence of Irish studies at home and abroad (see figure 0.1).[2]

The decades of conflict in Northern Ireland were characterised by national, ethnic, and sectarian passions – the hallmarks of a deeply divided society. Parts of the contemporary world are disfigured by similarly divisive forces. Multiculturalism may be fashionable, national conflicts may be less prevalent, peace processes may be in train, but that is only part of what is a largely Eurocentric story. Even within Europe, ethnonational tensions still simmer in Belgium, Spain, the Ukraine, the Urals, Macedonia, and the Balkans. Symbols, language, culture divide as well as unify. Beyond Europe but touching Europe also, the rise of Islamist extremism has brought politico-religious terror in its wake. There are many dissimilarities of course, but Northern Ireland in the later twentieth century, far from being an outlier or a throwback to the religious wars of the seventeenth century, finds its place all too easily within the modern world.

The Troubles are often conceived in terms of the headline events, the bombings, the killings, funerals, imprisonment, and hunger strikes, as in the first two chapters of this volume. But this is an impoverished agenda. To redress the balance and to aim for a more holistic account, two further chapters are devoted to a rebarbative aspect of the Troubles, that is, the practice of paramilitary punishments which is sometimes dignified with labels such as "informal policing" and "informal justice." The scale and severity of these attacks – orange-on-orange and green-on-green violence – has been largely obscured, in part because there has been so little media coverage down the years. To take but one example, Ed Moloney's *A Secret History of the IRA* is regarded by many as a brilliant achievement, and rightly so. A fine sense of history informs the narrative. It is psychologically acute, and the writing has the momentum of a good thriller. There are many insights and revelations, especially in relation to the "high politics" of Sinn Féin. Gerry Adams, the long-time president of Sinn Féin (who was

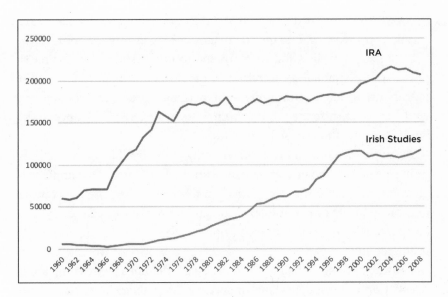

Figure 0.1 The frequency of printed references to "IRA" and "Irish Studies," 1960–2008

Source: Calculated using the Google Books Ngram online search engine.

"never a member of the IRA") emerges as an orchestrator of genius within the theatre of republican intrigue and is never far from centre stage. This undoubtedly gives the work coherence but at a cost. While my admiration for *A Secret History* remains undiminished, I have to say the approach misses out great swathes of IRA activity, quite possibly the most common forms of activity for so many IRA volunteers. There is only a single paragraph, that on page 153, mentioning paramilitary beatings and shootings in a book that is more than 700 pages long. Loyalist "policing" and intra-community terror, if anything, has received even less attention, yet these activities were intrinsic to the conduct of the Troubles.

For many republican volunteers their active service was that of maiming fellow nationalists, particularly so from the mid-1970s onwards. The same was true on the loyalist side where brute force also ensured neighbourhood compliance. Perhaps we need to reorient our understanding of the Troubles in some basic respects, particularly as to understanding the relative autonomy of social enclaves within society under conditions of conflict. Patterns of fear and terror persisted, and still persist, long after "peace" has been declared. More rounded treatments of the recent past would integrate the "Troubles from below" into the grand narrative. As also argued, social scientists (less so journalists and writers) tend to underestimate the degree of power over people's lives exercised by paramilitary organisations at the neighbourhood and community level, perhaps because of a disciplinary tendency to fetishize the powers of the state as well as a reluctance to delineate the limitations of state agencies.

A further weakness in the historiography of the Troubles, in part arising from a disproportionate engagement with "high politics," is the limited attention to distinctions along gender lines. It is true there are celebrations in some quarters of paramilitary women, the remorseless Dolours Price being a case in point, and masked women with guns featured periodically in the republican paper, *An Phobhlacht*.[3] A minority of women activists went to jail but unlike their male counterparts did not acquire comparable celebrity status (including sexual opportunities) on their release back home. Then there are the much-put-upon wives and partners of paramilitary fighters, enduring the daily grind of bringing up children on their own, arranging prison visits, and seeking to make ends meet.[4] But the Troubles added to the burdens of the generality of women, working-class mothers in particular, whose life struggle was securing the welfare, education, and safety of their families in the face of pressures of poverty while also facing harassment by the security forces and problems posed by paramilitaries in their neighbourhoods. "It was a woman shouldering everything."[5] The rhetoric that this was empowering for women, as some ideologues claimed, rings hollow.

If anything, sexual minorities fared less well. Homophobic values and prejudice against sexual minorities were ingrained in Irish nationalist and Ulster unionist culture.[6] Ian Paisley's bombastic campaign in the early 1980s to "Save Ulster from Sodomy" is perhaps the best-known illustration, but there were everyday manifestations that reached deeper into society. Not wholly surprisingly, therefore, the Troubles added a further layer of persecution. In the world of paramilitary braggadocio instances of homosexuality and other deviations from dominant values might be held to constitute antisocial behaviour. Those so stigmatised lived lives of fear, running the risk of physical and psychological harm.[7] These invisible minorities have yet to be integrated into the history of the Troubles.

On the twentieth anniversary of the signing of the Good Friday or Belfast Agreement of 1998 many commentators expressed surprise that the degree of polarisation in Northern Ireland was as pronounced as it was back then. If anything the spirit of mutual accommodation was weaker. Yet there had been two decades of relative peace. What could have gone wrong? Political scientists naturally parsed the various agreements, from the Belfast Agreement onwards, and made varying, often conflicting diagnoses. Perhaps it was the architecture of the agreements, perhaps it was their implementation (or nonimplementation), perhaps it was the indifference of London and Dublin. The list goes on, and some of the explanations presumably have some validity. But the burden of the thesis developed here is that more fundamental problems beset the peace process. It is necessary to go to a deeper level. The final chapter explores briefly, perhaps too briefly, ideological evasions, reflexive conscience-making (*conscientisation*), and the possibilities of atonement. The guiding principle, which is much influenced by varying European experiences in the aftermath of World War II, is that without an honest acknowledgement of the ugliness of the decades of terror, the possibilities of reconciliation across the communal divide in Northern Ireland are limited. If we look at present-day Northern Ireland, there is a (relative) absence of violence, what might be called a "negative peace," but this is not a society at peace with itself. What we have is an unstable equilibrium, the outcome of competing communal demands on the part of the two major ethnonational blocs in the North.

In the end, in seeking release from the past, we come back to responsibilities, which includes the making of responsible history. But engaging critically with one's own culture and taking responsibility for its sour fruits is about as painful as a barefooted ascent of the stony slopes of Croagh Patrick or one of the other holy mountains of Ireland. Fifty years after the outbreak of armed hostilities, is it not time to face the mountain?

Figure 1.1 Approach to Crisis

1

A Parade of Candidates

Question: Who was responsible for the Troubles?
Answer: Them 'uns!

INTRODUCTION

The play's the thing, they say. Well, actually no. The audience is the thing. It's a balmy evening in "internment week," August 1999. My ageing Skoda car, the survivor of at least four breakdowns, pootles along the Falls Road and turns right towards the Whiterock in West Belfast. I'm giving a lift to the writer and historian Ruth Dudley Edwards and the American novelist Lionel Shriver. Our purpose is to see a new play, "Forced Upon Us," featuring as part of *Féile an Phobail* or the West Belfast Festival. The play has already generated its own drama, being embroiled in controversy with the Arts Council of Northern Ireland. This is because of artistic or political considerations, depending on point of view.[1] We pass from evening sunlight into the shaded interior of a school building. The improvised theatre turns out to be a school hall; the stage is a platform in the centre surrounded by chairs and benches. We search out the last few seats. Most rows are within touching distance of the stage: this is intimate theatre-in-the-round. The atmosphere is heavy with anticipation and body heat. We are at the Belfast Institute of Further & Higher Education, on the edge of the fiercely nationalist Ballymurphy estate.

In my memory the name of the play is forever "On Our Knees."[2] Even as I write, I have to check again to retrieve the original title. The action opens on a note of macabre fantasy set in the Protestant-dominated, Belfast shipyards. A lone Catholic worker, imaginatively named "Paddy," is set upon by Protestant workers (one of whom is called "Billy"), beaten, and then bound by rope to a lamppost. A flammable liquid is poured over him, and he is set on fire by the loyalist thugs. This not so subtle allusion to burning crosses and the lynching of Blacks in the southern states of America is the prologue to a series of unrelentingly oppressive acts against northern Catholics, that is, the ethnonational group which in 1922 found itself trapped within the "Orange state" of Northern Ireland.[3]

History it ain't. But it must be in the running also for one of the worst plays ever written: dreary, monochromatic, and almost wholly lacking in dramatic tension. The director, the talented Pam Brighton, must have had some doubts as well. Every now and then one of the actors steps out of the play, into a pool of light, and belts out a rebel song. It is relief of a kind: he is, thankfully, a good balladeer. Towards the end of the performance the main protagonist, a Catholic mother, delivers a speech in which she recites the nationalist wrongs of ages, building to the climactic line "And that is why I vote Sinn Féin!"[4] All right, this is no Molly Bloom in sensuous raptures, but the significant point is that the audience was entranced throughout.

A little earlier or perhaps it was a little later – time and sequence mattered little to the drama – one of the match-stick characters, having recited a litany of woes, appeals to the heavens with words to this effect: Can we put up with this any longer? Out of the darkness, somewhere behind me, comes an audible whisper: "Can *we* put up with this much longer?" I dared not turn round but knew it was Ruth's voice. From further back, and almost immediately, another voice barked, "Why don't you fuck off then?"

The whisper had the shock value of laughter during the consecration of the host at a Catholic mass. The thing we ignorant outsiders, trapped in the hard chairs, failed to recognise was that this was sacred drama. Far from being bored, the congregation took deep, satisfied draughts from the cauldron of sorrows, wildly applauding the players at the end of the performance. This was collective catharsis. Or something. Had I had the chance to talk later with some of those sitting near me I imagine they would have reeled off, with characteristic Belfast directness and fluency, a series of incidents of British state violence, of discrimination, of slights to their culture, and much more. Moreover, much of this would have had a real, if selective basis in fact, including the Falls Curfew, the Ballymurphy killings, internment without trial, doors being kicked in, and sectarian murders during the Troubles.

Driving home, before dropping off Lionel Shriver in Notting Hill, on the other side of Belfast, I wondered, "might there not be some kind of guilt complex behind the intensity of the audience reaction?" "If there was," said Ruth almost dismissively, "I didn't see much sign of it." We talked on in the privacy of the car. "But couldn't that almost frantic desire to be reassured of the bigotry and inhumanity of the 'other' – the Protestant people – come from a sense of guilt about republican violence during the last three decades?" After some discussion, we let the idea drop. Yet it is a question that keeps coming back, growing more insistent as the years go by.

To place the conversation in context: the main republican armed force, the Provisional IRA, had ordered a "complete cessation of military operations" in August 1994.[5] Seven weeks later the combined loyalist paramilitary command declared its own ceasefire and ceased some but not all of its killings. Unlike the IRA statement, it had added the word "regret" for the pain and suffering caused by loyalist paramilitary violence. The IRA returned to "armed struggle" a year and a half later and continued until well into 1997 before declaring a ceasefire. Naturally emotions were still raw at the end of the decade, with accusations of bad faith on all sides and claims of security force complicity in loyalist killings. The IRA continued to execute and maim but only within the nationalist community, while loyalists did likewise within their community (as discussed in later chapters). Loyalists had also increased the frequency of random, or apparently random, sectarian attacks on Catholics.[6]

The intensity of that night – the anger and the hatred – stayed with me, as well as the half-conviction that we had been witnessing a glimmering of consciousness of another kind. There are the Troubles without, brought to us by voices, film footage and newsprint, and sometimes by direct experience. There are also the Troubles within, where consciousness connects obliquely with conscience. Even more circuitously, having wandered down different *boreens*, this brought me to the question, perhaps the most fundamental and frightening question about the Northern Ireland conflict.

It is this "Who was primarily responsible for the prosecution of the Troubles and its attendant toll of dead, injured, and the emotionally

traumatised?" I was afraid of the question, and its implications, so I sat
on it for a very, very long time. For some reason, rather like a subterranean
stream bubbling to the surface, now seems the time to revisit the question,
identify plausible candidates, and venture an answer.

HISTORY

> It is plain from what we have heard, read and observed that the train
> of events and incidents which began in Londonderry on 5th October
> 1968 has had as its background, on the one hand a widespread sense
> of political and social grievance for long unadmitted and therefore
> unaddressed by successive Governments of Northern Ireland, and
> on the other sentiments of fear and apprehension sincerely and ten-
> aciously felt and believed, of risks to the integrity and indeed con-
> tinued existence of the state.
> Cameron Report, 1969[7]

History is to blame. In a sense this has to be true. The conflict of ethnicity,
nationality, religion, and culture in these islands goes deep in time. The
structuring of intercommunal relations in the north of Ireland exemplifies
a degree of path dependence that is difficult to dispute.[8] Much of what happened in the 1960s was predictable; much was also unpredictable and con-
tingent. Sure enough, breaking out of inherited positions is both difficult
and painful. But an inevitability thesis will hardly suffice, however satisfying
such an interpretation may be to historians of a determinist bent. Those
who performed the action, and most did not, to take up arms at the end
of the 1960s were not automatons dumbly responding to ancestral voices.
To think so, is condescending to generations of loyalist and republican
paramilitaries (though curiously paramilitary self-presentation is sometimes in such Pavlovian terms). Moreover, paramilitaries were volunteers
– they rejoice in the very word "volunteer" – which, if it means anything,
signifies volition. Similarly the other armed forces, the members of the British army, the RUC, the Special Constabulary, and later the UDR, no more
than nationalist and unionist, Irish and British politicians, would hardly
subscribe to the self-caricature of being merely prisoners of history.

What has to be explained is not why there was struggle. There was struggle on the streets during the period of Civil Rights agitation, from roughly 1967 to 1971. There were pickets, demonstrations, counter-demonstrations, marches, sit-ins, as well as more conventional electioneering. The alternative to killing the "other" was not inertia. So, why did a period of intense political excitement in the second half of the 1960s spiral downwards into lethal communal and national conflict? More fundamentally, once ignited, why was this conflict maintained year after year for three decades or more. What group of organised actors was primarily responsible for propagating political violence over such an extended period of time?

WAS IT THE SECURITY FORCES?

Perhaps the root cause of the Troubles was repression by the security forces, the police, and the army. There is no doubt there was state repression, though it is also true that street agitators in the late 1960s sometimes went out of their way to provoke confrontation. As Eamon McCann candidly recalled, by the middle of 1968 "our conscious, if unspoken, strategy was to provoke the police into over-reaction and thus spark off mass reaction against the authorities."[9]

Nonetheless, the RUC did not cover itself in glory. The police attack on a civil rights march in Derry on 5 October 1968 galvanised a generation of street fighters. Less than a year later the police, aided by loyalists, were driving Catholic rioters back into the Bogside in Derry. The use of Shorland armoured cars with mounted machine guns during the associated rioting in Belfast in August 1969 resulted in the tragic death of a nine-year-old Catholic boy in Divis Flats in the west of the city.[10] Other demonstrations and counter-demonstrations, according to the Cameron Report, where the police found themselves as piggies-in-the-middle, were well-handled despite the best efforts of street politicians and demonstrators to contrive partisan advantage.[11]

The British army, which was welcomed with cups of tea into nationalist areas initially, made colossal mistakes early on. Whether the Irish army or indeed any other army thrust into the role of controlling stone-throwers, petrol-bombers, and eventually gunmen taking cover behind rioters would have reacted very differently is a moot point. An army is not designed for a policing role, and it may be, as the writer Dennis Kennedy has argued, the deployment of troops in Derry in August 1969 represented a fundamental error of judgement.[12] In any case, subsequent army operations, in particular the Falls Curfew – a blundering attempt to seize IRA weapons in July 1970 – were ill-conceived and served to alienate working-class Catholics. The full-blooded state violence of Bloody Sunday, January 1972, was an appalling crime, and the torture of some internees was a shameful episode in the life of a democratic state.[13] Internment without trial, largely directed at one community, served to further alienate Catholics. But the striking thing is that the British Army and the police learned over time. There were many Bloody Fridays, or the equivalent, but there were no further Bloody Sundays.[14] Though there were occasional unlawful shootings by state forces after 1972, including in all probability the shooting of several civilians in the New Lodge, Belfast, in 1973, in general the police and army operated under political control.[15] Had elected representatives not been in charge, deaths due to the army and the police would have been far greater (see the later discussion of agencies responsible for killings and the relative proportions of victims).

Moreover, one cannot get away from the fact that the police and the army, however ham-fisted or brutal their operations might be at times, were there to ensure law and order, not to elevate one community above another, nor to subvert the political process. Troops were stationed at communal interface areas. Troops stretched temporary barriers between loyalist and nationalist neighbourhoods. Clearly the objective was to contain conflict. Admittedly individuals and sometimes groupings within the security forces went beyond the bounds of the law but the institutions as a whole remained firm. Meanwhile, from late 1969 onwards, conspiratorial groups on the loyalist and nationalist sides were gathering arms and working overtime to undo these efforts.

It would be ungenerous, having acknowledged the dark side of army and police operations, not to acknowledge also the heroism of individual men and women in uniform. Five hundred British soldiers had lost their lives by 1999 and smaller numbers subsequently. Members of the RUC and the UDR lived particularly vulnerable lives within local communities in the face of booby-trap bombs, ambushes, and off-duty assassinations. More than 300 police lost their lives and thousands were injured in the course of their duties. Often it was only the thin green line of the RUC that helped contain savage communal violence. This was at terrible personal cost. Even when members had left the police force, they were still open to assassination, as was the case of nineteen former police officers.[16] In relation to the UDR and ex-UDR members, more than 200 suffered Troubles-related deaths, in most cases when off-duty.[17]

It is often objected that the RUC was an overwhelmingly Protestant force and hence served the interests only of the unionist community. However, there is very little evidence of this, at least from the early 1970s onwards, some individual cases excepted. Indeed the police found themselves in the eye of the loyalist storm on numerous occasions, enduring anger and attack from sections of loyalism. This was true during the two loyalist workers' strikes of the 1970s, the policing of the Anglo-Irish Agreement of 1985, and the policing of contentious Orange parades during much of the course of the Troubles. We may recall that Victor Arbuckle, the first constable to die in the Troubles, was shot by loyalists. That few Catholics, though there were brave exceptions, dared join the RUC during the 1970s, the 1980s, and the 1990s is understandable. Republicans made a point of assassinating Catholics in the force, these being perceived as double-traitors, first to their own community and second by aligning themselves with the British state. Conveniently, Catholic officers were more vulnerable than their Protestant counterparts to off-duty attack, at social or family events, enjoying a pint in a local pub, or attending a Catholic service.[18]

There is another dimension to the point about the denominational composition of the RUC and the UDR. It meant that one community bore the brunt of the casualties – some 500 deaths and thousands of life-changing injuries – in efforts over three decades to contain the crisis and maintain some degree of normalcy. For nationalists in Northern Ireland and in the Irish republic to have escaped this burden is not perhaps an advantage to be lightly dismissed.

It is surely significant that when the Provisional IRA issued what turned out to be its final ceasefire in 1997, the forces of the state were gradually relaxed in what were seen as overt acts of demilitarisation. Watchtowers along the border tumbled; army barracks closed; soldiers were redeployed abroad. Police numbers were cut back, and police stations were closed down. These were the very same police numbers and barracks that had been expanded in response to earlier paramilitary activity. Had there been permanent paramilitary ceasefires at any point from say 1972 onwards, the British army would have been recalled to barracks, albeit with a time lag, and there would have been no need for an expanded RUC and UDR. In other words, the security forces, as a collective entity, had not been independent agents promoting conflict but a reaction to the threat faced by civil society. The multiparty Belfast Agreement of 1998, further modified by the St Andrews Agreement of 2006, set the conditions for a more secure political environment in which the winding down of the security forces became possible.

THE SECURITY FORCES AND OTHERS

There is a more hybrid line of interpretation. Critics will object that there was collusion between members of the security forces and paramilitary organisations, particularly with loyalist paramilitaries who killed many Catholic civilians during the course of the conflict. This is true. The security forces had penetrated all the major paramilitary organisations, and in the murky underworld of espionage and counter-insurgency there seems little doubt that there were some appalling instances where a blind eye was turned to certain assassinations.[19] Astonishingly the security forces recruited the head of the IRA's internal security unit (the "nutting squad"). There are questions as to whether this key agent, Freddie Scappaticci, was allowed to kill nationalists suspected of informing as well as enforcing a brutal discipline in IRA-controlled areas (a discipline fully endorsed by the IRA command structure). The role of loyalist agents is also disquieting. These are aspects of the Troubles that need to be revealed more fully, though it is clear that the scale of these operations has been exaggerated. Moreover, when a rogue policeman or UDR soldiers participated in a killing, as was the case with the Miami Showband massacre in July 1975 for instance, they were acting as loyalist paramilitaries not as representatives of the security forces.[20] In fact, the RUC was successful in arresting two serving members of the UDR, as well as a former member of the UDR, all of who were involved in the killings. The three received lengthy jail sentences.

As we shall see later, the statistics of unlawful killings do not bear out the contention that the security forces made a major contribution on the killing front. Had there been widespread collusion it is difficult to explain why there were so few assassinations of well-known loyalist or republican gunmen. The case of the Provisional IRA, the paramilitary group that suffered the most casualties, is revealing. By 1999 the Provisional IRA had lost 293 of its members, representing some 8 per cent of all those killed violently.[21] Of these, 115 or on average between three and four each year were shot dead by the security forces. Surprisingly, less than half of the PIRA fatalities were due to the security forces. The remaining 178 died as a result of premature bomb explosions and accidental shootings (at least thirty of these), execution by former comrades (at least twenty-eight were killed as informers), due to internecine republican feuding, due to car crashes while on active service, due to hunger strikes, and due to loyalist attacks. Assassinations by loyalists, however, accounted for only a small fraction of the PIRA casualties. Thus had collusion with loyalist paramilitaries been a widespread practice, one is driven to the conclusion that it was a remarkably inefficient practice.

The real point is that the bulk of covert activity was designed to save lives. Collusion is a part of the intelligence story, and the smaller part. The intelligence services saved many lives – quite possibly hundreds, some would say thousands – by aborting loyalist and republican operations.[22] "Dead" men walking, as one agent, Martin McGartland, put it.[23] Some would go further and argue that it was the widespread penetration of the IRA by agents of the security forces ("touts" or informers) that forced the republican movement to adopt a "peace strategy." If this is correct, then the system of intelligence gathering not only saved lives during the time of the Troubles but saved innumerable lives *from 1994 onwards* by bringing the armed conflict to an end earlier than otherwise might have been the case. While this in no way exonerates individuals or groups operating outside the law, it bears restating that the system of espionage developed by the security forces, at some risk to the operators, saved many lives – some would claim hundreds and hundreds of lives – by disclosing in advance planned killings and bombings by loyalist and republican armed groups.[24] The balance lies with lives saved.

The myth of widespread collusion is useful in an ideological sense, in blurring the respective roles of loyalist paramilitaries and the agencies of the state and in directing attention away from some fearful possibilities. We might remind ourselves that in the absence of a vigorous security containment policy, the likelihood is that Northern Ireland would have slid over the precipice into the "doomsday" scenario of outright communal warfare at some point between the early 1970s and the 1990s. The likely loss of life hardly bears imagining, but the irresponsibility of those who diced with the death of civilian Catholics in the Belfast region and of civilian Protestants in outer Ulster should not be obscured. Though loyalists and republicans were probably sincere in protesting that they did not want all-out war, the logic of communal attack and retaliation would have tipped the two sides over the brink into civil war. The respective leaders, irrespective of initial intentions, would have been powerless to halt a downward spiral in which each twist of the communal screw reinforced the extremist tendencies within the other community. In the absence of a restraining force – the police, the army, the intelligence services – only one outcome seems possible.

Indeed there were moments when Northern Ireland seemed to teeter on the brink of civil war, despite the powerful restraining force of the police and British army.[25] The Garda and the Irish army also played a necessary supportive role in the politics of containment. Had the forces of restraint been withdrawn, there can be little doubt that the *further* casualties would have been in the thousands, more likely in the tens of thousands. Paramilitaries on both sides played Russian roulette with the nationalist and unionist communities, as did those who urged a "British withdrawal."[26] Fortunately the British and Irish governments set their face firmly against political adventurism.

WAS IT THE UNIONISTS?

There is the wider political movement that is unionism. Unionists had governed Northern Ireland through a single-party government since the foundation of the state in 1922.[27] Unionists at once abolished proportional representation in local government elections and set to work at manipulating electoral boundaries so as to ensure unionist majorities in local councils. Nationalists boycotted and sometimes attacked the new institutions. A monopoly of power bred a type of intolerance and arrogance, though the early years of the new state also witnessed some measures of generosity, as indeed was true of the Irish Free State as well.[28] Proportional representation in elections to the Northern Ireland parliament was legislated against in 1928, not so much to disadvantage nationalists as to counter the threat to unionist hegemony from breakaway factions within unionism.[29] (The dominant party in the Republic of Ireland, Fianna Fáil, also for electoral advantage, sought to abolish proportional representation in Irish parliamentary elections as late as 1968.) Unionist political representation was boosted further by the manipulation of electoral boundaries ("gerrymandering"), particularly in the west of the province, though hardly on the comprehensive scale implied by critics. Nationalists were disadvantaged by the property qualification applying to voting in *local* elections in Northern Ireland. This affected poorer Protestants as well, but the unionist leadership proved adept at warding off lower-class discontent, not least through its patronage of the "collaborationist" Ulster Unionist Labour Association.[30] A similar property qualification had been the norm in the United Kingdom before the Second World War but had been allowed to linger on in Northern Ireland in the postwar decades. (The property qualification, or disqualification, did not apply to General Elections in Northern Ireland, an important point lost in the clamour for "one man, one vote," to use the gender-inflected language of the civil rights movement of the 1960s.[31])

There was indeed electoral manipulation and politico-sectarian partiality in the allocation of housing and jobs, all with a view to weakening locally the Catholic and nationalist political position.[32] But we have to be careful about uncritically consuming narratives spun by civil rights activists and retailed, even less critically, in later academic writings. For instance, the 1971 Census of Northern Ireland shows Catholic households as overrepresented, not underrepresented, in local authority housing in Northern Ireland.[33] Most of the sixty-eight local councils, some of them tiny in size, would seem not to have discriminated actively along denominational grounds, though of course there were glaring exceptions. The celebrated study of the North on the eve of the Troubles by the American political

scientist Richard Rose concluded there was "no evidence of systematic discrimination against Catholics" in public housing provision, though he did
mention instances of bias "in areas controlled by Catholic councillors."[34]
The latter did not attract the ire of civil rights campaigners.

This may appear shockingly revisionist in view of the heat generated at
the time by housing and related problems. The paradox, if it be such, merits
a closer look. First, as in Britain and the Republic of Ireland, there was an
absolute shortage of housing in the 1960s, hence housing was an acute problem for many, irrespective of religious or national denomination. In all three
jurisdictions these shortages were politicised, but in Northern Ireland they
assumed an ethnically divisive colouration. Second, there was a *minority* of
instances of housing discrimination, some of a blatant kind, which served
to fuel anger and resentment within the Catholic community. Discrimination by nationalist-controlled councils did not suit the emerging (and now
orthodox) narrative nor did it attract much attention. Third, where houses
were located was used as a means of gerrymandering by some councils, and
this undoubted abuse could be generalised to suggest that unionist councils
did not wish to house Catholics. Fourth, and by and large unionists failed
to recognise this, the bedrock of grievance in the 1960s ultimately was not
reducible to issues of housing or jobs or even living standards: taking the
longer view, northern Catholic alienation stemmed from exclusion from
the Catholic nationalist state to the south and the involuntary incorporation
of northern Catholics within a Protestant, unionist state in the northeast
of Ireland. This was one in which the Unionist Party ruled in perpetuity.[35]
The result was a wounded nationalism and one that easily commanded
sympathy from the outside world. Issues of degree and scale might interest
social scientists – not all it would appear – but were an irrelevance to the
antiestablishment stone-throwing youth in the street. The collective hurt
of northern nationalists was further inflamed by prohibitions on the symbolic expression of Irish culture and aspirations. The Irish flag and *an
Ghaeilge* (the Gaelic language), to take only two instances, were seen by
many unionists as subversive of the status quo. Thus, while discriminatory
practices were real and apparent and not all on one side, the reality was
more complex than many nationalist and unionist commentators allowed.

In a sense this was all very Irish. The Cameron Report discerned a
"tradition that Protestant and Catholic representatives ought primarily to

look after 'their own people.'"[36] The political culture of Northern Ireland was not bounded by the border, as a peek across the divide from Derry into the neighbouring county of Donegal makes clear. One of the out-spoken critics of northern unionism was the Fianna Fáil minister and Donegal-born member of parliament, Mr Neil Blaney. He achieved a degree of national notoriety through his role in promoting Taca, a fund-raising body for Fianna Fáil. Taca had links to some of the shadier elements in Irish business life. Blaney was indefatigable in his criticisms of discrimination, for which he must be commended, but these criticisms only extended to Ulster unionists. In his own bailiwick discrimination along party political lines was an everyday reality. One study of the Blaney political machine is aptly titled *The Donegal Mafia*.[37] Local democracy in the north-west, it seems, bore more than a passing resemblance to the practices of ward bosses in Irish America. More to the point, few unionist bosses in the twentieth century could aspire to the kind of political patronage and control exercised by Blaney and his political associates at both national and local level. It may be that Donegal was the worst-case scenario in terms of clientelistic politics and the misuse of power, though later revelations about planning practices for Dublin city and county hardly bear out such a complacent assumption. To summon up the spectres of two notorious fixers, the names of the former Taoiseach Charles J. Haughey and his fellow minister Ray Burke were synonymous with graft and the abuse of power.[38]

Or to take the administration of justice, appointments to the Irish Supreme Court were heavily dependent on belonging to the party in power.[39] In local government, in view of the prevailing political culture, party membership tended to trump other qualifications when an appointment was in the gift of local councillors. The official rule was that canvassing resulted in automatic disqualification. On the contrary, as the historian Joe Lee caustically remarked, "no canvassing" meant automatic disqualification, while in the North the former civil servant Maurice Hayes judged, "The practice of canvassing which was prevalent at the time was both degrading and potentially an abuse."[40]

Sure enough, while the principle of political favouritism, manipulation of electoral boundaries, and job discrimination operated on both sides of the border, the effects were more acutely felt within the deeply divided society of Northern Ireland where more power resided with one political party. It is a nice question, though, as to which part of Ireland was the most assiduous in practising discrimination. There is also the awkward issue of projecting present-day standards backwards in time to an Ireland, north or south, where there was a tension between considerations of merit, in the modern sense, and a widespread presumption that one should favour members of the family, the extended family, and, by extension, those who thought similarly in politics, religion, and culture.[41]

So, was "unionist misrule," as distinct from "nationalist misrule," of such a character as to merit an insurrection of the kind apparent from 1970 onwards? Was the burden of social, political, and economic oppression such that it had become unbearable? The curious and unremarked fact is that the northern working classes, irrespective of religious or ethnic affiliation, had advanced their material interests substantially in the decades before 1969, not only relative to past standards but also relative to their counterparts in the Irish republic. The great reforms embodied in the postwar welfare state, in the spheres of health, education, and social security, did much to reduce absolute poverty and spread the benefits of education to more and more people.[42] It was a generation later before free-secondary education was introduced in the republic, a comprehensive national health service based on need rather than ability to pay has yet to emerge, and unemployment benefits and family income support were higher in the UK during the 1950s and the 1960s. When the discussion of social justice took off in Northern Ireland in the 1960s, there was little acknowledgement of this. Despite the best efforts of communists like Betty Sinclair and radicals in the labour and trade union movement, debate was quickly narrowed to concerns of communal and sectarian advantage.[43] At a populist level, relative deprivation and relative advantage, and a fair degree of mutual paranoia, mattered more.[44]

Yet the historical record on social advance is clear for the postwar decades. "Westminster rule" was broadening the opportunities for farmers, rural labourers, industrial workers, and their children. These changes were visible, even to newcomers like myself in the late 1970s. To give one seemingly insignificant image, I was struck by the small stature of the older men I saw in the working-class areas of Belfast – a legacy no doubt of the privations and poverty of industrial depression during the interwar period – as compared to the taller farmers of my home province of Munster.[45] Yet their children, some of whom I taught, were of good height and physique. Social reform had been made flesh, as it were.[46]

Some would argue that the Unionist Party under the leadership of Terence O'Neill was beginning to initiate further reforms at a provincial level. Be that as it may, few would argue that "unionist misrule" was intensifying in the 1960s.[47] Richard Rose's classic study of people's opinion in the late spring and early summer of 1968 found that 65 per cent of Catholics thought that relations between Catholics and Protestants were better than five years earlier.[48] To a surprising degree perhaps, the street politics of that decade, combined with external pressure from London and Dublin, succeeded in wringing electoral reform, changes to policing, and reform of housing from a reluctant unionist establishment. The case, therefore, for a crushing burden of grievance, incapable of change except by resort to the gun, is simply not tenable. As that wisest of civil servants has remarked, "I think the movement [for reform] did effect real change, and would have achieved more and produced a new society at ease with itself over a decade or so."[49]

WAS IT THE "ORANGE STATE"?

Yet one of the most cherished notions in popular discourse is that reform was not possible.[50] This is so at variance with the historical facts that it bears detailed scrutiny. It is true that unionists controlled the Stormont parliament from 1922 to 1972 when the regional parliament was prorogued. Still, opposition politicians, who were made up of a varied collection of nationalists, independent unionists, and the Northern Ireland Labour Party, exercised a limited countervailing power, as did the Catholic Church operating in public and even more effectively in private.

During the 1960s, one-party rule was challenged increasingly effectively on the streets of Northern Ireland. Under the leadership of the civil rights movement, pressure was exerted simultaneously at the local, regional, and national levels. True enough, leading members of the Ulster Unionist Party such as William Craig and Harry West resisted change, as did many back-bench unionist MPs. The Orange Order, dully predictable in most matters, set its face and its bowler hat against "concessions" to "disloyal elements."[51]

But they failed. The inventory of reforms for the later 1960s, shown in table 1.1, included a widening of the franchise, reform of the housing allocation system, and, *mirabile dictu*, the creation of an unarmed police force. Reform was not only possible; it was an actuality. The notion that politics within Northern Ireland was beyond reform always rested on a fallacy, on the assumption that fundamental powers resided at Stormont rather than with parliament at Westminster. Westminster might slumber but once it roused itself, as it did in the later 1960s and subsequently, there wasn't much unionists of the "Little Ulster" variety could do about it. Moreover, some unionists favoured reform. To maintain the original and partisan thesis it is necessary to argue that the operations of the British state, and its role in Northern Ireland, were beyond reform. One might as well argue that the Irish state or other West European states were beyond reform.

The later 1960s and the 1970s constituted a period of remarkable social change in Irish, British, and European societies. Laws discriminating against women were repealed, censorship of books and magazines was relaxed, and prejudices against sexual and racial minorities were beginning to be tackled. Reform was in the air. In the Republic of Ireland there was a questioning of some of the foundational assumptions of Irish society, including elements of the Irish constitution, unequal pay for women, prohibition on divorce, and even the special position of the Roman Catholic Church.[52] As in Northern Ireland, some of these progressive tendencies were deflected or delayed by the resort to arms and its polarising implications. The effect of the early flash flood of violence was to strengthen traditional and reactionary political forces north and south of the border.

It seems to me no accident that those wedded to the impossibility thesis were often committed to militarist solutions. Demands for reform in the 1960s slipped, almost unconsciously, into demands for the destruction of the Northern state. Achieving a United Ireland held an almost utopian appeal for many on the northern nationalist side, despite the fact that public services and living standards were lower in southern Ireland. This failed to take account of the fact that a substantial minority of people on the island were vehemently opposed to a one-state solution. Even the nationalist people of Northern Ireland have been divided on the issue.[53] There is also a long-standing doubt about the appetite of southern nationalists for unification, should this involve costs, as it undoubtedly would. The British state might have succumbed to withdrawal from Northern Ireland, as some extremist nationalists and ultraleft adventurers advocated, but far from leaving a *united people* in its wake – the essential basis for a united Ireland – such action would have led to civil war and a further harvest of communal hatred. An Ireland united by coercion rather than consensus is a contradiction in terms, something long acknowledged by progressive nationalists. Nowadays, a more enlightened understanding, based on acceptance of the principle of consent, finds expression in the Good Friday Agreement.[54]

When evolving historical processes are heavily disrupted it is easy to lose sight of the likelihood that reforms would have continued to flow, albeit on a timescale that is not precisely predictable. In other words, there is no reason to believe the reforms implemented by Stormont under pressure from Westminster and a committed civil rights movement would have suddenly dried up circa 1970. The international context was also favourable to change as the influence of European social democracy was working in the direction of social equality, gender equality, and human rights. Short of the end of history, pressures would continue to be exerted by London and, perhaps increasingly, Dublin and Washington throughout the 1970s and beyond. To the surprise of both critics and die-hard supporters, the so-called Orange State proved to be highly vulnerable to forces for reform.

ANTI-CATHOLICISM: BRING ON THE BIGOTED, FRENZIED, PROTESTANT PREACHERS

There is a deep strain of anti-Catholicism within northern Protestant culture and, in the not-too-distant past, within the larger British society.[55] The eminent sociologist and Protestant layman John Brewer has catalogued a series of displays of anti-Catholicism in Ireland from the seventeenth to the twentieth century.[56] It is a remarkably honest and dispassionate account of unchristian acts in a Christian society, viewed exclusively from one side of the fence. There is, as yet, no equivalent Catholic recognition which frankly documents instances of Catholic intolerance of "non-Catholics" though the list must surely extend from the 1641 atrocities to the burning of Protestant civilians in a barn at Scullabogue during the 1798 insurrection and onwards to the 1820s and the Rockite disturbances that, among other things, targeted "Protestant heretics."[57] One could go on, but there is clearly a parallel history of Catholic sectarianism that extends to the present day.[58]

In Ulster there was no shortage of inflammatory street preachers. From Roaring Hugh Hanna to the Rev. Ian Paisley, there were ministers who mixed fundamentalist Protestantism and virulent antipopery rhetoric with unionist politics. This is a combustible mix in a divided society. A loyalist, Hugh McClean, when charged in 1966 with involvement in the sectarian killing of a Catholic man in Malvern Street off the Shankill Road, is said to have confessed, "I am sorry I ever heard tell of that man Paisley or decided to follow him."[59] No doubt some loyalists in *their reception* of the Paisleyite creed of faith and fatherland felt incitement to communal hatred. But one suspects that a motivation to kill required more complex motives. Dr Paisley denied any connection to the Malvern Street murder, while Gusty Spence, one of the founders of the self-styled UVF of the mid-1960s and no admirer of Paisley, was dismissive of any suggestion that the firebrand preacher had played a role in the formation of this Protestant paramilitary group. Taking the longer view, Paisley made clear in a number of public statements, and from quite early on, that he condemned the murder of Catholics.[60]

My friendly solicitor David Cook, the first nonunionist mayor of Belfast, impressed on me during the course of conversations spanning the 1980s and 1990s the malign nature of Paisley, as man, minister, and politician. He preached an old-time religion of hatred; he fomented confrontation; his intransigence was legendary (until compromise happened to suit his own insatiable ambition).[61] He helped amplify anger within the nationalist community and some would see him as, in effect, a recruiting sergeant for the IRA. I have little or no difficulty with such assessments. Paisley was a hugely bigoted and destabilising force in politics during the 1960s and 1970s.[62] I am also conscious that in Irish and Ulster history the distinction between constitutional and violent political action was not always clear-cut: think of the Ulster Covenanters in 1912, or at least a minority of them, and Carson's Volunteers.[63] Ambiguities, posturing, and on occasion collaboration existed in Paisley's relationship with Protestant paramilitary organisations.[64]

For instance, during the second loyalist workers strike, in the year 1977, Paisley was prepared to collaborate with the UDA to add muscle to the direct action and street politics that the strike involved.[65] But there was no sustained involvement on his part in promoting paramilitarism nor an equivalent to the IRA's unambiguous resort to arms, with consistent Sinn Féin backing it has to be said. The street preacher and rabble-rouser did not make the quantum leap to becoming an advocate, still less a director, of Protestant terrorism. Many of its advocates scorned the "Big Man." Arguably Paisley's major contribution to the motivation of paramilitarism was at the green rather than the orange end of the spectrum. The best-selling writer and journalist Ed Moloney goes so far as to suggest that Paisley was the "midwife" who gave birth to the Provisional IRA.[66] Certainly the primitive communal ideology of the early northern Provisional IRA was reinforced and validated by the bogeyman that was Paisley.

We might also remember that Paisley and his followers constituted a minority within unionism for most of his political career. This was especially so in the 1960s, before the mutually reinforcing dynamic that bound the extremes of nationalism and unionism came into fully charged contact. To liberal unionists, in the age of the Beatles and the Rolling Stones, Paisley and his followers were a grotesque throwback to another age. On two occasions the Northern Irish state committed him to prison. For those of us growing up in southern Ireland, Paisley's booming voice was a source of both bewilderment and amusement. References to the Pope as "old red socks" seemed almost naughtily beguiling, that is, if you were far removed from the tinderbox that was the North. The entertainment value of the Big Man, for a southern Irish audience, was recognised by the national broadcasting station Radio Telefís Éireann, which lavished air time on the exotic indigene from the Far North. The Hollywood star Liam Neeson, from a Catholic background in Ballymena, was drawn to hear Paisley for rather different reasons. Neeson has related how he would sneak into church to hear Paisley perform. It was Paisley the bible thumper and pulpit performer who helped inspire Neeson to fashion a career in acting. So the Paisley phenomenon, and its reception, is a complex one. In a further perverse twist, the reactionary stance of Paisley and his associates, it could be argued, actually aided the passage of civil rights legislation in the 1960s. Nor should we forget that Paisley spent at least as much time attacking other Protestant denominations as he devoted to criticising the Church of Rome.

Paisley was rightly singled out for criticism by the Cameron Report in 1969 for his tactic of counterdemonstration and use of public prayer meetings to draw together crowds of belligerent loyalists.[67] Nor should it be forgotten that in the early confrontations with civil rights marchers some of his raggle-taggle admirers and supporters were armed with billhooks, cudgels, and even the occasional revolver.[68] But for all the violence of the word, for all his thundering denunciations of Pope and popery, of treachery and traitors, of ecumenists and Lundys, there is no evidence of Paisley promoting violence against his Catholic neighbours. The sociologist Steve Bruce has raked through Paisley's public career and can find no basis for such claims.[69] For what it's worth, my own occasional glimpses of the man suggest a similar conclusion. From the late 1970s, I would once in a while drop into the Martyrs Memorial Church on the Ravenhill Road in Belfast to listen to the Big Man. As he harangued, cajoled, and led his people in prayer, he struck me as first and foremost a man of the cloth. Sure enough, his was a preaching that blended old-time religion with waspish asides about contemporary politics. But I was left in little doubt as to which was the wellspring for this overbearing son of the Protestant Reformation.

Paisley would go to the brink, like some civil rights agitators, but largely within the limits of violent street theatre, not that of armed insurgency or counterinsurgency. And that is a really important distinction. He did not advocate the use of the gun to settle the question of the union. So far as I know, only a few members of his religious congregation, the Free Presbyterians, were convicted of terrorist offences. Had Paisley been a full-blooded militarist, like the leaders of loyalist and republican paramilitary organisations, such was his charisma, the Troubles would have been far bloodier. But he wasn't. Paisleyism, particularly through its tactic of counterdemonstrations, contributed to the descent into chaos, but in terms of advocating, directing and, above all, perpetuating armed violence Paisley failed to cut the mustard.

THE MAIN CHURCHES

Where the hell was Jesus Christ during the Troubles, even as the God-fearing Christians of Ulster assailed heaven with their divided prayers? It may be more appropriate to address his representatives on earth. Some people, taking the long view, see the mainstream churches as making a decisive contribution to the Troubles. There are important distinctions to be made here. It would be difficult to dispute the claim that the churches played an important role in maintaining segregated structures in Irish life, affecting education, healthcare, marriage, and intercommunal socialising. The influence of the churches went into the making of a divided society. Much more could be said about that in historical time but the fundamental truth remains that during the modern conflict all of the Christian churches resolutely opposed the use of violence. Indeed alongside the march of the militant men – it was men by and large – went the quieter tramp of peace-making initiatives by men and women of the clergy. One day we will have time to appreciate the depth of the work of the Corrymeela Community, of the Quakers, of the Glencree Reconciliation Centre, and of the endeavours of individual clergy such as John Dunlop, Edward Daly, Denis Faul, Cathal Daly, Sister Anna, Robin Eames, and so many others.

It is true that a small number of priests and pastors acted as chaplains and cheerleaders to paramilitary groups.[70] The less than usually authoritative *Protestant Telegraph* warned its readers in August 1974 that the Roman Catholic Church supported the IRA and was engaged in a "Holy War" against "pagans".[71] But dissident priests and pastors were the exception. Had the Catholic Church, for instance, blessed the activities of republican paramilitaries, which after all was an option, then there is no doubt the conflict would have been immeasurably worse. Had the Presbyterian Church or the Church of Ireland adopted a similar jihadist stance alongside loyalist paramilitaries the bloodletting would have been on an appalling scale. Indeed when we pause to consider why the killings and maimings were not on a larger scale, part of the answer must lie with the peaceful messages and moral concerns inculcated by the main body of Christian churches.

LOYALISTS: THE DEMOCRATIC UNIONIST PARTY

Then there are the organised political forces – wider than simply Paisleyite followers – of uncompromising loyalism that coalesced in the Democratic Unionist Party in 1971.[72] The DUP opposed power sharing and was strident in its attacks on Irish nationalism. It demonised the Irish republic as a "safe haven" for nationalist terrorists and was almost equally critical of the British government for its "soft" security policies in relation to the IRA. Among its more fatuous demands was the call that the border with the Republic of Ireland, with its hundreds of crossings along its 500 kilometres length, be sealed. Members of the DUP took prominent positions in the two Ulster loyalist workers' strikes: that of 1974 that helped bring down the then power-sharing executive and that of 1977 which ended in humiliating defeat for Paisley in particular. The 1977 strike was my first experience of street politics in Ulster. I joined other left-wing comrades outside the Harland and Wolff shipyards exhorting workers to cross the politico-sectarian picket lines and return to work. We needn't have bothered. The police, the army, and the secretary of state for Northern Ireland, Roy Mason, stood firm. Unlike some industrial action in Britain in this period that also had political undertones – the 1974 British coal miners' strike comes to mind – the loyalist strike crumbled.[73]

Leading members of the DUP were involved in various attempts to create paramilitary-style organisations in support of the security forces. These included the Third Force in 1981 when the heightened political rhetoric of the DUP spilled over into more sinister activity. A photograph of the time shows loyalists on an Ulster hillside holding aloft gun certificates.[74] (These were legally held guns, of the kind often found in farming households.) Fortunately, these adventures on the part of Paisley's Third Force did not lead directly to paramilitary action. As was said at the time, and despite a backdrop of IRA bombings and shootings, Paisley marched his men to the top of the hill and like the Grand Old Duke of York he marched them down again. While this may have helped radicalise a small number of loyalists, its net effect may well have been to dissipate loyalist anger in the hills around Ballymena. Ulster Resistance was another failed initiative of leaders of the DUP. In late 1986, in angry reaction to the Anglo-Irish Agreement of the previous year, Paisley and his deputy Peter Robinson donned red berets and organised paramilitary-style rallies. But a year later the DUP severed its links with Ulster Resistance when it became clear that some members were involved in importing weaponry.[75]

The Anglo-Irish Agreement signed on the 15 November 1985 by British prime minister Margaret Thatcher and Garret FitzGerald the Irish *taoiseach* (prime minister) was in some respects the precursor of the Good Friday Agreement. For the first time it gave the Republic of Ireland an official consultative role in the governance of Northern Ireland.[76] Ulster unionist opinion was predictably outraged. On the first anniversary of the signing of the agreement I joined my friend David Wilson, who was then working for the Canadian Broadcasting Corporation, on one of the feeder marches from the Donegall Road, on the edge of the loyalist Sandy Row, heading into the centre of the city. My recollection is that we were behind a large banner in blue lettering spelling out "Castlewellan True Blues." I felt a little uneasy. Dave and I had already practised my temporary name change: William it was, not the more Gaelic-sounding Liam. As the speeches ended at Belfast City Hall, Orange bands struck up their marching airs and began peeling away, one by one, from the main demonstration on their homeward route. By then stone-throwing loyalist youths, who had little interest in the speeches, were attacking the police cordon stretched across lower Chichester Street. The grand Robinson & Cleaver building was looted, with one rioter emerging to cheers through the broken plate glass clutching a full-sized model in fashionable dress. Shades of Easter Week, Dublin 1916, I thought. Dave and I were close to the police line but at a safe angle. I was astonished at the calm and discipline of the riot police as stones and chunks of paving stone bounced off their riot shields and Land Rovers. In an almost surreal scene, the music of the departing Orange bands provided a soundtrack for the waves of advancing and retreating rioting youths. This was *son et lumière* of a sort. The mob was eventually dispersed as the police, having soaked up loyalist punishment for what felt like a long time, advanced slowly into Donegall Square. Meanwhile most of the crowd had already dispersed.

This is revealing. The rioters were a youthful minority within the assemblage. There were no guns. There were no petrol bombs. It was clear from the efforts of several Orangemen who tried to persuade the rioters to stop that they were appalled by the street violence. I recall vividly a member of the Loyal Orders, in regalia and with arms outstretched waving a furled umbrella in one hand, standing between the police lines and the advancing rioters, appealing for calm. (It may have been MP Ken Maginnis, but I wasn't sure.) It was a brave and dangerous stand but to no avail. Significantly also, this was the last massive demonstration against the Anglo-Irish Agreement that had Ulster unionist and DUP politicians on the same platform. Even an angered unionist population had little time for reckless street violence.

There had, however, been serious rioting and strike action during that first year and also a comic-opera "invasion" of Clontibret, a village in County Monaghan close to the border. Peter Robinson, deputy leader of the DUP, led a band of militant followers along a border road that wound its way through a village in the Republic of Ireland and then back into Northern Ireland. Whether this was an occupation of sorts or simply noisy, threatening street behaviour is not clear. No doubt some local people were frightened by the incursion. In view of the temper of the period, some may have feared that this was the prelude to something more dangerous. But the republic's unarmed police force, the Gárda, arrived and promptly arrested Peter Robinson. And that was that.

This street theatre might be contrasted with the actual operations of loyalist paramilitary organisations. On a Saturday evening three weeks before Christmas 1971, a four-man UVF gang placed a bomb at McGurk's Bar, on the corner of North Queen Street and Great George's Street, on the edge of the nationalist New Lodge area in north Belfast. The pub owner was a Catholic, Patrick McGurk, as were most of the customers. The bomb exploded almost immediately, killing the owner's wife Philomena and their twelve-year-old daughter Maria. Such was the lethal nature of the bombing of the crowded bar that thirteen others died as well.[77] This was one of the earliest and bloodiest of the mass killings during the Troubles. These human tragedies continued to unfold. The UVF, and its subsidiary known as the Red Hand Commando, murdered 547 people up to the end of the year 1999.

There have been flirtations at times between the DUP, or at least some of its members, and loyalist paramilitaries. The same is true of some Ulster unionist politicians. But it has usually not gone beyond that. Some will recall the histrionic Rev. William McCrea appearing on a platform with the loyalist murderer Billy Wright at the height of the Drumcree crisis.[80] But such disgraceful episodes were not characteristic of DUP or Ulster unionist activity during the thirty or so years of the Troubles, and McCrea's maverick behaviour seems not to have enjoyed much support within the DUP.

McGurk's Bar

The bombing of McGurk's Bar, close to the Catholic New Lodge Road in North Belfast, ranks as one of the worst atrocities of the Troubles. This was the handiwork of the UVF. The bomb was placed hurriedly inside the doorway to the pub and exploded almost immediately. This caused the building to collapse. The scene was a horrific one. The dead and the wounded had to be dragged from the rubble. Fifteen Catholics were murdered and many others injured.

Robert McClenaghan, for one, did not know that his grandfather – one of the customers in the bar – had been killed until he saw his name appear in a news bulletin on television. Not only was the scene of the tragedy chaotic, all kinds of rumours circulated as to which organisation had been responsible. It was claimed by some government sources that a bomb was being prepared in the pub by republicans and had gone off prematurely. This false claim was propagated by the security forces and the intelligence services despite evidence to the contrary. This added to the grief and anger of the survivors and their relatives.

Figure 1.2 McGurk's Bar. John's grandfather, Bernard, is first left, while his father, Patrick McGurk, is third in the row behind the bar.

The owner of the bar, Patrick McGurk, appealed for no retaliation, even as he mourned the death of his wife and daughter. "It doesn't matter who planted the bomb. What's done can't be undone. I've been trying to keep bitterness out of it." His forgiving words fell on deaf ears. A week later, in swift retaliation, a no-warning bomb destroyed the lives of four others, including two infants, on the Shankill Road, Belfast. The distraught child, Robert McClenaghan, grew up to become an IRA bomber. So it goes, across and down the generations. Patrick McGurk, heroically forgiving to the end, survived his injuries and died in 2007.[78]

Robert James Campbell was the only UVF man convicted of the murders. In 2011 John McGurk, the youngest son of Patrick and Philomena McGurk, who himself underwent the terrifying ordeal of being trapped under concrete and rubble on that fateful night, visited the killer in his small terrace house in North Belfast.[79] "Eight times I asked him to tell me more about what happened and about the others who carried out the barbaric bombing with him. But eight times he refused – repeating over and over: 'I can't' or 'I won't.'"

The killer was aged seventy-five years at this stage, had spent fifteen years in prison, and was in poor health. He used the word "sorry" over and over again but resolutely refused to name the other killers (now believed to be dead) or to meet other children of his victims. In the end, this old man, in the shadow of death, dressed in a shabby jumper and grey sweat pants could only whisper: "I can't Mr McGurk. I am very, very sorry … You are going to [have to] leave me alone."

More typically, the confrontational tactics of the DUP, not unlike civil rights demonstrations in the 1960s, were confined to pickets, open-air demonstrations, and support for strikes, marches, and verbal shouting matches against a backdrop, let it be said, of appalling shootings, killings, and maimings that rolled on year after year. No doubt individual members harboured ambivalence towards violence. But the DUP did not advocate the assassination of its political opponents, though members of its party were assassinated. It did not bomb city centres or isolated villages, though unionist business premises were disproportionately destroyed. More generally, as a party it did not advocate violence as a means of achieving political ends.

It does not have the unblemished record of the SDLP, for instance, which has been unwavering in its pursuit of radical change by purely peaceful and democratic means.[81] But for all its street theatre, its blustering, its hard-line political stance, the DUP has a commitment to law and order, an adherence to democratic values, and an abhorrence of political violence. These values place it firmly within the democratic fold. Had this not been the case, then the resort to the gun would have been far more popular within working-class loyalism and beyond. Though I am reluctant to concede as much, the same seems true of the Orange Order, particularly in rural areas.

It is surprising, therefore, to see a simple equation being made between the DUP and Sinn Féin. Nor is this of recent vintage. I remember talking to the late John Whyte after a seminar at the Institute of Irish Studies in 1981. This was at the height of the Hunger Strike in the Maze Prison. Professor Whyte was arguably the finest scholar of the Northern Ireland Troubles and someone I respected enormously. I remarked that I was dismayed by the large numbers of Catholics and nationalists who had voted for Owen Carron, a reputed gunman, standing for Sinn Féin. "But the loyalists have got the DUP," he responded. I was so astonished by John's reply that I fell into silence. I needed to think further about the equivalence or otherwise of these two political parties.

Whether this represented John's considered opinion I have severe doubts. But there is no doubt it is a widely held view, both in the past and especially in the wake of the St Andrews Agreement. The two political extremes, one orange, the other green, were coming in from the cold to unhappily cohabit in an enforced power-sharing government. Viewed along one dimension, that of ethnic identity and national aspiration, this was indeed true: these were the extremes. But there are other dimensions to the comparison, the most important of which is adherence to democratic means in advancing a political program, and there the comparison breaks down. In Northern Ireland this was no abstract principle. It was at the heart of day-to-day existence. Sinn Féin, by contrast, exulted in the actions of the IRA.[82] If this meant setting off car bombs in built-up areas, so be it.

If this meant the assassination of political opponents, so be it. If this meant intimidating fellow nationalists, so be it. Overlapping membership between the two organisations sealed the deal.

Thus, while it is convenient to reach for equivalences – it has become almost obligatory in polite political discourse to pull one strip off the green and one strip off the orange – this rhetorical posture (decent and all as it is in ordinary conversation) does serve to cloud fundamental differences.[83] It may be a convenient fiction at times to view the DUP as the equivalent of Sinn Féin, historically speaking, but the bomb, the Armalite, the rocket launcher never formed part of the DUP kit.

PROTESTANT PARAMILITARIES

It is instructive to note that 30 years ago the IRA and the loyalist para-militaries were routinely described as "maniacs", "crazy", "blood-thirsty" or "psychopaths". This was nonsense. Politically motivated violence/terrorism is by definition mindful; it is designed to achieve a political end.
Consultant Psychiatrist, Dr Philip McGarry[84]

The first killings in the current round of the Troubles were by a gang of loyalists centred on Gusty Spence.[85] This was as far back as 1966. In some circles this is seen as the start of the Troubles, as we know them. The year 1966 also marked the fiftieth anniversary of the Easter Rising and a re-grouping of sections of the IRA round a new strategy of pursuing social as well as military struggle.[86] It is a somewhat arbitrary starting point for the latest phase of the Troubles, but it will do. Any one of the following few years might work as well. What will not do is to assume that this was the cause of the massive violence of the 1970s and beyond. The whole course of the Troubles can hardly be attributed to one set of grisly killings. There had been politico-sectarian killings of civilians in every decade since the 1920s, carried out either by loyalists or by the IRA. It is also a mug's game to try to think in terms of who started the conflict and attribute responsibility on that basis, the answer being of course "them'uns," and Irish history can be ransacked for any number of start dates to justify one set of assertions or another. We might as well go back to the sibling rivalries of Cain and Abel. The approach taken here is to view the modern Troubles as qualitatively different, with human agency kicking in at every stage of the unfurling events.

The loyalist paramilitaries, the UDA, the UVF, the Ulster Freedom Fighters, the Red Hand Commando inflicted terrible suffering on the nationalist community and to a considerable extent on their own community. "Save us from our defenders" must have been a heartfelt wish on many a Protestant housing estate, particularly during times of internecine warfare between different loyalist factions. The statistics are horrendous. Loyalist paramilitary groups were responsible for more than a thousand murders between 1966 and 1999. While they managed to kill a small number of republican militants, and a larger number of fellow loyalists, the great majority were Catholic civilians. Overall, they were responsible for almost 30 per cent of all deaths during the period.[87]

How this came about is revealing. The descent from sporadic street violence to mob violence, including the burning out of Catholic homes in the Lower Falls–Grosvenor area in 1969, led in turn to the formation of local defence associations, on both sides of the communal divide. These associations, in a short space of time, metamorphosed into armed paramilitary factions. But the really important point is why loyalist paramilitarism, from the tiniest of beginnings – Spence's 1966 gang could have been fitted inside a minibus – assumed a massive, semi-permanent form. At its height the UDA may have had 30,000 members, while several thousand volunteers passed through the ranks of the more secretive UVF.[88]

The answer is uncomfortable but simple. Loyalist paramilitarism was largely *reactive*. The response of many, which includes my own earlier views, will be to deny this. Of course loyalist violence was not purely reactive. The communal invasions of Catholic areas in the late summer of 1969, the house burnings and the expulsions were proactive, as were Catholic attacks on the police, business premises, and on some minority Protestant neighbourhoods during the same period.[89] It is also true that those under the influence of psychopathic leaders like Lenny Murphy, the head of the Shankill Butchers, would have operated until dead or imprisoned.[90] Others would have assassinated lone, vulnerable Catholics to satiate their communal hatreds, even under idealised political conditions post-1969. But nothing like the scale, intensity, and longevity of loyalist killings would have materialised without the emergence of an armed threat to the union.

With orange and green locked into a structure of mutual antagonism, violent action on the part of republicans or loyalists led to violent reaction, which fed into further action and reaction, and so the spiral of violence was reproduced through time. In this reactionary dance of death, the one energised the other. In the process, the political extremes within unionism and nationalism were strengthened and reform-oriented organisations such as the Northern Ireland Civil Rights Association, the Northern Ireland Labour Party, and the trade unions were swept aside.[91] That said, the loyalist paramilitary tradition has always been marked by ambivalence. Unlike republicanism, it has had no clear objective other than the defeat of armed nationalists, though individuals and factions within have on occasion entertained ideas of an independent Ulster, of a return to the status quo ante, or other fantastical notions. There was also the fear of sellout, the fear that Britain might conclude a deal with the neighbouring Irish republic to the detriment of the unionist people. But once the armed republican threat to unionists and the United Kingdom state was withdrawn following the Provisional IRA cessation of violence in August 1994, loyalist violence was largely switched off.[92] It is revealing that the return to bombings and killings by the Provisional IRA in 1996, as the "total cessation" of violence turned into a "temporary cessation," did not result in an immediate break in the loyalist ceasefire. These various ceasefires were "imperfect," to use the language of the times. The killing machines could not be turned off so easily: republican groups were responsible for sixty-six murders in the five-year period, 1995–99, and loyalist groups were responsible for a further forty murder victims. Many of the latter were random sectarian assassinations.[93] Loyalists and republicans also engaged in an orgy of punishment beatings and shootings during those ceasefire years.

Still the central argument remains intact, that of the reactive character of loyalist paramilitarism. Following the IRA statement of August 1994, loyalist paramilitaries lost their *raison d'etre* of "defending" loyalist areas or "taking the war" to the IRA. Even the sporadic attacks, including killings, by new IRA groupings in the quarter century since then have failed to induce a loyalist paramilitary backlash. Not that this worried unduly those within armed loyalism who were attracted by the gains to be made from drug dealing, racketeering, and a bit of gratuitous violence. Similarly, some former republican fighters found new callings in fuel laundering, drink and cigarette smuggling, as guns for hire, and even in people trafficking.

THE NORTHERN IRELAND CIVIL RIGHTS ASSOCIATION

Officially, the Association [NICRA] campaigned only on civil rights issues, but in practice its activities tended to polarise the Northern Ireland community in traditional directions.
Cameron Report[94]

In the eyes of some loyalists the Northern Ireland Civil Rights Association (NICRA) was responsible for the Troubles or at the very least its outbreak. William Craig, the authoritarian minister for Home Affairs, characterised the campaign as driven by republicans and communists.[95] Formed at the start of 1967 in Belfast, NICRA was a coalition of forces, composed of radical younger nationalists impatient for change, a smattering of reform-minded unionists, republicans (old and new style), and a small but active gaggle of communists and socialists.[96] Hard-line unionists missed the gradations of ideological colour and played into the hands of the more militant elements within NICRA and associated groupings.

The demands for reform by NICRA included "one man, one vote" (in local elections), an end to the gerrymandering of electoral boundaries, and fairness in the allocation of housing and employment in the public sector. All these demands were consistent with "British rights for British citizens" and were skilfully deployed to outmanoeuvre unionist backwoodsmen in the Stormont parliament. Two other demands, the abolition of the Special Powers Acts, which had been used repeatedly to counter the IRA, and the disbandment of the all-Protestant "B Specials" (Ulster Special Constabulary), had more of a nationalist colouration but were acceptable to some liberal unionists.

As the agitation gathered force it became both more aggressive and more communally based in the Catholic and nationalist population. This was in response to the use of excessive force by the RUC, most notably in Derry on the 5 October 1968; it was partly in response to the ratchetting up of communal tensions as a result of the Paisleyite tactic of counter demonstrations; it was also because some of the more youthful demonstrators were high on adrenaline and transported by the prospect of stone-throwing, petrol-bombing, and rioting. Others, on the even higher plane of ideology, particularly would-be student revolutionaries, saw provoking violence and inducing counterviolence from the police as essential to their objectives, be it the achievement of a socialist society or a United Ireland of one kind or another.[97]

The important point here is that the NICRA was not a single coherent entity but rather an amalgam of disparate elements, straining in different directions, that was successfully channelling deeply held grievances within the Catholic and nationalist community.[98] Not surprisingly, in view of the limited central control, the localities assumed increasing importance as time went on and some civil rights demonstrations degenerated into occasions for communal rioting.

Needless to say, this was not a movement instructed in the philosophy of nonviolence, as espoused by Mahatma Gandhi or Martin Luther King, despite the best efforts of John Hume, Austin Currie, and others. In view of the deep traditions of sectarian rioting in Ulster, it is not wholly surprising that street demonstrations spilled over into violence. This was precisely what some civil rights individuals and factions desired.[99] As time passed some seemed not to notice that the early support from a minority of liberal unionists was ebbing. These were unionists who supported civil rights but were alienated by the growing street violence and also by what they perceived as the growing convergence of civil rights and traditional Irish nationalist demands. This was true also of a number of mainstream socialists who began to withdraw.[100]

Nonetheless, the success of NICRA in winning reforms from a reluctant Stormont executive that was under intense pressure from Westminster resulted in a spectacular series of changes within a short space of time. More might well have followed. One activist feared the civil rights campaign might run out of demands, such was the initial success of their endeavours.

The question hanging in the air is this: did the activities of NICRA, in bringing thousands of essentially nationalists and Catholics out on to the streets, result in violence? Undoubtedly so, with the police and extreme loyalists making their own complementary contributions to the process

Reforms and initiatives due primarily to the civil rights movement: Northern Ireland 1968–69.

- Housing reform: a fairer, points-based system for the allocation of local-authority housing inaugurated.
- The discredited, unionist-controlled Londonderry Corporation abolished and its role taken over by a Development Commission.
- Special Powers Act: those emergency powers at variance with the European Convention on Human Rights to be abolished once security conditions permitted (but widespread disorder and the emergence of armed groups prevented the introduction of these changes).
- The company vote in local elections abolished, 22 November 1968 (but universal adult suffrage ["one man, one vote"] in local elections not conceded).
- "One man, one vote": universal adult voting rights in local government elections granted (23 April 1969).
- Local government electoral boundaries to be drawn up by an independent commission.
- An independent commissioner for complaints to investigate complaints against government departments.
- Ministry for Home Affairs: hard-line Stormont minister William Craig dismissed from office.
- Hunt Committee set up to consider reforms to the RUC.
- The Cameron Report on disturbances in Northern Ireland finds many of the grievances complained of by NICRA had validity.
- Hunt Committee recommends that the RUC becomes an unarmed civilian force and also recommends the abolition of the B Specials (a Protestant auxiliary force much resented by nationalists).
- A London Police officer, Sir Arthur Young, sent in to head up the RUC and to implement the Hunt policing reforms.
- The new post of a minister for community relations established.
- Issues of fair employment in Northern Ireland find their way onto political agendas at Westminster and Stormont (in that order). The long and tortuous journey of promoting equal opportunity in the labour market, irrespective of political, religious, or gender considerations is set in motion.

of communal confrontation. But Northern Ireland had witnessed sectarian confrontations before. From at least the late eighteenth century onwards, communal riots and sometimes killings had long disturbed public order in the north of Ireland.[101] But these had been contained historically. There was neither a necessary nor an inevitable descent into widespread and prolonged gun violence and killings in the later twentieth century. Had wiser counsels prevailed within unionism and loyalism, the reforms sought and achieved by NICRA would have helped stabilise Northern Ireland. But even without that hindsight wisdom, the NICRA effect need not have ignited decades of political violence. We need to escape the mental straitjacket of determinism and bear in mind the various *transitions* during the late 1960s from peaceful civil rights demonstrations, to civil rights demonstrations with elements of violence, to communal confrontations, and finally the descent into prolonged warfare. The last was qualitatively different and required something more as we shall discover later.

For those desiring more fundamental change, including advancing social class solidarity across the communal divide, it has to be admitted there was a downside to the later course of the largely Catholic civil rights agitation. In the words of Aaron Edwards, the late 1960s witnessed "a revitalised sectarian brinkmanship on the streets of Northern Ireland."[102] The increased communal polarisation, even before the resort to the gun, did not augur well for socialist and labour politics. One revealing index of this polarisation was the once respectable and then declining electoral fortunes of the Northern Ireland Labour Party, which drew support from both sides of the communal divide. The collapse of democratic socialism and the disintegration of cross community politics proceeded with startling pace, as is illustrated by the following figure.[103] Ethnonationalism, be it of an orange or of a green variety, not only trumped left-wing politics every time, it undermined intercommunal and class solidarity (though there is much wishful thinking then and now that asserts the opposite).

PEOPLE'S DEMOCRACY AND TROTSKYITE GROUPS

William Craig, the minister for home affairs at Stormont, caricatured the civil rights movement in Northern Ireland as a communist and republican conspiracy and did much to ensure that at least part of that claim become

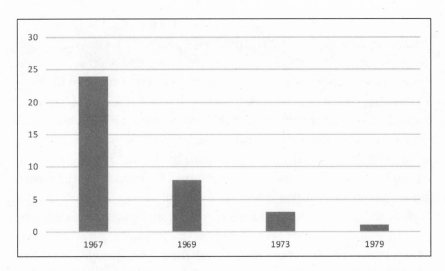

Figure 1.3 Collapse in the share of votes (%) for the Northern Ireland Labour Party, 1967–79

Source: Calculated from data sets compiled by Nicholas Whyte and published at the ARK website, http://www.ark.ac.uk/elections.
Note: The authoritative ARK website receives funding from the Economic & Social Research Council (UK). It is "a resource providing access to social and political material on Northern Ireland."

self-fulfilling.[104] Still, small, unrepresentative ultraleft groups were important catalysts in the increasing polarisation of northern society for a brief interval between 1968 and 1970. The coat-trailing People's Democracy march from Belfast to Derry in January 1969 proved to be especially effective in stoking communal fires.[105] Despite the youthful idealism and the confident assertions that Protestant–Catholic differences were merely red herrings strewn across the road to social revolution in Ireland, the reality proved bitterly disappointing. Communal rather than class conflict was the immediate and the enduring effect. Good intentions, it seems, are rarely enough.

Some of the tactics espoused by leading agitators were by times devious and self-deluding. The Cameron Report was of the opinion that youthful, would-be revolutionaries such as Eamonn McCann, Michael Farrell, and Kevin Boyle had a different notion of "nonviolence" as compared to the official position of the civil rights movement. Thus it was permissible to engage in "defensive" violent reaction to the police.[106] This was in line with the thinking of New Left groups in western Europe more generally at this time, where student leaders argued the merits of provocation in the hope of inducing violent over reaction from state forces. In the case of Northern Ireland such adventurism opened the door to a dark place where communal hatreds lurked. By no stretch of the imagination, however, can these forays into street politics be held responsible for the recrudescence of armed violence and the semipermanent form it assumed. It may be a harsh judgement but it is difficult to escape the conclusion that the youthful ideologues, many of them students or former students, had proved to be "useful idiots," to use that Leninist phrase, in a political drama they largely misunderstood.[107] The irony does not stop there. It was the *old* men – men like Billy McKee and Seán Mac Stiofáin, devout Catholics and devotees of the gun in politics – *not* the long-haired radicals who were about to command the future.[108]

THE BRITISH STATE

> The Prime Minister, on behalf of the British Government, reaffirms that they will uphold the democratic wish of the greater number of the people of Northern Ireland on the issue of whether they prefer to support the union or a sovereign united Ireland. On this basis, he reiterates, on the behalf of the British Government, that they have no selfish strategic or economic interest in Northern Ireland.
> Downing Street Declaration, 15 December 1993[109]

The conquest of Ireland, or more precisely the subjugation of the different principalities, chieftainships, and lordships that constituted the Irish polity before 1700, was at the hands of the more centralised power of first the Welsh Normans, later the English, and later still the British. The inflows in the seventeenth century of Protestant settlers, who were concentrated heavily in the northern province of Ulster, proved momentous in the long run. Imperial domination was completed and consolidated by 1700. Jumping radically forward in time, the opposition in Ulster to Daniel O'Connell's demonstrations for Catholic emancipation in the 1820s and for repeal of the union in the 1840s signalled that two of the three major ethnoreligious blocs on the island – Presbyterians and Anglicans – were following a different evolutionary trajectory to that of Irish Catholics and Irish protonationalists. The home rule controversies of the late nineteenth and early twentieth centuries only confirmed what had long been evident to even casual observers: Protestant Ulster was different and saw itself as separate from the predominantly Catholic drift towards Irish nationalism.[110]

Much ink has been spilled on the issue of whether or not the United Kingdom had economic, political, and strategic interests in Northern Ireland in the twentieth century. There is little doubt that British politicians, and particularly the Conservative Party, were committed to maintaining the constitutional link with the Protestant north, or what became the state of Northern Ireland in 1922. Whether Britain had an economic interest in Northern Ireland in the depressed interwar period is debatable (though strategic considerations would have trumped any financial considerations), but this was certainly not true from the 1970s onwards when the region was propped up by massive subsidies from the British exchequer. Moreover, as the technology of warfare changed in the postwar decades, particularly with the advent of nuclear weaponry, the military and strategic interest of Northern Ireland to Britain became peripheral at best.

As a part of the United Kingdom, though with some semidetached features, Northern Irish politicians were ultimately responsible to Westminster. Like it or not, Britain was party to the conflict, both in historical and in contemporary times. This conflict had national as well as communal dimensions. The most visible expression of this involvement was the deployment of British troops on the streets of Belfast and Derry in August 1969 and across all parts of Northern Ireland in the months and years that followed. A related and also costly corollary of the British involvement in Northern Ireland was massive subsidies to prop up living standards, not to mention dealing with deaths (seventy civilian deaths), injuries, and bomb damage in Britain itself. Public expenditure in the region was consistently much higher than tax revenue, with the result that the British exchequer was obliged to meet the gap. The subvention in recent decades ran to many billions of pounds; in the financial year 2013–14 alone it was in excess of nine billion sterling.[111] Nor is it the case that Northern Ireland had natural resources such as oil or gas or indeed other kinds of resources that were in limited supply in Britain and that might have been of some economic or strategic value.

The more detailed picture for Northern Ireland for the financial year 2013–14 is as follows (and is indicative of earlier drains on the British exchequer dating back to the 1970s):

Public sector revenue: £14.9 billion
Public sector expenditure: £24.1 billion
Deficit: £9.2 billion

This subsidy amounts to the equivalent of £5,000 per head of population in Northern Ireland, or on average £13,250 per household. The British subvention represents a huge boost to living standards in the province. Thus, in recent decades, although Britain had interests in Northern Ireland, perversely these seem to have been embedded in mainly *negative* assets. It is simply a fiction to believe that Westminster was clinging to some remnant of empire, as the more polemical critiques of British policy put it. It is also clear that British politicians wavered in their determination to retain Northern Ireland within the United Kingdom. The British prime minister Harold Wilson, we now know, seriously entertained the idea of a British withdrawal from Northern Ireland, much to the consternation of the Irish government.[112] A later prime minister, Margaret Thatcher, wondered if repartition might be a possible solution. We thus have the double irony of Irish politicians who were bound by *Bunreacht na hÉireann* (Irish constitution) to work for an all-island republic who were desperately seeking to stave off such an eventuality, while British politicians charged with upholding the integrity of the UK state were exploring means of offloading its troublesome Irish province.[113] Until a power-sharing agreement was worked out at the end of the 1990s, direct rule from Westminster remained the least-worst option as viewed by London and Dublin. The British dimension to the Northern Ireland conflict needs to be recognised, but the core constitutional problem revolves round the differing national aspirations of people within a deeply divided region. To paint an utterly imaginary scenario: if most northerners had been willing to enter a geographically enlarged Irish state in the 1970s there would have been little opposition from the British parliament, a handful of ideologues like Enoch Powell notwithstanding. (Arguably the same might have applied in 1922.) The steely resolve undergirding the British presence in Northern Ireland was the 900,000 indigenous British and Ulster unionists, not politicians sitting in the Westminster parliament or British troops on the streets of Northern Ireland.

The Belfast or Good Friday Agreement of 1998 crystallised what had long been the thinking of policy makers and politicians: while a majority of the people of Northern Ireland favoured remaining within the United Kingdom, the constitutional status quo would remain. As far back as 1973 the Sunningdale Agreement, involving Dublin, London, the SDLP and the Ulster Unionist Party, signalled the direction of change. Viewed in international terms, the British position on the Belfast Agreement was a remarkably liberal stance, as unlike most states faced with secessionist movements, ranging from Spain and France to the Russian Federation and Ukraine, the UK state has long accepted the right of a section of its citizenry to exit collectively and take a part of its sovereign territory with it.

THE IRISH STATE

As in the best detective stories, perhaps the Irish state is the shadowy suspect we tend to overlook? It is true that in the early days of the Irish Free State, the charismatic military and political leader Michael Collins authorised the smuggling of guns to northern nationalists, with a view to undermining the nascent state of Northern Ireland.[114] A little earlier Dan Breen, a leading gunman from my own county, had gone north to instruct the northern IRA in the art of killing.[115] Northern nationalists had initially boycotted many of the institutions of the unwelcome political entity within which they now found themselves. They had the support of the Irish Free State for this truculent response.[116] But this stance was not maintained, Irish taxpayers being noticeably less indulgent in matters financial than their British counterparts. Down the years there were bellicose speeches from southern political platforms, a little shriller when the main political party, Fianna Fáil, was out of office. But all major political parties, from Labour to Fianna

Fáil, subscribed to anti-Partitionist rhetoric of one kind or another. Irredentism ruled, in the Irish constitution and in public discourse.

During the 1960s, under the guidance of progressive nationalists such as Sean Lemass and Jack Lynch and with the advice of top civil servants like Ken Whitaker, the republic's northern policy had taken on a more constructive aspect.[117] This evolutionary pathway was intersected by the civil disturbances at the end of the 1960s. Several members of the Irish government were implicated in a plot to smuggle arms to the emerging Provisional IRA. These included Charles J. Haughey, later to feature in some of the worst corruption scandals in the history of the state, and Neil Blaney, the boss of bosses in the "rotten borough" of north Donegal. Neither was found guilty, but there seems little doubt that some high-ranking members of the Irish political elite were involved in smuggling weapons to the Provisionals.[118]

I had some sense of this myself. On holidays in the fishing village of Ballycotton, in County Cork, in the summer of 1973 with my Cork-born father-in-law, Gerry Barry, and his family and relatives, we were enjoying a lively conversation on socialism in the public bar of Paddy Flynn's small hotel. We were vaguely aware of a young guitar player and a companion of about the same age in another corner of the bar. My in-laws knew the musician as one of the locals; he had played with their children as a boy during summer vacations by the sea. Not long into his session, the guitar player turned angrily on our group, singling out my father-in-law for particular attention. Though the evening was still young, he had just delivered "Kevin Barry," which is a song usually associated with closing time in many an Irish pub. The charge was that our group had failed to pay due attention.

"Ye won't even listen to patriotic songs. You've sold out on your country. You go over to England and get good jobs, and then come back here in your big cars." I was fascinated by the mixture of class and national resentment. As it happened, Dr Gerry was a general practitioner in York, a Labour voter, and great supporter of the National Health Service. He refused to take on private patients on principle. He kept close ties with his native city of Cork and with his extended kin network back home.

Then the pub confrontation took a totally unexpected turn. A nephew of Dr Gerry, Dr Paddy O'Brien from Dublin, jumped to his feet, clearly stung on his uncle's behalf. "You talk about patriotism! Who here is a member of the Provisional IRA?" Complete silence. Adding to the tension, some of us, including Paddy, were aware of the off-duty Garda drinking quietly on his own in a corner of the bar. Paddy stood so smartly to attention it looked as if he was on a parade ground. "Well, *I am*. And what have *you* done for your country?" Complete silence once again. The guitar player had not only lost his voice, he seemed to shrink in size. His companion's eyes were downcast. Mrs Flynn, the owner's wife, then intervened and asked the young men to leave, which they did without fuss. Paddy I knew to be a staunch supporter of Fianna Fáil and a friend of Charlie Haughey – his daughter married one of Haughey's sons – but I wasn't aware of his connections to the IRA. Later, in the privacy of the residents' lounge, he told us how he had ferried arms in the boot of his car from Dublin to Dundalk, for the use of the Provisional IRA.[119]

There were many such examples of gun smuggling. A Belfast-born friend of mine Seán Ó Cearnaigh (Sean Kearney), a fluent Irish speaker, militant trade unionist, and veteran of the IRA campaign of the 1950s, told me how in 1970 he had driven from Donegal to the Falls Road in Belfast with a carload of weapons.[120] The deadly cargo he had received directly from a well-known Fianna Fáil senator. Seán later bitterly regretted his role in the gunrunning. Driven by emotion, he had felt defensive action against Protestant mobs was necessary. But as defensive postures translated into offensive action, with gun and bomb attacks on the security forces, on Protestant businesses, and civilians, he became an outspoken and courageous critic of the Provisional IRA, in not one but two languages.[121]

Another was the great trade union and labour organiser Paddy Devlin, whom I came to know in his later career. Pugnacious as ever, Paddy had stood up to the Provisional IRA over the hunger strikes, which he saw as having sectarian undertones. Though we never discussed it, I knew Paddy had been seeking guns to defend Catholic areas way back in 1969. Like Seán, he had rethought his political position as the northern conflict took on a distinctly tribal colouration.

No doubt there were many such acts during the confusion and mayhem of 1969 and 1970. But it has to be acknowledged that the Irish state, as distinct from some powerful individuals therein, did not engage in such adventurism, and the wise counsels of Jack Lynch and Liam Cosgrave, both *taoisigh* during the 1970s, prevailed.[122] The ship of state remained on the conciliatory course charted in the mid-1960s by Lemass and Whitaker.[123]

Unionist critics would no doubt object that there were some absurd decisions on extradition handed down by Irish judges, that there is evidence of collusion between a few members of the Garda and republican paramilitaries, and that the Irish security forces were less than diligent at times in picking up IRA suspects.[124] There is little doubt that these acts of commission and omission led to tragedy north of the border. Moreover, the Fianna Fail-supporting daily newspaper the *Irish Press* sometimes descended into a variant of green jingoism. This must have provided some comfort for Sinn Féin and the IRA.

All this may well be true, indeed it would be difficult to deny the charges, but they relate to individuals and groups rather than to the state itself. It is clear that throughout the period of the Troubles, the Irish state and the main political parties – Fianna Fáil, Fine Gael and Labour – insisted that Irish unity could only come about by agreement, not by force of arms, thus robbing republican paramilitary organisations of any claims to democratic legitimacy. Where republicans transgressed the laws of the Republic of Ireland, they were imprisoned. Portlaoise Jail is a tangible reminder of that.[125] And a creaky extradition system did exist between the Irish and British states. While more could have been done, Ireland was not the safe haven for fugitive IRA members so frequently alleged by angry and frustrated unionists. I suspect future historians will judge more harshly the fumbling of the Irish state during the Troubles and the ambivalence of sections of southern society more generally (in part a failure to rethink traditional narratives), but none will assert that the dynamic of violence was deliberately promoted and sustained across the decades by the Irish state.[126]

THE INLA, THE IPLO, PLA, AND OTHER REPUBLICAN SPLINTER GROUPS

The INLA was formed as a breakaway from the official republican movement. The INLA and its various offshoots were responsible for large numbers of killings, as well as bombings and injuries, but they were not the principal agencies of death. The INLA and the later IPLO – a breakaway

Dominic McGlinchey: the "finest republican of them all"

The career of Dominic McGlinchey epitomised in extreme form the almost nihilistic quality of republican socialist terror. He admitted, almost casually it seems, that he could not recall precisely how many people he had killed but it was "around the thirty mark."[129] Slight of stature, he was a commanding figure when holding a gun in his hand. In the same interview, asked what he felt about his victims, he added, "I do what has to be done and don't think about it thereafter." On another occasion he revealed that he liked to "get in close" when dispatching his victims. Some were UDR men and RUC men, or ex-members of the security forces, or civilians; some were his comrades or former comrades. He also allegedly carried out interrogations with a red-hot poker of members of the INLA he suspected of disloyalty.[130] He "masterminded" the bombing of the Droppin Well Inn in 1982 in which eleven soldiers and seven civilians were killed. Though he condemned the action, he admitted the INLA was indirectly linked to an attack in 1983 on a Protestant mission hall at Darkley in South Armagh, close to the Irish border.[131] Three members of an evangelical prayer group were shot dead and others wounded as they sang out "Are you washed in the Blood of the Lamb?"[132]

Mary McGlinchey, his wife, was also a member of the INLA and is said to have played her part in the execution of two fellow republicans, as well as in other operations. In 1987 she came close to being washed in the blood of her own children. A gunman entered her house in Dundalk and then pushed his way into the bathroom where she was bathing her two sons. The ten-year-old Declan recalled his mother saying, "Not in front of my children."[133] In all probability, the murder was an act of vengeance carried out by former comrades.

At the time of his wife's execution Dominic was in prison in Portlaoise Jail in the Republic of Ireland. Seemingly inevitably due to the nature of extremist conspiratorial groups, Dominic McGlinchey was shot dead by former associates after his release from the Irish prison a few years later. In a graveside oration Bernadette McAliskey, who had campaigned for civil rights in the 1960s, described him as "the finest Republican of them all."[134] She added, to cheers, "This man never in the whole of his life dishonoured the cause he believed in." According to his own lights, that was probably true.

from the parent body – seem to have attracted more than their fair share of brutish individuals and much energy was ploughed into executing fellow volunteers, sometimes after torture, in the name of fighting "imperialism."[127] By the close of the twentieth century they had killed 150 people, a fair number of whom were their own members.[128]

Prone to fracturing, and in later years heavily involved in drug dealing and racketeering, the INLA disintegrated into feuding factions. One grouping, the IPLO, was forced to disband by the Provisional IRA in November 1992, following what was dubbed the "night of the long knives." Some former members of the INLA took up full-time criminal careers with Dublin-based drug gangs and as gunmen for hire. Despite the viciousness of these groupings and their penchant for violence, they were largely incidental to the trajectory of the wider conflict.

THE OFFICIAL IRA

We stand not on the brink of victory, but on the brink of sectarian disaster.
Liam McMillen, Official IRA, 1973[135]

The IRA had been undergoing a process of politicisation in the later 1960s under the influence of a Marxist-leaning leadership. The principal ideologue, urging a shift away from militarism towards social activism, was the Dublin-based academic Roy Johnston. (He features briefly again in the final chapter of this book.) In the process, this conspiratorial organisation lost some of its more socially conservative activists, some of whom, such as Seamus Twomey and Joe Cahill, became active again when street clashes erupted during the summer and autumn of 1969. The civil rights agitation meshed readily with the IRA leadership's critique of conservative political structures, north and south. It offered the opportunity, as its strategists saw it, to link social and economic demands to the "national question."[136]

Members of the IRA participated in the early civil rights movement but, it is important to emphasise, the IRA did not in any sense control the movement. At the early demonstrations it supplied stewards who sought to contain attacks on police lines.[137] It is no accident though that IRA men were attracted to the role of providing "muscle" on the demonstrations. It is no surprise either, as time went by, that members of the IRA switched to more aggressive roles. At a civil rights march in Newry in early 1969, the IRA stewards attacked the police after they had attempted to reroute the march. Six police vehicles were burned. Seamus Costello, a leading member of the IRA, was arrested after helping push an RUC Land Rover into the Newry Canal. There were other instances. So it goes.

The IRA split in 1969 over the direction of the leadership and the deteriorating situation in Northern Ireland. Among the charges levelled by the dissidents was the "extreme socialism" of the organisation, its recognition of "foreign parliaments," and letting down nationalists in the north.[138] Out of this thinking was born the Provisional IRA in December 1969. In the following month the political wing of the IRA, the Sinn Féin party, also split. There were now two IRAs, known to the public as the Official IRA and the Provisional IRA and each had its corresponding political wing, labelled with pleasing symmetry Official Sinn Féin and Provisional Sinn Féin. The old names are best, it seems.

The Official IRA was involved in what it termed "defensive" military action in Northern Ireland in 1970 and 1971 and this included killing a number of British soldiers and police and bombing a variety of targets. It was also involved in feuding with the now competing Provisional IRA. The Official IRA, at least at leadership level, was concerned that its actions should not aggravate Protestant–Catholic divisions. The breakaway or dissident Provisional IRA was much more comfortable with riding the dragon of communal sectarianism. But it is also fair to say that in the early stages of the Troubles the Official IRA did much to advance the militarisation of the conflict and of course it had no mandate for its actions from the Irish peoples, north or south.

As Northern Ireland slipped deeper into a three-cornered shooting match involving republican paramilitaries, loyalist paramilitaries, and the security forces (RUC, UDR, and regular British troops), with associated communal rioting and mob violence, the Official IRA did a radical rethink of its strategy. It declared a unilateral ceasefire on 29 May 1972.[139] Earlier attempts to limit the range of targets – members of the RUC and the UDR were not to be shot at except in cases of retaliation – had fallen into chaos. The fears underlying this volte-face were summed up the following year in the chilling words of a leading republican and civil rights campaigner: "We stand not on the brink of victory, but on the brink of sectarian disaster."[140]

The truce did not mark an end to armed hostilities. Later killings and so-called punishment attacks were carried out by the organisation, there were feuds with other republican groups, and there was criminal activity on a large scale. But an ideology that stressed antisectarianism and working-class solidarity meant that the scale of armed action was severely curbed in the aftermath of its ceasefire. The ceasefire proved to be permanent, though some disgruntled volunteers, seeking action, drifted off into alternative paramilitary groups. As one restless northerner asked plaintively during the arguments leading up to the ceasefire, "who can we shoot?" [if not the police or army].[141]

This winding down of military action by the Official IRA is hugely significant in terms of illuminating alternative possibilities within the northern conflict. Had other republican groups emulated the Official IRA in its radical rethink of armed struggle, then there is every reason to believe that loyalist violence towards the nationalist community would have assumed a downward trend during the 1970s and eventually would have fizzled out. Freed from the dilemma of fighting on two fronts, the security forces would have been well positioned to bear down on residual loyalist terror and also offer more effective protection to Catholics and nationalists.[142]

Almost 400 people had lost their lives between 1966 and the end of May 1972. But we now know that more than three thousand others, mainly civilians, would follow them to the grave. That harrowing requiem to the Troubles, *Lost Lives*, calculates that there were 3,636 Troubles-related deaths by 1999 and at the time of writing the total is approaching 4,000.[143] Most of these lives could have been *saved* had other armed republican groups followed the lead presented by the Official republicans. This is a shocking realisation. It bears repeating. Had all republican groups called off their armed offensives in the early summer of 1972, then in the region of 3,000 lives could have been saved.[144] Tens of thousands would have escaped injury in shootings and bomb explosions.[145] Thousands more would have escaped the wrath of paramilitary vigilantes. Billions of pounds worth of damage to homes, businesses, and infrastructure could have been averted, while the trauma of many tens of thousands of relatives of victims need not have been experienced. Moreover, the lives and families of thousands of volunteers within loyalist and republican paramilitary organisations would also have benefited, as many of these would go on to experience jail, disrupted personal and kin relationships, mental health problems, alcoholism, and drug addiction.[146] Their partners, wives and children might also have escaped some of the domestic violence that has been linked to paramilitarism.[147] Research by Ulster University points to almost a quarter of a million adults in Northern Ireland suffering from mental health problems, with at least half of these being directly related to the Troubles.[148] The chain of trauma doesn't end there. In some, perhaps most, families the consequences of Troubles-related trauma are transmitted down the generations, to children and grandchildren, adding further layers of suffering to the toll of what, in the final resort, was *avoidable* loss.[149] As has been said, the bullets keep on travelling.

Figure 2.1 *Authoring Insurrection*: Martin Meehan mural, North Belfast

2

Responsibility and Its Burdens

It takes after all very few people to kill enough people to frighten
a very large number.
Frank Wright, *Northern Ireland*

INTRODUCTION

The opening chapter assessed the role of a range of historical actors in igniting, driving, and perpetuating the conflict in Northern Ireland. The elephant in the room begins to come into focus. The IRA split into two organisations at the end of 1969, comprising those who came to be known as the Official IRA and the breakaway grouping of the Provisional IRA. Shortly afterwards, in January 1970, the political front for the IRA, Sinn Féin, split along parallel lines. The Provisional IRA was mainly northern based, imbued with the fears of a beleaguered Catholic minority – a Defenderist mentality – but at leadership level also aspiring to a united Ireland secured by force of arms.[1] As with loyalist mobs, it could also tap into deep traditions of communal sectarianism and was uninhibited in switching on rioting when it suited in the early years of the conflict.[2]

A united Ireland promised not only a fairer future for northern Catholics and the realisation of their dreams of nationhood. Such an outcome carried the primal satisfaction of a decisive victory over the communal enemy, the northern Protestants and unionists. A variety of emotions, those of fear, anger, hatred, coexisted and sometimes predominated over more abstract political ideals. Interestingly, southern republicans, even of the Provisional persuasion, seem not to have shared this visceral dislike of unionists and unionism.[3]

It may be unfair to appear to be reserving the leading role in the drama that was the Troubles for the Provisional IRA. Its self-understanding is quite different and deserves to be given serious consideration. Might its activism not be understood as a quest for social justice? That is a more straightforward explanation and one that has been given repeated emphasis by the republican leadership in the decades since the end of the "armed struggle."

The trouble with this line of argument is that many of the key reforms in housing, local government, and voting had been conceded by the time the Provisional IRA went on the offensive. Even a largely unarmed police force, the RUC, was on the cards following the reforms proposed in the Hunt Report on policing.[4] The remarkable record of success of the civil rights movement and other reform groups, as argued earlier, showed the potential for further reform. But the new game in town was not reform. Henceforth, and for three grim decades, the progression from rioting, petrol bombing, tarring-and-feathering to torture, car bombings, assassinations, and mass killings, under the direction of the Provisional IRA, served to sideline conventional politics and street agitation.

The word equality was an oft-repeated mantra in Sinn Féin statements during the 1990s and beyond. However, in a speech to members in Enniskillen in November 2014, the president of Sinn Féin, Gerry Adams, seemed to suggest that pressing for equality was merely "the Trojan horse of the entire republican strategy."[5] This was qualified in subsequent statements. Irrespective of the precise meaning, the historical record as revealed in republican publications such as *An Phoblacht* does not suggest that demands for equality or social justice were the principal motivating factors in the Provisionals' campaign.

Communal Defence

If the Provisionals were not primarily about reforms targeting social justice and equality, perhaps they were about communal defence. There is little doubt that the notion of being defenders of the people is hugely important in terms of the self-image of both republican and loyalist paramilitaries. Strangely it is an almost wholly mythical conception, which is why the same few examples taken from 1969–70 tend to be recycled in republican and loyalist narratives.[6] If one looks across the period of the Troubles as a whole it is quickly evident that neither loyalist nor republican paramilitaries had the capabilities to defend their respective communities from attack.[7] Otherwise how was it that a handful of people were murdered in

intercommunal violence in the generation before paramilitary organisations adopted the role of *defenders*, whereas thousands died after 1969?
How was it that so few republican paramilitaries were killed by loyalists
and so few loyalist paramilitaries were killed by republicans once the
Troubles got under way?

Three Catholic civilians were murdered by loyalists between 1966 and
the end of 1969, that is before the Provisional IRA became the ostentatious
defenders of the Catholic and nationalist people.[8] But three decades of
"defensive" endeavour thereafter resulted in the murders of well over 500
Catholics by loyalist killers. The IRA had a hopeless record in preventing
deaths such as these: less than 2 per cent of IRA killings, or twenty-eight to
be precise, were of loyalist paramilitaries.[9] The story doesn't end there. The
IRA added hundreds to the Catholic death toll through its own murderous
attacks on Catholic civilians. From time to time it also executed republicans
from other factions or, more usually, from within its own ranks. In addition, and right through the Troubles and beyond, Catholics were subjected
to paramilitary-style shootings or maimings, mainly at the hands of the
IRA. A number of Catholics were simply "disappeared." To add a further
macabre fact: a majority of violent deaths within the ranks of the IRA itself
was inflicted not by the RUC, the UDR, or the British Army, as one might
have expected, but was due to other agencies.[10] In fact only 40 per cent of
the deaths suffered by the IRA were due to the security forces. A major
danger facing an IRA volunteer, it turns out, came from other comrades
within the republican movement, either by accident or by design. Many
met violent ends because they were executed by their fellow-volunteers,
because of internecine feuding, because inexperienced volunteers died
handling guns or explosives. Remarkably, one out of every two deaths of
IRA volunteers was due to the IRA itself.[11]

Ending the "British Presence" in Ireland

So, if the *casus belli* was not social justice and it was not defence, then what
was it? The simple and incontrovertible fact is that Sinn Féin and its "cut-
ting-edge," the IRA, sought to coerce the Protestants and unionists of the
north into an enlarged nationalist state. The sanitised version of the three
decades of armed struggle, one that was propagated with particular fervour

during the fortieth anniversary marking the start of the civil rights movement, was that the Provisional IRA's campaign was little more than a continuation of the campaign for civil rights by other means. The reality was
very different. Back in 1970 at the formation of the Provisional republican
movement its foundational principle was set out: "On this the first issue
of this paper we wish to say bluntly and openly that we are standing on
the 'Rock of the Republic.'"[12] It went on to assure its readers that the IRA
"will not be diverted into the parliamentary blind-alleys of Westminster,
Leinster House and Stormont." The first leader of the Provisional IRA,
London-born John Stephenson (later rendered as Séan Mac Stiofáin), recorded in his memoir, "we believe that only by force of arms can Ireland
achieve her complete freedom."[13] Writing in 1975, he promised that the
renewed IRA campaign would be prosecuted with "the utmost ferocity
and ruthlessness" to win Irish freedom.[14] In his world view, "revolutionary
violence is the only way for an oppressed people to win their freedom."[15]

Mac Stiofáin was stating no more than the obvious for the faithful. A
policy statement by (Provisional) Sinn Féin in 1972, the most lethal year
of the entire Troubles, read as follows: "Ever since Tone, Republicans have
always recognised that the only ultimate factor influencing the imperialists
is force or the threat of force."[16] When the IRA declared a ceasefire in 1997,
effectively marking the end of armed hostilities against the British state
(but not the wider community), it reminded everyone that the IRA was
still "committed to ending British rule in Ireland. It is the root cause of divisions and conflict in our society."[17] Civil rights, equality, and so much
else were more incidental concerns.

It takes a considerable communal blindness and a huge propaganda
machine to drive these uncomfortable truths to the edge of consciousness.
Moreover, the militarism of the IRA served to induce murderous attacks
on Catholics, thereby increasing rather than reducing the vulnerability of
Catholics to politico-sectarian attack. (For some, a convenient misreading
was that the cumulatively rising death toll of Catholic civilians was a demonstration of the continuing need for the IRA.) But the IRA was by no
means impotent. What the IRA could offer on the road to a united Ireland
was the sweet odour of *vengeance*.

What the "Struggle" meant

We will erect the Irish Republic again in all its glory no matter what it costs and like Pearse "We know of no way by which freedom can be obtained and when obtained, maintained, except by armed men."
An Phobhlacht, February 1970

We can only have peace and justice in our land when the last vestige of British Imperialism has been driven from our shores, and driven from our shores they will by the Volunteer Soldiers of Óglaigh na hÉireann.
Joe Cahill, *An Phobhlacht,* July 1971

Sinn Féin leaders "have said and will continue to say that a real peace process has to end partition and Britain's role in Ireland."
Editorial, *An Phobhlacht* 15 April 1993 on the occasion of the Sinn Féin Annual Commemoration of the 1916 Rising, Easter 1993. Similar sentiments may be found at virtually any Easter commemoration before or since.

In particular, we pay tribute to those who have given their lives in the last 25 years to ensure that this generation of Irish people will be the last to live or die under British rule. It is our generation and the many young people in front of us here who will begin to shape a free and independent Ireland, ruled by the men and women of Ireland and not by the laws or the guns of a foreign government.
Bairbre de Brún (later a Sinn Féin MEP), *An Phobhlacht,* 15 April 1993

There has never been a generation of republicans like this one. This is the only generation not to have been beaten … the only generation committed to carrying on the struggle until a democratic Ireland is in place.
Jim McAllister, Sinn Féin councillor, *An Phobhlacht,* 15 April 1993.

We are especially proud of our republican patriot dead and each of our fallen comrades with whom we are gathered to remember, honour and whose lives we celebrate here today.
Michelle O'Neill, leader of Sinn Féin in the "North," at the "Loughgall Martyrs" 30th Anniversary Commemorative Parade, April 2017.[18]

Vengeance

Both sets of paramilitaries were pretty good at vengeance, as the tally of intercommunal killings testifies. Innocent-sounding place names like Monaghan, Kingsmill, Enniskillen, Teebane Cross, Poyntzpass, Greysteel, Loughinisland, Ormeau Road, Omagh are inscribed in the memories of the survivors of mass killings. Tombstones across the province bear cold witness. The bombing of McGurk's Bar on the corner of North Queen Street in Belfast in 1971 and the carnage at Frizzell's fish shop on the nearby Shankill Road a generation later were prime expressions of communal sectarianism, albeit framed in terms of wider political motivations. These bookended a grim catalogue of other multiple killings.

The unpalatable, unacknowledged truth on both sides of the paramilitary divide was that these organisations could only inflict *vengeance* on the other side, the odd exception notwithstanding. The Troubles claimed close on four thousand lives, most of them civilians, and the vast majority of killings were due to agencies other than the police and the army. The stark facts are set out in the table below (which does not cover the later years). As defenders – self-styled, self-deluded, or otherwise – paramilitaries proved not only ineffectual but counterproductive in terms of communal defence. Each *invited* vengeance killings from the other side and thus unionist and nationalist working-class neighbourhoods were trapped in a world of mutually assured terror. The inevitable outcome was an ever-rising death toll on both sides of the communal divide. This was true of the communal conflicts of the 1920s; it was true again in the 1970s, the 1980s, and the 1990s.

The table above is as good a thumbnail sketch of the Troubles as any, drawing on what is possibly the most disturbing book ever published on this complex conflict. Still, a hugely important observation must be added. *Lost Lives* catalogues *deaths* only, thereby capturing a fraction of the Troubles' impact. More than 40,000 others, mainly civilians, suffered injuries, some of the most life-changing kind, with knock-on effects for their close relatives and friends. Most of these injuries were due to paramilitary organisations; some were from shootings but more often were due to bomb explosions. To appreciate the sheer intensity of these attacks within a small population, it may be more meaningful for some readers to see the

Table 2.1
Agencies Responsible for Deaths During the Troubles, 1966–99

All deaths:
The number of Troubles-related deaths: 3,636
Republicans were responsible for six out of every ten deaths (59%)
The Provisional IRA was responsible for half of all deaths (49%)
Loyalist were responsible for three out of every ten deaths (29%)
The security forces were responsible for one out of every ten deaths (10%).

Civilian deaths:
The number of Troubles-related civilian deaths: 2,037
as a proportion of all deaths: 56%
Number of Catholic civilian deaths: 1,232
Number of Protestant civilian deaths: 698
Number of civilian deaths due to the IRA: 636

Combatant deaths:
Deaths suffered by republican volunteers: 392
Deaths suffered by loyalist volunteers: 144
Deaths suffered by the security forces: 1,012
Paramilitary deaths as a proportion of combatant deaths: 35%
Paramilitary deaths as a proportion of all deaths: 15%

Deaths by Religion:
The number of Catholic civilian deaths: 1,232
The number of Protestant civilian deaths: 698
Most Catholic civilian deaths were at the hands of loyalists
Most Protestant civilian deaths were at the hands of republicans.

Provisional IRA deaths:
Number of PIRA volunteers killed in the Troubles: 293
as a proportion of all deaths: 8%
Deaths of PIRA volunteers: proportion due to the Security forces: 40%
Deaths of PIRA volunteers: proportion *not* due to the Security forces: 60%

Loyalist paramilitaries killed by the Provisional IRA: 28
As a proportion of all PIRA killings: less than 2%

Irish-born persons as a proportion of all deaths: greater than 80%

Source: Calculated from McKittrick et al., *Lost Lives* (1999), 1473–84

deaths and injuries projected onto a British or an American scale. Relative to the population size of Britain, for instance, we are speaking, in round figures, of 130,000 deaths and one and a half million injuries. This number of deaths is three times that experienced by Britons during the Blitz of the Second World War.

A number of fundamental points emerge from table 2.1. There is the sheer longevity of the conflict, which was some five times the duration of World War II. Ethnic conflicts, where there isn't a decisive winner, tend to have that characteristic. Most of the casualties were civilian and most were killed by paramilitary organisations. Contrary to populist accounts, only a small minority of civilian casualties were due to the security forces. The RUC, despite being the object of much ideological and communal hatred, was responsible for less than 2 per cent of *civilian* deaths and also less than 2 per cent of Troubles-related deaths more generally. Most civilian deaths were Catholic, which is in accordance with popular impressions of the Troubles. Most suffered at the hands of loyalist assassins, but substantial numbers were sent to the graveyard by armed groups from within the Catholic community. The Provisional IRA, for one, killed 198 Catholic civilians up to 1999 and well over 200 for later end dates. It was also responsible for the deaths, for one reason or another, of 161 republican volunteers. The families of these victims might be surprised to learn that this was more than five times its kill-rate against loyalist paramilitaries, who were ostensibly enemies of the IRA. There are no statistics that I know of for the ethnoreligious breakdown of the tens of thousands injured, though the likelihood is that the majority of victims were Protestant since Protestant town centres and businesses were disproportionately targeted.

Security force deaths were two and a half times more frequent than those of republican paramilitaries and seven times more frequent than those of loyalist paramilitaries. This sets Northern Ireland apart from many insurgencies in the twentieth-century world where state forces typically inflicted disproportionate casualties on other armed groups. During the Algerian struggle for independence, 1954–62, for instance, at least 300,000 people were killed – some estimates are much higher – and most of those slaughtered were Muslims.[19] Or to take a single incident, when an Arab demonstration turned violent in May 1945, in a prefiguration of later atrocities, mobs attacked and killed more than a hundred white Europeans. The French army and French vigilantes retaliated by killing more than a thousand Algerian Muslims, a disproportion of ten-to-one or the reverse of the Northern Ireland pattern.[20]

Civilian Deaths

The highly-respected writer and journalist Peter Taylor has compared the Provisional IRA and Islamist extremists and has come to the conclusion that while the latter sought to attack and kill civilians indiscriminately, the IRA did not set out to kill civilians, with a few notable exceptions such as the killing of five Orangemen, and the attempted killing of others, at Tullyvallen Orange Hall in 1975 and the group execution of Protestant workers at Kingsmill the following year.[21] The first contention is undoubtedly true but the second has to be questioned. In fact, the Provisional IRA, as well as the Official IRA and republican splinter groups, was responsible for the deaths of hundreds of civilians and the wounding of many others whom they *deliberately* rather than accidentally targeted. Civilians were targeted for a variety of motives: it could be because they were politicians, because they lived in border areas, because they supplied building work, food or other services to the security forces, because they were former police or soldiers, because they were industrialists, because they were judges, lawyers, magistrates, because they were witnesses to an incident, because they drank in certain pubs, because they had personal differences with paramilitary "hard men," because they were presumed to be spies, because they were alleged drug dealers. The list is a long one, even if one does not include (though some would) the twenty-nine prison staff who were also killed. The Provisional IRA was reluctant to admit publicly some of these "hits." Others it was more than happy to acknowledge: "In a brilliantly planned and firmly disciplined operation two members of the judiciary were simultaneously executed as top agents of the system which has oppressed the Irish people for so many centuries."[22] These were Judge Rory Conaghan and Martin McBirney, a resident magistrate. Conaghan came from the Catholic community and McBirney was a former chairman of the Northern Ireland Labour Party.

An alternative reading of this event is offered by the poet Paul Durcan who possesses authority beyond that of poet, at least for some (and assuming that is possible), by virtue of his blood relationship to John McBride, one of the executed leaders of the Rising in Dublin, Easter 1916. Durcan, a living member of the patriotic dynasty, links the death of his aunt, Sara Mary, to contemporaneous deaths in Belfast. The poem is entitled "At the grave of my Aunt Sara Mary" and is from his collection *The Laughter of Mothers*.[23]

On the morning she died two heroes of the IRA,
September 16th, 1974,
separately arriving at the houses of two judges in Belfast,
shot them both dead in front of their daughters
as they were eating their breakfasts, cornflakes and sugar,
so that old daily Ireland might be a nation once again.

An Phobhlacht might also exude an air of nonchalance on civilian death and injury, as in its report of the killing of a former UDR man and worker at St Luke's Hospital, Armagh. "The booby trap bomb attack on the former UDR soldier ... took place on Friday, February 19th, just after lunch time as he left work, where he was a foreman engineer in the maintenance of St Luke's hospital in Armagh city. The car, a blue Vauxhall Chevette, had travelled about five hundred yards when the explosion occurred, blowing off both his legs." *An Phobhlacht* mentioned in parentheses, perhaps by way of exculpation, that the victim had "left the regiment only two months earlier."[24] The incidental detail serves to give the impression of a professional and entirely legitimate operation.

Taylor is right to insist that the IRA was not like Islamist terrorists and right to say attacking civilians was not the dominant aspect of the republican insurgency. (He might perhaps have allowed a qualification or two to his argument in that many of the attacks on serving members of the UDR and the RUC took place in a *civilian context*, when off-duty and out farming, shopping, visiting sick relatives or enjoying a drink.[25]) Furthermore, one of the IRA's favourite weapons, the bomb, was unlikely to distinguish between security forces and civilians. In any case, as indicated above, he is wrong to believe that the direct targeting of civilians was not a significant part of republican activity. Moreover, when we consider that republicans, and loyalists for that matter, targeted thousands of civilians in punishment shootings or mutilations, some of which resulted in death, what looks like a plausible hypothesis to begin with simply collapses under the weight of a multitude of "exceptions."

There are other aspects to the killings of the Troubles. Viewed through the prisms of social class and gender, of those meeting violent deaths a disproportionate number (and in all likelihood a majority) were working-class and male. This is as might be expected. But there are two further findings from the analysis of the data on deaths that, for me at least, packed a surprise. The first is perverse, though of course only if one takes the rhetoric of republicanism at face value. According to the script, the "war" was not against the Protestant and unionist people of Northern Ireland. After all, they were simply misguided members of the Irish nation who would one day wake up to this realisation and embrace their true identity. The "war" was against the British army of occupation and its withdrawal from Northern Ireland was a necessary condition for unionist self-realisation. If so, one might imagine that soldiers of the British Army would be the principal targets and would be heavily represented among the casualties. Was this the case? The fact is that of the 3,600 or so Troubles-related deaths in Northern Ireland, less than 15 per cent of this total – 13.8 per cent to be precise – were soldiers of the regular British Army.[26] The equally startling or perhaps more startling fact is that more than *four-fifths* of the fatal casualties of the Troubles were *Irish* (in the sense of being born on the island of Ireland). In practice it would seem the Troubles was a form of communal and civil war, man against man, fought out largely within the confines of Northern society.[27]

THE RISE OF THE PARAMILITARIES

In Northern Ireland paramilitary casualties in the conflict were relatively light in what must have been one of the most luxuriously conducted and concluded insurgencies of modern times. The typical fate of a volunteer was imprisonment. Most surrendered easily, whether loyalist or republican, and that was that. Many became informants. Most prisoners were released soon after the Belfast Agreement in 1998. Some who had not been apprehended were give royal pardons. But the two sets of paramilitaries inflicted heavy suffering on their host communities, as well as on members of their own organisations or on competing organisations within their own ethno-religious bloc. The most lethal "killing machine" by far was the Provisional IRA.

The Provisional IRA also spearheaded the early paramilitary killings, those of 1966 excepted. This is another aspect of the Troubles that is insufficiently realised. Loyalist retaliation was of course highly likely in such circumstances, but it is worth noting that loyalist paramilitaries got into the killing game fairly slowly (see table 2.2). In 1970, for instance, the Provisionals killed eighteen people, which contrasts with the one victim who was murdered by loyalist paramilitaries. In *bliain an áir* (year of destruction) of the modern Troubles – the year 1972 – the killing ratio narrowed but the republican rate was still more than double that of loyalists. It is true the British army was responsible for one particularly dreadful atrocity in that year, Bloody Sunday in Derry, and this had catastrophic implications for public order. The year 1972 was the worst year for killings by the British army. These numbered seventy-nine, or eighty if one includes the one killing by the UDR. This was less than one-third of the number of lives extinguished by republicans in the same year.

Sociologists and political scientists have a tendency to work their way from the summit of state power down to lower levels in attempting to explain local political disorder. The laudable ambition to offer structural interpretations that encompass the totality of relationships might begin with the international order, or in the case of the Troubles it might begin with Irish–British relations. Some come close to fetishizing state structures and betray a naïve view of power hierarchies. There is no doubt there is something satisfying, not least aesthetically, in moving from the general to the specific. What could be more natural than tracing lines of causation from the apex of the power structures downwards to the lower level, constituent units. In terms of explanatory weight the higher levels of the power structure are presumed to enjoy disproportionate influence and those impacts are more-or-less transitive from one level to the next. These assumptions, often of an implicit kind, permeate much writing on Northern Ireland and possibly on divided societies elsewhere. They might

Table 2.2
Number of Killings by Republican and Loyalist Paramilitary Organisations, 1969–72

	By Republicans	By Loyalists
1969	5	3
1970	21	1
1971	107	22
1972	280	121

Source: Calculated from McKittrick et al., *Lost Lives* (1999), 1475–6.

be valid if we were talking about a Stalinist, a Nazi, or a highly authoritarian power structure. We are not.

Restraints on the exercise and transmission of crude power are built into democratic societies. For these and other reasons people in the localities exercise considerable autonomy, sometimes even countervailing power when it comes to reproducing or aggravating national, racial, ethnic, or sectarian relationships in a local setting. The quicksilver quality of social difference or social prejudice allows it to slip the institutional restraints. This is true, *a fortiori*, when national, ethnic, or sectarian difference crystallises into armed insurgencies. When state forces overreact with lethal power the problems are compounded, paradoxically strengthening the power and autonomy of locally based insurgents operating within a host community. One of the lessons of the Northern Ireland conflict is not only the degree of agency but the degree of effective power exercised by paramilitary organisations in the localities, despite the attentions of the apparently all-powerful state.

WAS THE "LONG WAR" INEVITABLE?

There were long-standing historical conditions, structures of inequality, and patterns of symbolic negation, as well as much else that made social discontent and conflict possible and even likely in Northern Ireland.[28] But an insurgency wasn't remotely inevitable. This required agency and entrepreneurial activity on the part of men and women at the end of the 1960s.

In the United States, where the grossest abuses of power – economic discrimination, political discrimination, segregated schools and segregated public spaces, vigilante attacks, and mob killings – had rained down on the African American population, a widespread insurgency never materialised. Comparisons between the plight of African Americans and Catholics in Northern Ireland, as deployed by some civil rights campaigners and still reproduced by extreme nationalist groups in Ireland and America, while wide of the mark, were polemically useful. Black America did not, however, follow Northern Ireland over the precipice into armed communal confrontation. Demonstrations and other forms of nonviolent protest proved far more potent than posturing with guns.[29] As in Northern Ireland, there were other ways.

AN ANALOGUE: THE OPPRESSION OF WOMEN

There is another parallel that might be invoked that is much nearer home. In the 1960s a majority of the Northern Irish population was discriminated against in the workplace, in the legal system, in the civil service, in teaching, in virtually every aspect of public life. These were the women of the north. That there were more oppressive burdens on women in the Republic of Ireland was small comfort. Contraception and divorce were prohibited in the republic in the early 1970s and a report a few years earlier had found that only 1 per cent of women occupied posts in the higher professions and just 6 per cent were in managerial roles).[30] A raft of legislative and other changes in Britain and Ireland in the 1970s removed the major formal obstacles to women's advancement, though it is the case that much remains to be done to redress inequalities in relation to income differentials, opportunities for promotion, and participation in politics. It is also true that more controversial areas of policy and morality, such as access to abortion, are still the subject of debate, though not only between politicians and people but also between different groups of women. Nonetheless progress has been steady and cumulative. In view of the pervasive inequalities along gender lines in Northern Irish society in the 1960s, might women not have taken up the gun and the bomb to accelerate the pace of reform, in a more militarist version of the Suffragettes of the early twentieth century?

The Status of Women in Northern Ireland

In the pivotal decade of the 1960s there was a yawning gender pay gap in Northern Ireland. The average hourly pay of women, relative to men, was between a half and two-thirds. But change was on the way, in the shape of the Equal Pay Act of 1970 and other reforms. By 1994 average hourly pay was 80 per cent of the male level, indicating a significant closing of the gap.[31] The continuing differential arose in part from the concentration of women in lower-paid sectors of the economy so of course more still needed to be done. In addition, it was reported that women had made striking progress in terms of their labour market participation and employment levels.[32]

While the "marriage bar" in the public sector, which obliged women to resign their posts on marriage, had been abolished in Britain (but not Ireland) in 1946, other officially sanctioned forms of discrimination affecting women persisted. These were dismantled by the Sex Discrimination Act of 1975.[33] Women were to be treated in the same way as men in education, personal finance, housing, and employment.

Limited family planning services were available in Northern Ireland during the postwar decades. However, there was strong social pressure, particularly in Catholic communities in the north, against the use of such services. Nonetheless, at the end of the 1960s, reforms at a UK level allowed local authorities to provide contraception on social and medical grounds, with no restriction on marital status.[34] Such reforms were slow to materialise south of the border.

More generally, women were discriminated against in the public sphere and particularly in the political arena. Progress has been slow and uneven, though it is hardly without significance that the leaders of the two largest political parties in Northern Ireland in 2018 were women, as is the leader of the smaller Alliance Party of Northern Ireland.

I was a sideline supporter of the new women's movement or what is sometimes referred to as second-wave feminism. This was while I was a student at University College, Cork, which became a centre of feminist activism at the end of the 1960s. I was impressed by the commitment, the youthful radicalism, and the clear-sighted analysis of the status of women in Irish society.[35] There were no emotional appeals to a misty past or exaggerated claims about the present though in a sense this was about identity politics, the identity of women in society. There was a commitment to radical reform, and indeed the 1970s and the 1980s witnessed massive social change in relation to the status of women. The striking point is how much the women's movement and an altered public consciousness had secured in terms of reforms for women (and indirectly for men) by means of lobbying, protest, and persuasion. Again this is the trajectory the Northern Ireland Civil Rights Association, the Northern Ireland Labour Party, trade unions, and other reform-minded organisations might have traced out, building on the many reforms that had already been won in a remarkably short space of time. Moreover, these organisations were more established than the women's movement, had deeper financial pockets, more extensive social connections, and dealt with governments in London and Dublin that were by no means implacably opposed to reform. But by the early 1970s the lights had gone out in the north.

What NICRA or the People's Democracy, or other militant groups, could not deliver was a united Ireland. Neither, for that matter, could the Provisional IRA. Even after a thirty-year campaign of violence it had to accept, not publicly of course, that its primary object remained unfulfilled. The former deputy leader of the SDLP Seamus Mallon put it more bluntly: the IRA had suffered "total failure."[36] And to boot, it had left in its wake a society more deeply divided along ethnonational lines than was the case before 1969 (though it is not clear if this was a cause for much concern within its ranks).

THE ROAD NOT TAKEN

The rise of the Provisional IRA succeeded in diverting the course of Irish history. In a peculiar sense that was a signal achievement. But the course not taken was a more promising one. The conditions for radical reform were good at the end of the 1960s, not just for women and other social groups but for ethnic minorities as well. Reform was in the air, to the chagrin of some doctrinaire revolutionaries. What were termed student revolts spread out from France and Germany, anti-Vietnam and anti-Apartheid demonstrations rocked European cities, women were organising and pressurizing as never before, and the labour and trade union movements were in an assertive mood.[37] Discourses of rights and opportunities for minorities – black Britons, gay men and women, children's rights, Scottish and Welsh cultural concerns – were coming to the fore in the 1970s. Instead of embracing the future, Northern Irish society found itself deflected into a siding where reaction reigned. An alternative Northern Irish politics was possible but not with gunmen and barricades at the end of the street. Progressive movements were rendered impotent by the rise of armed groups and simply retreated into the shadows. Little wonder that feminist groups in the north lagged behind their southern counterparts in terms of organisation and coherence. There was the complication some women activists were "green" (less frequently "orange") before they were feminist. In any case it was simply impossible to compete with the new and more primitive politics of the street, featuring bombings, shootings, rioting, and the funereal trappings of death.

The remembrances of the Belfast-born poet, Gerald Dawe, *In Another World*, a title with multilayered meanings, evokes a world of lost opportunity.[38] Seen through the eyes of a teenager, Belfast in the 1960s was a city full of music. But the "curtain fell with the beginning of the Troubles." Coming back to Belfast after a few years of student life elsewhere, Dawe was shocked by the abrupt transformation of place and mood.

"I remember walking through the city one night – it would have been about 1972 or 1973 – and it was like walking through a ghost town … The pubs shut at about 6 or 7pm, the cinemas were closed and the buses stopped early. It was like walking through a city at war with itself. People withdrew into their own districts and then, inside their own districts, back into their own homes; they didn't look out. It was bleak."[39]

We can only guess as to what that other world might have been. The point is there were alternative pathways that were radical, reformist, and nonviolent. The music might have been just as good. In July 2005 the IRA dumped arms, committed itself to exclusively peaceful means, and made known what many had long realised: "We believe there is now an alternative way to achieve this [a united Ireland] and to end British rule in our country."[40] We may agree or disagree over objectives but it is hard to visualise an outcome that would have been more dystopian than the society produced by the thirty years of terror.

POWER FROM ABOVE BUT NOT ONLY FROM ABOVE

The emphasis in this work is very much on the lower-level politics of the period, on the role of pressure groups, communities, and paramilitaries in shaping history. This is not to say that high politics was not relevant or to deny that Irish–British relations helped structure the conflict. But the United Kingdom and the Republic of Ireland, though out of tune with each other on some issues, were committed to damping communal tensions and combating volunteer armies of orange and green during the 1970s and beyond. Thus the striking thing is that communal violence and attacks on the northern statelet, as well as on the British state more generally, flourished despite the efforts of these higher-level agencies seeking to enforce their *apparent* monopoly of coercive power. In fact, for most of the period of the Troubles, the British and Irish states were reacting to the initiatives of armed groups and seeking to contain the conflagration. Historical actors in the northern localities, with the support of extremist nationalists south of the border and westwards in Irish America, waged an offensive struggle that was deliberate, that was reviewed from time to time, that was self-reflexive, and that was committed to ultimate victory, irrespective of the human costs involved.[41] That the campaign flouted the wishes of the majority of Irish nationalists hardly troubled the fanatic heart.

To develop this theme into a more general observation, Northern Ireland illustrates the relative autonomy of the localities when it comes to identity politics. Just as Marxists or at least some Marxists in the 1960s came to appreciate the relative autonomy of the superstructure from the economic base of society, so social theorists need to come to terms with the relative autonomy of the localities and the powerful role of individuals and groups within these in propagating political violence. This is especially true of a deeply divided society where militant groups exercise disproportionate leverage. Northern Ireland was just such a society.[42]

This brings the spotlight back to where it truly belongs, trained on the individuals and groups who were primarily responsible for political violence and the promotion of armed struggle. Enter, stage right, the Provisional IRA and its political wing, Sinn Féin. The initiative and the continuing commitment to engage in "armed struggle," extending over three decades, lay with the "invisible army," the Provisional IRA, and more specifically with its secret Army Council. Not that the decision makers – no mere instruments of history who decreed year in and year out that the armed offensive should continue – were invisible. The names are well known, and they would not wish it otherwise (though perhaps for rather different reasons). The roll call of orchestrators and entrepreneurs of the Troubles – almost exclusively men – includes Seán Mac Stiofáin, Seamus Twomey, Joe Cahill, Daithí O'Connell, Ruairí Ó Brádaigh, Máire Drumm, Bobby Sands, "Darkie" Hughes, Dolours Price, Brian Keenan, Billy McKee, J.B. O'Hagan, and so on right down to the foot soldiers who did their stuff in humbler capacities. Some were unreconstructed militarists, often socially conservative, from earlier IRA campaigns; others were new entrants who became radicalised during the course of the Troubles.

The primary objective of armed struggle was to achieve a united Ireland. Thus the IRA would force a withdrawal of the British state from the northern counties of Ireland and incorporate forcibly the unionist population in an all-island nationalist state. This polity would be united in a geographical sense but of course divided at the level of people and community, which is where the fundamental divisions of the island lie. While there are complexities to the Provisionals' "war," there being secondary objectives as well,[43] the primary objective dominated all other considerations. The fact that Sinn Féin looked forward to marking the hundredth anniversary of the Easter Rising of 1916 with an all-island state, either achieved or round the corner, is at least a measure of the consistency of this ambition. The rest of the ideological baggage, relating to social and economic affairs, was not only incidental but sometimes internally contradictory.

For example, Provisional Sinn Féin was fiercely opposed to membership of the European Economic Community, viewing it as a threat to Irish sovereignty, yet when a referendum was held in Britain and Northern Ireland in 2016 on membership of the more intrusive European Union Sinn Féin advocated a pro-EU stance.[44] While railing against unemployment, particularly for Catholics, the Provisionals'"economic war," that is bombing work-places and selectively assassinating businessmen, had the effect of destroying jobs, reducing external investment in the province, and preventing the cre-ation of new jobs (the reverse of what was happening so successfully in the Republic of Ireland during the 1970s and later).[45] Combined with other shocks emanating from the international economy, the result was to push up unemployment in working-class areas and to reduce living standards relative to the levels that might have been enjoyed. In effect, the "economic war" blighted working-class lives in republican and loyalist areas.

Or to take a more symbolic issue, though one with important material implications as well, there was the repeated bombing of the rail link be-tween Dublin and Belfast by the Provisional IRA. For those of us involved in the Peace Train initiative, which aimed at keeping the lines of communi-cation open, we could not fathom how destroying one of the major trans-port corridors serving communities north and south of the border could possibly advance the cause of a united Ireland. Such bombing also had the almost inevitable tragic consequence: a fifty-five-year-old Dubliner, Letitia McCrory, travelling to Belfast, was blown apart by an explosive device placed on the train.[46] She left behind her, in the wake of the explosion, five motherless daughters.

THE CHOICE

There have been the almost unconscious expressions of ethnic hatred on both sides of the house. I had the privilege of teaching adults, including a fair number of republican ex-prisoners at Magee University College at the beginning of the 1980s. Social life in the city in those dark days could hardly be described as inviting, so I frequently found myself chatting in the college restaurant to students or in Andy Cole's pub at the bottom of the nearby Rock Road. One evening I recall talking to possibly the bright-est student of the year, a young married man and a republican. His idea of the place of northern Protestants in Irish society did not shock me. I had heard the view many times before. But it was the ease and taken-for-grantedness of what he had to say, coupled with the fact that he was such an impressive student – working class, Catholic, and a drop-out from St Columb's College as it happened – that disturbed me. The melting away of Protestants from city-side Derry since 1969, with the exception of the tiny Protestant Fountain area just outside the city walls, becomes more understandable against this ideological backdrop.[47]

"Protestants should accept that they are Irish."

"And if they don't?"

"Well, that's up to them, but the future is a united Ireland."

"But they don't want a united Ireland."

"They have to accept it or get out. That's the choice."

This sentiment echoes the words of the IRA leader Ernie O'Malley during the closing phase of the Irish revolution. He foresaw "what hardening had to come" and he warned that if unionists could not support the idea of an Irish republic they could "clear out and serve the empire elsewhere."[48] Even the great statesman of Irish nationalism Eamon de Valera had entertained similar ideas of ethnic purging. "His deepest belief," according to John Bowman, "was that Ulster unionists were only entitled to remain in Ireland on the condition that they renounced their unionism and opted for Irish citizenship."[49] At a Fianna Fáil Árd Fheis in 1939 he floated the idea of a reverse plantation: that Ulster unionists would be encouraged to emigrate to Britain and Irish emigrants to Britain would be brought back to replace them. The only surprise is that he was still articulating such views as late as 1962. "If in the north there are people who spiritually want to be English [*sic*] rather than Irish, they can go and we will see that they get the adequate, right compensation for their property."[50] The crudity of the terminology – English instead of British; the exclusiveness of the idea of Irishness – is consonant with the sinister undertones to the proposition itself. I would like to think that this was not de Valera's considered position at the end of his life but the more important point is that the sentiments themselves had a wider currency.

This expulsive propensity is present in both political communities. Historically it has been associated more with Protestantism and loyalism: witness the Armagh disturbances of the 1780s, attacks on Catholic homes before and after the defeat of the second home rule bill in 1893, and the mass expulsion of Catholic workers from the shipyards in July 1920.[51] But it is also present in Catholic protonationalist and nationalist tradition, from peasant atrocities during the rebellion in Wexford in 1798, through the Rockite insurgency of the 1820s, to attacks on isolated Protestants during the Troubles. In view of these traditions, it is worth reflecting that expulsions amounting to ethnic cleansing would have been the probable by-product of the Provisional IRA's campaign of violence, had it succeeded.

This is not the place to unfold the arguments in detail but there is a de-gree of ambivalence towards the moral worth of Protestants within north-ern nationalism. In part it is a debate about historic origins. Protestants are planters or settlers, alien in origin and hence not due the same status as the indigenous people, whoever they might be. Many years ago in Belfast I put it to a republican acquaintance of mine that Protestants, and latter-day unionists, had been in Ireland for much longer than most people of Irish descent in the United States and had come for much the same economic reasons. Did he favour their repatriation in the same way as the National Front in England wanted the Black British repatriated? "That's different," he snapped.

I might have added but didn't remember to that while some Protestants trace their lineage back to the plantations, many others do not. Tens of thousands of immigrants in the 1690s, for instance, were economic refu-gees fleeing famine in Scotland (in a quirk of history, many Catholic and Protestant refugees fled Ulster for Scotland a century and a half later dur-ing a great famine in Ireland), while in the later nineteenth century skilled workers from the west of Scotland and the north of England streamed into the Belfast shipyards. Moreover, from the seventeenth century onwards, there were conversions from Catholicism to Protestantism, and vice versa, in each of the sixteen or so generations since the defeat of Gaelic Ulster in the early 1600s. The racially pure Ulster Planter and the racially pure Ulster Gael is almost as rare as the four-leafed shamrock in many parts of the north.[52] In contemporary times, and depending on context, tone, and motivation, the terms "planter" and "settler" can be part of a quasi-racist discourse that, intentionally or otherwise, serves to feed ethnic animosity.[53]

FOSTERING SEGREGATION

Major institutions within the nationalist and unionist communities have also fostered difference and division. The Gaelic Athletic Association and the Orange Order are outstanding examples.[54] Up until 1972 the GAA for-bade its members from attending soccer or rugby games, presumably lest their sense of Irish nationality be compromised, thereby staking out a political, ethnic, and cultural border.[55] The naming of GAA clubs after nationalist heroes such as the racist John Mitchel or the 1916 revolutionary Patrick Pearse drove the message home. This was taken farther in the north in recent decades, where Gaelic sports grounds were used for nationalist rallies such as the quarter-century Hunger Strike commemorations in 2006. The one at Casement Park that I attended had a militaristic air, with men (mainly men) in dark uniforms marching on to the pitch. Images of the gun and the camán merged (as was literally the case in some punishment attacks carried out by the Provisional IRA). The Orange Order served a comparable purpose, that of reinforcing ethnic boundaries within the unionist community, even if far fewer members were implicated in paramilitarism as compared to members of the GAA. Intentionally or not, the effect of Orange exclusiveness was to entrench hostile attitudes that were part of the raw materials for racialist attitudes and sometimes actions. It should be acknowledged that reform proved possible within the GAA and less obviously so within the Orange Order. The GAA has done much to rid itself of archaic rules, though it was noticeable that on contentious issues such as disallowing members of the PSNI from participating in Gaelic games (Rule 21), northern GAA officials formed part of the reactionary rear guard.[56]

At the root of segregation in Northern Ireland lie largely exclusive marriage patterns and the separation of children during the formative years of childhood. No one is born a Catholic or a Protestant. All the major churches in Northern Ireland bear a heavy responsibility for segregationist practices and the lack of contact, understanding, and tolerance that flows from the separation of young people. The churches, and the Orange Order, torpedoed attempts at integrated education embodied in one of the earliest and boldest initiatives of the newly formed Northern Ireland government, the educational reforms proposed by Lord Londonderry.[57] Particularly vexatious was the *Ne Temere* decree promulgated by the Catholic Church, which insisted that children in religiously mixed marriages had to be brought up as Catholics. Such supremacist thinking served to deepen the communal divide, increasing clerical control of people's lives and inflicting intense emotional pressure on couples, their families, and their wider kin networks.[58]

These were but some of the cultural institutions that sustained segregation, sectarianism, ethnic and national conflict. But the point is that these elements of civil society were long standing and were not sufficient in themselves to produce a conflagration. What was needed by the late 1960s for the initiation of armed conflict and the perpetuation of that conflict were organisations dedicated to the gun rather than the ballot box as the arbiter of political futures.

RESPONSIBILITIES

There were structural forces at play that shaped the deterioration in communal relations in the north in the late 1960s.[59] But much more was at play. As always there were chance occurrences that could not have been predicted such as the death of Samuel Devenney in Derry in July 1969, which served to inflame local opinion against the RUC.[60] There was the international context that intersected with the local, most notably the progress of the American civil rights movement for racial equality and the more amorphous student revolts of 1968. The demonstration effect of both movements was electrifying within the parish society that was Northern Ireland. Then there was the changing communications context that projected vivid television images as well as the fruits of investigative journalism to a wide and intensely engaged public. These conjunctural factors highlighted discriminatory practices used against the Catholic community as never before. They also helped to energise popular resistance and gain national and international political attention. But initiatives for reform need not have taken the violent form they eventually assumed. That required human agency, including agency of a kind that also elbowed aside people and politicians committed to more pacific courses of action.

This chapter confronts questions about the Troubles that are at once obvious yet go largely unanswered within the academy.[61] They are absolutely fundamental in that they bear on the denial of the most sacred of rights, the right to life. In particular this chapter wants to know why the armed hostilities extended over such a long time period and the identity of the actors and agencies primarily responsible for ensuring that state of affairs. It seeks to attribute responsibility to the principal collective of historical actors, while aware that others bear varying degrees of responsibility for particular actions and reactions. It is also acknowledged that social structures as well as human agency are involved and that the two inter-penetrate.[62] But even deeply embedded traditions and habitual actions, never mind radical initiatives, require decision making by historical actors, most obviously so when these actors are confronted by many potential turning points along a road of three-decades duration.

How might we identify such actors or more specifically the actions of those actors that resulted in the descent into large-scale violence and at times its seemingly endless nature? This is a historical task, and there are a number of criteria that may be invoked to ease the work. Some are quan-tifiable; all are open to evidence.[63] First, the human agents in question must have been responsible for a significant share of the killings and other forms of extreme violence (otherwise they would have had only a limited impact on the scale and longevity of the conflict). Second, they must have been resolved not only to use political violence but possessed of the will and the resources to fight for the long term ("for as long as it takes," as one leading proponent of the "long war" put it). Third, they must have been willing to ignore evidence of disquiet or opposition, as expressed in elections, peace demonstrations, appeals by individuals and clergy, or other signs of op-position to violence (otherwise, as with the case of the Official IRA, the military campaign would have been vulnerable to public opinion). Finally, they must have had the ideological coherence and sense of legitimacy, de-spite the lack of a conventional mandate from the peoples of Ireland for "war," to take over important functions of the state, including the admin-istration of justice and the punishment of alleged antisocial elements in areas they controlled (as detailed later in this volume). Such control was vital to the long-run viability of the campaign.

The actions of the Provisional IRA, and only the Provisional IRA, hit all of these bells. This critique of the Provisional IRA and of Sinn Féin, for such it is, is not primarily a moral critique, though one is certainly poss-ible.[64] Looking back, the critical event was the formation of the Provisional IRA at the end of 1969 and the determination of its leaders to unleash the latest phase of armed opposition to the British state. The 1970s and beyond could have been very different as the existing conflicts could have been handled differently within the existing and *still evolving* political structures, as argued earlier. The decision to turn away from politics and resort to arms

– first in a defensive posture for tactical reasons, later as part of an offensive strategy (in pursuit of an Ireland united by force) – by Daithí O'Connell, Ruairí Ó Brádaigh, Sean Mac Stiofáin, Joe Cahill, Billy McKee, Brian Keenan, and other traditionalists brought into being a military machine that younger militants such as Martin McGuinness, Ivor Bell, Kevin McKenna, among others, steered remorselessly through the decades of terror. There were many armed groups in Northern Ireland but only one had the capability to impose its authoritarian will on so many over such an extended time scale. It revelled in its own power and sense of entitlement, and proclaimed responsibility for the actions of its members while remaining impervious to much of public opinion. Even as the "peace party" within Sinn Féin struggled to gain ascendancy in the later 1990s, the majority of IRA activists still favoured a continuation of the "armed struggle."[65] Had their will prevailed, the era of political violence might have been prolonged indefinitely. Only Sinn Féin and the IRA could, by taking unilateral action, wind down the conflict, as was demonstrated by their "cessation of violence" in 1994.

This is a strong proposition. Fortunately we have a means to test it. If the proposition is true, then when the principal agents of conflict shut up shop on armed action, the Troubles should have fizzled out. Thus, the aftermath of the IRA's declaration in 1994 furnishes something of a natural experiment for this prediction. We know in fact that when the "undefeated army" of the IRA departed the field, still with arms intact, the level of violence shifted onto a much lower plane. The British army wound down its operations, as did loyalist paramilitary groups. This followed in the wake of the withdrawal of the military threat to the British state and Ulster loyalism posed by the IRA. It could have happened sooner. The conclusion must be that the Provisional IRA was primarily responsible for the direction, methods of engagement, scale, and, above all, the longevity of the Troubles.[66]

THE ARC OF RESPONSIBILITY

The portrait of the Provisional IRA presented here is an unflattering one. But should the arc of responsibility extend only to the Provisional IRA and the various republican splinter groups? That is the strong case in relation to responsibility. But is there a weaker, more diffuse case for suggesting a wider collective Catholic and nationalist responsibility? Or at least a secondary responsibility that goes beyond those actively involved in the republican movement in the years before the final Provisional IRA ceasefire of 1997?

Of course there were tens of thousands of *individuals* who cannot be accorded any responsibility at all. First and foremost there were the morally courageous men and women associated with the mainly Catholic Social Democratic and Labour Party. Many of the older members had been involved in the civil rights movement and had campaigned for reform. Crucially they were committed to nonviolent action. The same can be said of those from a Catholic, sometimes nationalist background within the Alliance Party and the struggling labour movement. Members and former members of the official republican movement after 1972 might also be included on the side of those who sought to slow the advances of politico-sectarianism.

Still we are faced with some uncomfortable facts. First, the Provisional offensive enjoyed high if varying levels of support throughout the Troubles. The year 2001 is a watershed date. In that year the nationalist population shifted allegiance to make Sinn Féin the largest political party in the north. This was after the Belfast Agreement of 1998 but well before the IRA decommissioned weaponry and when organised criminal activity and punishment attacks were still in full swing.

Second, the likelihood is that throughout most of the Troubles support for northern republicanism was available to varying degrees from at least a large minority of the nationalist people. This varied by social class, by region, and possibly by gender. No doubt, at different moments in time, feelings of support shifted backwards and forwards at an individual and a communal level in response to state repression, loyalist violence, or revulsion at a particularly gruesome loyalist or IRA action. The essential point, though, is that the extent of tacit support or sympathy is likely to have been wider than voting figures alone suggest, revealing as those statistics themselves are. Certainly this has been claimed by republican activists, and there is some evidence for this, at the very least on particularly emotive occasions. During the hunger strikes of 1980–81, a flash flood of emotion engulfed much of northern nationalism. (Others of course interpreted the

Table 2.3
Support within the nationalist electorate for Sinn Féin, 1982–2017,
as measured by Westminster elections

Year	SF share of vote (%)	Type of election
1982	32	Assembly N.I.
1983	39	Westminster
1987	32	Westminster
1992	29	Westminster
1997	39	Westminster
2001	50	Westminster
2005	56	Westminster
2010	61	Westminster
2017	70	Westminster

Source: Calculated from election data on the ARK website, http://www.ark.ac.uk/elections.

hunger-to-death strike not in terms of heroism or martyrdom but as self-killing by starvation or as suicide by self-starvation.[67]) On occasion this took on a politico-religious garb as crowds gathered in the streets to recite Catholic devotional prayers, the Rosary in particular. A friend of mine, Gráinne, who taught in a Catholic secondary school off the Falls Road, Belfast during the period of the hunger strikes found that she was one of the few teachers in the school who declined to go outside and attend a hunger strike street meeting involving the recitation of the Rosary. Most of her fellow teachers did not support the IRA, but the strike had become an issue of communal identity and solidarity. Another friend, James, a farmer from County Armagh, recalls that he enthusiastically attended funerals of hunger strikers, though his family were SDLP supporters and had reservations. The supreme example of an outpouring of communal grief was the funeral of Bobby Sands, the IRA man whose hunger strike ended in death by self-starvation. The funeral is said to have attracted a crowd of 100,000.[68] Other IRA funerals attracted large if not comparable assemblies.

These displays of public emotion – in effect physical and emotional support around the bodies, symbols, and rituals of republican militarism – contrast sharply with reaction to the treatment of labour democrats from within the Catholic ethnos. Gerry Fitt, MP for West Belfast and veteran of the civil rights movement, was hounded out of his north Belfast home by a republican mob and voted out of parliamentary life soon after. Under similar communal pressure, Paddy Devlin, the trade union leader and former minister in the short-lived power-sharing executive (1973–74), was forced to flee the family home in West Belfast before being rejected at the polls a few years later by nationalist voters.[69] "Get out to fuck you Protestant lover," was one of the phrases that stuck with him.[70] So the paradox: to advocate political violence or to be ambivalent about terror was no necessary barrier to political approval within nationalist politics. But to step outside communal boundaries, to violate the invisible unity of the ethnos, was to invite political annihilation. It is not easy to understand these internal dynamics in which some lives from within the ethnic group mattered much more than others.

VOTING PATTERNS AND WHAT THEY TELL US

Today a clear majority of northern nationalists support Sinn Féin, for long the political wing of the Provisional IRA and unambiguously committed to the armed insurgency. Once Sinn Féin, under the direction of the IRA Army Council, decided seriously to contest elections in Northern Ireland, the extent of that support became visible.

In its first province-wide electoral outing, the Assembly elections of 1982, Sinn Féin received just more than 30 per cent of the nationalist vote, exceeding what many had thought of as the underlying support for militarist republicanism. There is some ambiguity as to what constitutes the nationalist section of the electorate, so it is worth dwelling on this for a moment. It approximates but does not coincide with the Catholic share of the population (which has been rising in recent decades), as some Catholics in this period voted for the noncommunal Alliance Party and sometimes for independent candidates or tiny labour parties. For the purposes of the calculations in tables 2.3 and 2.4 it is assumed that the Irish nationalist electorate was composed of those who voted for parties with the explicit aim of achieving a united Ireland, that is, the SDLP, Sinn Féin, Workers Party, New Agenda/Democratic Left, People's Democracy, Irish Independence Party. Slightly different figures might be obtained, for instance, by adding in 40 per cent of the Alliance vote to the nationalist share, as this was roughly the proportion of Catholics in the party. This has not been done for two reasons: the most important is that many Catholic members of Alliance would be affronted at such a presumption in relation to their political and national affiliations; secondly, it makes little difference to the trends apparent in the two tables. As regards independents and some tiny parties, these pop up from time to time but in quantitative terms they are not significant. The brush strokes presented in the two tables are sufficiently indicative as they stand.

It is striking how quickly further support surfaced, whether latent or newly persuaded, as Sinn Féin and the IRA extended their investment in the twin-track strategy: an armalite in one hand and a ballot box in the other. In the Westminster election of 1983 Sinn Féin garnered close to 40 per cent of the nationalist vote, an astonishing achievement for a party that had relatively little experience of electioneering.[71] Admittedly this was in the emotional aftermath of the hunger strikes, the phase of the armalite and the rosary beads, but it does show deep foundations of support for armed struggle within the nationalist population (as indeed Sinn Féin claimed). The local elections of May 1985 demonstrated that this was no momentary spasm. With 36 per cent of the vote, Sinn Féin had been accorded widespread legitimacy within northern nationalism.

The communal bloodletting of the early 1990s depressed the Sinn Féin vote somewhat. I recall canvassing for Dr Joe Hendron because of his social democratic rather than his nationalist credentials in the UK general election of 1992. West Belfast had been transformed into "Tricolour City" in support of the sitting MP Gerry Adams, president of Sinn Féin. As we left the campaign office in the Lower Falls one evening, a carload of Sinn Féin supporters, one holding a tricolour out the window, swept by. "Brit lovers," they shouted, in a variation of the white American racist chant. On polling day I was standing with a female colleague outside the gates of a Catholic school in West Belfast handing out election literature. As afternoon turned to evening and darkness approached, we were the only election workers apart from a large gathering of Adams' supporters outside the polling station. Suddenly a figure immediately recognisable to me pushed through the throng, bore down on me, and in a loud voice demanded to know, "why don't you fuck off back to the Free State where you come from?" Such thoughts *had* occurred to me but there wasn't a chance to compliment him on his prescience. A flood of accusations poured forth. When he paused for breath I mentioned I too had a few things to say. "I'm not fucking listening to you." He then disappeared back into the crowd (but happily not from public view as he was later elected as an MLA for Sinn Féin).

This was the election in which Gerry Adams lost his Westminster seat due to an informal alliance of SDLP and unionist voters. This was the unity of Catholic, Protestant, and Dissenter, so long celebrated in republican rhetoric but apparently not welcome in practice. The loss of the West Belfast stronghold was especially painful for the party leadership and may well have accelerated progress in the Hume–Adams talks. But the electoral setback was short lived.[72] In the local elections of the following year the Sinn Féin share of the nationalist vote was back up to 36 per cent.

The elections of the later 1990s are particularly interesting in terms of what they tell us about popular opinion within northern nationalism in relation to "armed struggle." In August 1994 the IRA had declared a cease-fire but it returned to bombings, shootings, and killings in February 1996.[73] This renewed military campaign was in progress when the people of Northern Ireland went to vote in the UK general election of May 1997. Some expected Sinn Féin to suffer reverses as a consequence of the return to violence. This was not so. Support for Sinn Féin had solidified, with the party securing 40 per cent of the nationalist vote.[74] This was confirmed in the local elections later that month (21 May 1997), when Sinn Féin garnered more than a hundred thousand votes and took 44 per cent of the nationalist vote. In other words, against a soundtrack of resumed republican violence, almost half of the nationalist population was still prepared to countenance a political party that worked hand in glove with armed paramilitaries.[75] In the Assembly elections of the following year the SDLP vote was only marginally ahead of that of Sinn Féin.

By now paramilitary nationalism had the wind in its sails. In June 2001, in the landmark Westminster election of that year, Sinn Féin overhauled its main nationalist rival, the SDLP, for the first time. What was threatened in the early 1980s, following the hunger strikes, had finally come to pass. In the local government elections on the same day in 2001, the Sinn Féin victory was even more decisive as it took 21 per cent of the votes as against

19 per cent for its rival. The pattern was set for Sinn Féin electoral dominance in the north in the new century. By May 2005 Sinn Féin had pulled
farther ahead despite the IRA's continuing involvement in punishment attacks, despite the multimillion pound robbery of the Northern Bank in
Donegall Square, Belfast, and despite the semipublic execution, more or
less on a whim, of a Catholic from the Short Strand, Belfast. That man was
Robert McCartney.[76] These incidents featured a few months before the
election, showing at least the indifference of a majority of northern nationalists to the use of political violence, now on a much reduced scale.
Currently Sinn Féin is endorsed by a clear majority of northern nationalists, more than six out of every ten (tables 2.3 and 2.4). Indeed at the 2017
Assembly elections the party achieved stunning results, securing 70 per
cent of the nationalist vote.[77] John Hume might travel to Oslo in 1998 to
collect a Nobel Peace Prize but back home Sinn Féin was the triumphant
face of Northern nationalism.

People support political parties for a variety of motives. Not every vote
for Sinn Féin before the temporary ceasefire of August 1994 was a vote for
the campaign of violence. But even for those who placed an emphasis on
other policies there was at best a relaxed attitude to political violence and
its victims (presumed to be the "other side"). It would be difficult to argue
voters for Sinn Féin were sometimes confused or hardly noticed, as the consistently distinctive feature of the party's policy was support for the IRA.
That carried consequences that were visible for all to see. The IRA campaign
dominated day-to-day life in the province, from security searches to shootings, to bomb attacks on "economic targets," and neighbourhood "policing." Social encounters across the communal divide dwindled. For many
Sinn Féin voters supporting the party must have been an endorsement of
the armed struggle. As Martin McGuinness memorably put it in 1986, in
his dual role as an elected representative of Sinn Féin and as a member of
the northern command of the IRA:

> We don't believe that winning elections and winning any amount of
> votes will bring freedom. At the end of the day it will be the cutting
> edge of the IRA which will bring freedom.[78]

Table 2.4
Support within the Nationalist Electorate for Sinn Féin, 1982–2017,
as Measured by Local Government and Assembly Elections

Year	SF share of vote (%)	Type of election
1982	31	Assembly N.I.
1985	36	Local Government
1993	35	Local Government
1997	44	Local Government
2001	51	Local Government
2005	57	Local Government
2011	61	Local Government
2014	63	Local Government
2017	70	Assembly N.I.

Source: Calculated from election data on the ARK website, http://www.ark.ac.uk/
elections, and newspaper reports for 2017.

THE OTHER SIDE OF THE FENCE

By contrast there has been only limited support for political parties linked
to loyalist paramilitary organisations. The most successful of these in recent years, the Progressive Unionist Party, has typically taken less than 2
per cent of the combined unionist vote. The fact that loyalist parties with
direct links to paramilitary organisations, like the Ulster Volunteer Force
and the Ulster Defence Association, haven't even contested many elections
is itself significant, as is the degree of *unacceptance* of former loyalist
prisoners in some Protestant areas.[79]

The pattern from 1982 onwards, as revealed in table 2.5, could not be
much clearer. Electoral support within the unionist population for political
parties associated with loyalist paramilitary organisations has been slight,
irrespective of whether we are talking about local, regional, or national
elections. The big hitters throughout the period since 1982 were the Ulster
Unionist Party and the Democratic Unionist Party, whose combined vote
in the Assembly elections of 1982, for instance, accounted for 90 per cent of
the unionist vote. Support for paramilitary-linked unionist parties peaked
at the Stormont Assembly Elections of 1998 in the afterglow of the signing

of the Good Friday Agreement. The Progressive Unionist Party and the Ulster Democratic Party together secured 7 per cent of the unionist vote on a large turnout.[80] Both supported the agreement, which no doubt helped, but this degree of popularity proved short lived.

The position in the 1970s is more complicated. This was when political and constitutional uncertainty was at its height. Some unionist politicians flirted with paramilitary "hard men," particularly during the loyalist workers strikes of 1974 and 1977, but in general kept them at arms length. The year 1974, which featured widespread unionist reaction against a power-sharing executive for Northern Ireland and a Council of Ireland, represented something of a high-water mark for paramilitary politics within the unionist population. The Westminster election of October 1974 offers some guidance but even then the picture is blurred. Ken Gibson, of the Ulster Volunteer Party and a onetime head of the UVF, had a poor election, securing less than three thousand votes. However, the Vanguard Unionist Progressive Party, or more simply the Vanguard Party, which might be viewed as having paramilitary tendencies, achieved a vote just short of 100,000 (92,622 to be precise). If one puts these two together, they represent 22 per cent of the unionist votes cast in that election. This is an upper-bound estimate, almost certainly grossly so. Some members of Vanguard had links to loyalist paramilitary organisations and the movement had some militarist trappings, but rhetoric and street demonstrations substituted for military action. Within two or three years of the October election, Vanguard had largely lost its electoral force. Thus even in the 1970s there was no equivalent to the Sinn Féin party arguing consistently for a campaign of violence against their political opponents.

One by-election in particular demonstrates the limits of electoral support for Protestant paramilitarism. This was the 1982 by-election to find a replacement for the assassinated unionist MP and clergyman, the Rev. Robert Bradford. I lived in the constituency, South Belfast, and recall the intense fear and emotion in the aftermath of the murder. The times seemed propitious for a hard-line loyalist response at the polls. The Ulster Democratic Loyalist Party nominated its charismatic leader "Big John" McMichael (later assassinated by the IRA) as its flag bearer. McMichael was also a leading figure in the UDA. When the votes were counted it emerged that McMichael had got less than 2 per cent of the vote.

Table 2.5
Support within the Unionist electorate for paramilitary-linked political
parties, 1982–2016

Year	Share of the Unionist vote (%)	Type of election
1982	4	Assembly N.I.
1985	2	Local Government
1993	3	Local Government
1997	6	Local Government
1998	7	Assembly N.I.
2001	1	Westminster
2005	1	Local Government
2011	1	Local Government
2016	2	Assembly N.I.

Source: Calculated from election data on the ARK website, http://www.ark.ac.uk/elections

This narrative might be nuanced a bit further. Some DUP supporters must have had a "sneaking regard" for loyalist paramilitarism, and this is likely to have varied through time. A few may have been actively involved in terrorist groups, though there isn't much evidence of this. The Rev. William McCrea, hardly one of the bright sparks of the party, once notoriously shared a platform with the loyalist killer Billy Wright at the height of the political hysteria surrounding the Drumcree protests.[81] As already noted, loyalists and some unionist politicians, including Dr Ian Paisley, collaborated during the first and second Ulster workers strikes of 1974 and 1977. These are episodic moments, however. For all the ambiguities and the inflammatory rhetoric, there is precious little indication of the full-blooded and consistent participation that one finds on the part of Sinn Féin members, then and now, in supporting the IRA. Nor do we see the same overlapping membership. The striking fact is that when unionist voters were offered the choice of a candidate linked to loyalist paramilitarism, the offer was decisively rejected, over and over again. That is one huge difference between the two political communities. It is one that has been insufficiently recognised.

AN OPPRESSIVE MINORITY?

This brings us, at least those of us from a nationalist background, to some uncomfortable conclusions. So uncomfortable that I have been sitting on many of the arguments of this book for many years. We may sum up by saying that the spectrum of tolerance for violent actions against the British state and the unionist community was an extended one. At one pole there was the minority of hard-core insurrectionists, determined to drive the "British" out of Ireland by military force. In the broad middle of the spectrum were those who were critical of particular IRA actions but who drew a certain satisfaction from the discomfort of unionists, including the exacting of historical vengeance. Then there were the bystanders who were indifferent to or taciturn on the subject of violence – violence directed not just against the British state but against the unionist "other" in the main. The unpalatable possibility is that, when lumped together, these constituted close to a majority of northern nationalists during periods of the Troubles. At moments, as prisoners were on hunger strike in the Maze prison – the assassination of prison officers during the same period went largely unremarked – they may well have constituted a majority of the nationalist people.[82] At the very least we are talking about a large and disproportionately influential minority who countenanced terror, albeit with varying qualifications.

This perspective radically reshapes our understanding of the Troubles. Counterintuitive as it may seem, this suggests that the nationalist community, with varying degrees of responsibility, has constituted an oppressive minority from the early 1970s until the end of the century. Given the historic coherence of the nationalist community, in terms of religious, social, and political values, it is perhaps not wholly surprising that communal responses came to the fore at times. In any case, while support might fluctuate, consistently large, and sometimes very large numbers were prepared to countenance the coercion and killing of their fellow citizens. These numbers expanded as the Troubles rolled on, paused at the beginning of the 1990s, and then built cumulatively through time.

An oppressive minority? Surely not. But oppressive minorities are all too well known in history. The phrase the "Norman yoke," embedded in English popular culture, recalls an episode in the history of the neighbouring island when a small military elite superimposed itself politically on a larger society. Nearer home, and roughly a half-century earlier, Brian Boru and the O'Briens of Clare – relatively minor chieftains to begin with – succeeded, albeit temporarily, in a similar-type venture of conquest and domination over much of Ireland. Switching to a larger canvas, there are innumerable instances of oppressive minorities, down to contemporary times. There was, for example, the Alawite political dominance of Syria, the Sunni control of Iraq under Saddam Hussein, and the Tutsi control of Burundi until fairly recent times. The white apartheid regime of South Africa that almost saw out the twentieth century is the best known example of all.

Minorities can repress. Of that there can be no doubt. Circumstances may be all. But surely in the Irish case any suggestion of nationalist oppression skates over the icy reality of unionist control of Northern Ireland between 1922 and 1970? Unionists, despite the many layers of internal difference, might be said to have constituted a mildly oppressive majority at most. Or in the nuanced opinion of a leading member of the Northern Ireland Labour Party, "the Catholic grievances did not amount to oppression" but "the Catholic minority received less than fair treatment from the Protestant majority."[83] This majority operated within political, legal, and constitutional constraints, and unlike authoritarian regimes elsewhere movement into and out of the territory was unrestricted. Security policies in the neighbouring Irish state between 1922 and 1969 were little different in terms of the use of state coercive powers and for much the same reason (the existence of armed threats to the state). It is striking that in one month in 1972 more people met violent deaths at the hands of the IRA than in the whole period from the stabilisation of the Northern and Southern Irish states, stretching that is from the mid-1920s through to 1969. Moreover, even under "unionist misrule" cognisance was sometimes taken by Stormont of Catholic and (less so) of nationalist sensibilities.[84] The more exclusivist Orange demands were sometimes resisted – in itself significant – though unhappily not always successfully.[85] This was devolved government in a divided society. With some change of detail the Stormont record is not terribly different from that of the other state on the island of Ireland, which also, as it happens, faced political conspiracies from within in each decade of the twentieth century (though not from its Protestant minority).

The Irish state is surely a more relevant comparative reference point than
the anachronistic comparisons sometimes made with twenty-first century
pluralist and multicultural societies.[86]

THE FAILURE OF POLITICAL VIOLENCE

It is time to sum up the successes and the failures. The Irish Women's Liberation Movement, formed at roughly the same time as the Provisional
IRA, as well as the more broadly based Irish Country Women's Association
and the Irish Housewives Association, carried off triumphantly major reforms to state and society in the Republic of Ireland.[87] The change wrought
by these organisations illustrates one of the central themes of this work,
which is the feasibility of reform within the Irish and British political
systems. In relation to northern policy, the Irish and British states, the
SDLP, and Alliance parties had chalked up constitutional achievements
such as the Sunningdale Agreement of 1973 – stillborn but pointing towards a future settlement – the Anglo-Irish Agreement of 1985, and of
course the Good Friday Agreement of 1998, as well as a series of social and
economic initiatives that ranged from the provision of public housing and
healthcare to employment law and an expansion of individual rights. By
contrast, as argued earlier, the IRA in its various incarnations had little to
show by way of positive achievement after almost three decades of violence. This is not to deny that the British state made dreadful mistakes
or that there were inexcusable instances of the use of lethal power. The
tragedy of Bloody Sunday and the debacle of internment spring immediately to mind. But remarkably there was no repeat of Bloody Sunday, and
by and large the security forces worked to contain the crisis within the
constraints set by a liberal democratic state.

   While the state operated under certain restraints, few inhibitions, other
than residual Catholic moral codes, guided the Provisionals' offensive.[88]
Town centres were blasted; civilians were placed at risk; children (boy
soldiers) were exploited as part of "armed struggle,"[89] in itself an internationally recognised war crime; suspects were tortured and sometimes
"disappeared"; opponents were executed. Internal opposition was snuffed
out. This was communal power with a vengeance: the power of life and
death over others, with virtually no accountability. The "Provisionals' war"

was engineered from within the Catholic and nationalist community and prosecuted across three decades with ingenuity and ruthlessness. While the degree of complicity in this communal and national aggression must remain a matter of controversy, there seems little doubt of the substantial popular Catholic support afforded the Provisional IRA and Sinn Féin during the course of the Troubles. The extent to which northern nationalists cohabited with terror and then developed a selective Troubles' memory is a troubling thought. The irony is that this is a community that prides itself on its sense of history.

Figure 3.1 Freedom of a Kind

3
The Terror Within

They beat me with poles. They said they were going to fill the bath [for torture
by half-drowning]. They made me write a last letter to my kids. My hands were
tied, but I managed to lift the blindfold and saw the window. I ran for it but
bounced off. I never prayed as hard. I was drifting in and out. They finally took
me outside. They shouted "Lie down. Lie down." There was a bang and that's
the last thing I remember.

Andrew Peden[1]

BACKGROUND

Andrew Peden has been described as a "victim of the peace." Less than a
year after the signing of the Good Friday Agreement and five years after
the loyalist and IRA paramilitary ceasefires of 1994, his home was invaded
early one morning, he was abducted, and taken to a flat in the Shankill
Road, interrogated and beaten during the course of the day, and finally
shot in the legs by the UDA.[2] This was justice paramilitary-style. The usual
calibre of weapon used in such punishment attacks is a handgun. This time
it was the more fearsome shotgun and only after the torture party had
gone on for twelve hours. The parting shot, as it were, was the blast to his
legs from the shotgun.[3]

Andrew Peden was taken to the Royal Victoria Hospital in Belfast. His
left leg was amputated immediately – it felt like "raw steak" – and his right
leg had to be taken off three months later. Both legs were amputated close
to his groin. In addition to his own trauma and being condemned to life
in a wheelchair, there was the transgenerational effect: "My two wee lads
are growing up with so much anger." There was one other detail: he was
entirely innocent of the charge levelled against him, that of aiding a rival
paramilitary group.

The phenomenon of paramilitary punishment beatings and shootings has to be seen in the context of the Troubles in Northern Ireland. Beginning in 1970 a dissident wing of the Irish Republican Army, the Provisional IRA, began rearming for a sustained assault on the British state and the unionist-dominated statelet of Northern Ireland. Loyalist paramilitary action and reaction added fuel to the conflict, and the attempts by the security forces – the police and army – to contain the insurgency met with limited success, and indeed in some instances the indiscriminate use of force by the security forces had the effect of exacerbating the crisis. The supreme example is that of Bloody Sunday in Derry in 1972 when the parachute regiment of the British army opened fire on a nationalist civil rights march and killed, some would say murdered, fourteen innocent civilians.

There is disagreement as to the duration of the Troubles, but the IRA ceasefire of 1997 and the Good Friday Agreement of the following year marked an end to major hostilities, though sporadic political violence continues to this day. The legitimacy of the police force, the Royal Ulster Constabulary, was suspect in the eyes of many Irish nationalists even before the civil upheavals began, and this was further undermined by the intensity of the crisis.[4] The result was a partial policing vacuum in relation to "ordinary" crime, particularly on working-class estates in Northern Ireland.

Having as a matter of policy made conventional policing inoperative, or at least much less effective, loyalist and republican paramilitaries – essentially Protestant and Catholic militias – proceeded to administer their own form of "alternative justice" or "rough justice" as the former leader of Sinn Féin, Gerry Adams has put it.[5] The Ulster Volunteer Force, the Ulster Defence Association, and the Provisional IRA were the principal organisations involved.[6] As viewed through the dark glasses of these paramilitary organisations, their punitive actions were in response to community pressure to deal with car crime, break-ins, drink and drugs offences, and other forms of antisocial behaviour. A particularly dangerous form of "antisocial" behaviour was to cross a member of a paramilitary organisation, in a pub, a betting shop, or on the street.

A TRADITION OF VIGILANTISM?

Vigilante-style methods of control and punishment in certain localities were not unique to late twentieth-century Northern Ireland. The history of secret societies in the eighteenth and nineteenth centuries might seem to offer some precedents.[7] Whiteboys, Hearts of Oak, Hearts of Steel, Rightboys, Rockites, Terry Alts, Peep O'Day Boys, Ribbonmen, and other clandestine groupings were quick to visit punishments on fellow farmers, traders, and labourers in addition to representatives of the landed elite or the state. These ranged from threatening letters to the cutting of ears or tongues, other forms of mutilation, and sometimes death. The victims were held to have violated presumed community norms, usually in relation to issues such as the occupation of land, rent levels, tithe exactions, renewal of leases, wage rates, evictions, and land grabbing. Sometimes attempts at economic redress were mixed with sectarian bigotry.[8] Or the nocturnal exploits of local gangs or lodges might amount to little more than gangsterism for vindictive purposes or personal gain.[9] Moving to more recent times, the period 1919 to 1923 was one of intensified political conflict, land seizures, intimidation, sectarianism, and expulsions, with sometimes violent consequences for those who did not submit to the wishes of armed militants. Republican courts were set up as part of a wider campaign to supplant the British state in Ireland. There was a faint echo of this in 1930s Belfast when a republican vigilante group is said to have terrorised local nationalists. According to a former IRA volunteer and ex-internee from the 1950s, Seán Ó Cearnaigh, the faction was led by a notorious duo, the Hicks brothers, who administered violence in a largely gratuitous fashion.[10]

These antecedents might suggest historical continuity[11] or some form of path dependence but that is hardly the case. For one thing there is a yawning gap between the 1920s and the 1970s. Furthermore, the heavy involvement of loyalist paramilitaries in the shooting and beating of fellow loyalists is not easily related back to the history of unionism. While it is true that the relationship between loyalists and the police and court system deteriorated during the 1970s, and still further after the Anglo-Irish Agreement of 1985, this was due to force of circumstances. Loyalists in principle favoured the existing institutions of the state, including the police and court system, and more generally the British connection, as of course did unionists more generally.

It seems reasonable to conclude that it was the conditions of the time that gave rise to vigilante activity, independently of traditions of violence. Moreover, other conflict zones have thrown up forms of collective violence associated with paramilitary groups similar to those observed in Northern Ireland in recent decades. Black townships during the period of apartheid in South Africa furnish perhaps the best-known examples. The image of "necklace killing" – placing a tyre round the neck of a victim, pouring on petrol and setting it alight – is forever associated with the name of Winnie Mandela and the so-called Mandela United Football Supporters Club. The legal processes of the white racist regime in South Africa had little to commend them either, so victims of rumour and accusation within the Black community were placed in a position of extreme jeopardy. So-called popular or summary justice directed against alleged collaborators and sexual minorities has also featured in Hamas-controlled areas of Palestine.

Nonetheless, once paramilitaries found themselves adopting a "policing" role in the north, and this is more the case in relation to republican vigilantes, it is not surprising that historical precedents such as the republican courts of 1920–22 were invoked, in part to legitimise the practices of the moment. In that sense, history mattered. Thus, while the impetus for punishment attacks by loyalists and republicans (or protorepublicans) in the early days of the Troubles derived from the immediacy of conflict, these instances of past behaviour smoothed the pathway to more ambitious schemes for community control.[12] An initially inchoate set of practices when no-go areas were established in 1969 evolved into more systematic forms of repression that were coloured by and rationalised in terms of earlier precedents and the building of alternative state structures.

These acts and practices might also be placed within the long-run history of judicial punishments. If Michel Foucault is to be believed, by the beginning of the nineteenth century physical punishments were dying out: "The body as the major target of penal repression disappeared."[13] He also notes an associated shift in thinking, and presumably in sensibility, in Europe and the United States, resulting in the decline of punishment as a public spectacle. Public hangings came under critical scrutiny; displaying tortured bodies to the crowd became less acceptable; the public inspection and ridicule of wrong doers (as when displayed in pillories for example), was discountenanced. Viewed against that backdrop, the methods of "informal justice" practised in Northern Ireland represent a regression to pre-Enlightenment punishment practices. Or to invert Foucault:[14] in the late twentieth century, the spectacle of physical punishment reappeared; the body became the focus of extreme punishments; and public manifestations of wounding, mutilation, and tarring were all too apparent in some urban working-class and rural localities.

FORMS OF "PUNISHMENT"

The repertoire of paramilitary punishments was a varied one. But first a word of warning to the unwary. "Punishment" is placed in inverted commas because the word is a euphemism for extreme forms of physical violence directed against defenceless victims and not a slap on the wrist as some might imagine. The term is also objectionable as it carries a presumption of guilt.

Warnings

Frequently, though by no means invariably, the process began with a warning or a threat of violence.[15] This could be in written or in verbal form.[16] The deliberate propagation of rumours about drug dealing, sexual deviance, or other forms of antisocial behaviour might precede or accompany overt paramilitary attention. Blackening the name of a "suspect," often referred to as a "scumbag," was sometimes done with a view to setting up the individual for more harmful attention later on. These forms of psychological pressure could be terrifying because of the uncertainty and because "The Boys" could come at any time of the day or night.[17]

Curfews and fines

That is, being confined to home for certain hours of the day and night under threat of greater retaliation, was sometimes the corollary of a warning. A further variant was to impose fines on the alleged offender or his or her family.[18] According to Joe Austin, a Sinn Féin councillor who often

acted as a spokesman for the party on justice issues, a visit from the paramilitaries was in virtually all cases sufficient to ensure compliance, and
there the matter ended.[19] This claim merits closer attention.

Public humiliation

The iconic image of public shaming is of a woman, head bowed, tied to a
lamppost, with a dark substance poured over her head. This was not
simply shaming but abduction, verbal abuse, and assault, a scene seemingly
more redolent of medieval village life than that of a modern welfare society. In fact Seamus Heaney drew on early history and mythology to evoke
images of a condemned woman:[20]

> Her shaved head
> like a stubble of black corn,
> her blindfold a soiled bandage,
> her noose a ring
> to store
> the memories of love.

In late 1971 both the Official IRA and the Provisional IRA in Derry issued
warnings against young women fraternising with soldiers of the British
Army (the same army that had been welcomed with cups of tea into the
Bogside in Derry a few years earlier). Possibly the earliest of these attacks
involved a twenty-year-old factory worker. On the night of the 8 November
1971 a group of women, perhaps half a dozen, invaded her home in the
Bogside, seized her, blindfolded her, tied her hands behind her back, questioned her, and demanded to know the names of other girls who had gone
out with soldiers. They then shaved her head.[21] The following night Martha
Doherty, a nineteen-year-old girl, also from the Bogside, was dragged to
an open space within view of Free Derry Corner ("You are now entering
Free Derry," the gable end wall proclaimed). A crowd of around eighty
people watched the spectacle, some cheering and shouting "soldier lover."
Martha Doherty's hair was first cut roughly with a scissors, then by razors.
Finally cold tar was poured over her head and feathers dumped on the
sticky substance to complete the humiliation.[22]

A third incident quickly followed. The *Irish Times* reported on its front page of the ordeal of Deirdre Duffy, another factory girl:

> She was tied with wire to the same lamp-post as Miss Martha Doherty, aged 19, who was tarred on Tuesday night. A cardboard placard – "Soldier Doll" – was hung from her neck. A crowd of about 200 watched in silence as a woman cropped her dark hair with scissors and then poured red and black liquid – either paint or tar – over her head. The girl, who lives in Westway, Creggan, was tied to the post by her chest and feet.[23]

These three attacks took place within a stone's throw of Free Derry Corner. One might wonder if any of these factory girls, or the onlookers for that matter, either then or later puzzled over the slogan "You are now entering Free Derry."

So much for Foucault's generalisations. The practice of tarring – a generic term for some closely related assaults on the female body – soon spread to west Belfast, where severe beatings sometimes preceded the final acts of humiliation. Groups of Cumann na mBan women, originally the female section of the IRA, distinguished themselves in policing their sisters. The instruments for beating "offending" girls and women included hurley sticks and iron bars. One social scientist is of the view that, "in comparison with the methods of other resistance movements" head shaving, tarring and feathering, and kneecapping were, as he puts it, "quite mild."[24]

Women and men were involved in these assaults. Nor was this intra-community violence confined to nationalist areas. The public parading of victims, with labels attached, was also used against boys and adolescents by loyalist and republican paramilitaries. In 2003, the Ulster Defence Association forced two youths to stand in a busy shopping area on the Ligoniel Road in north Belfast holding placards proclaiming, "We are scum who robbed our own people."[25] According to John Bunting of the Ulster Political Research Group, a decision had been taken by the UDA to "move away from punishment shootings" in favour of "naming and shaming." The organisation felt this was a progressive and more humane approach to juvenile delinquency.

Though often identified almost exclusively with women in popular memory, tarring and feathering was used against both men and women during the Troubles and extended sporadically into the twenty-first century. However, the cropping or shaving of women's heads has a particular gender dimension, and this requires some explanation. In the view of the German feminist researcher, Juliane Roleke

> The shaving of women's heads was a "punishment" technique which had clear sexual overtones and was used especially against women. The perceived "dishonourable" behaviour of the attacked women led to their symbolic degradation by shaving the traditional core symbol of "true" femininity, the head hair.[26]

The public and ritualised nature of these humiliations – victims (male and female) were sometimes tied to posts near a church or other public building and placards tied round their necks to advertise their "crimes" – was a means not only of punishing the victims but of signalling to the wider community the new power realities. Enemies of "the people" beware.

Shootings and beatings

These came to be the preferred methods of both loyalist and republican paramilitaries. The prelude to such attacks sometimes involved the invasion of a victim's family home and threats against other members of the family. The "site of justice" was often a piece of waste ground, an alleyway, a playground, or the home or backyard of the victim's family. The implements used in the assaults included baseball bats, hurley sticks, clubs (sometimes studded with nails), concrete blocks, sledge hammers, iron bars and spikes, and other improvised weapons. The usual objective was to crush bones and joints and thereby incapacitate the victim. Thus the injuries were scattered round the body. Paramilitary-style shootings, by contrast, targeted specific parts of the body, including bullets to the ankle, leg, knee, arm, elbow, or in extreme cases a shot to the lower back (risking spinal injury). Though it may seem counterintuitive, beatings could be worse than shootings because, according to orthopaedic surgeons, the shattering of bones and joints could do irreparable damage. Medical research into the shooting of one hundred victims between 1986 and 1989 found that "the possibility of a complicated injury involving bone, blood vessel, or nerve (either alone or in combination) occurred in approximately 40% of knee injuries, 70% of ankle injuries, and 30% of elbow injuries."[27] If the injuries were to the head, the prognosis could be even worse. A UVF victim, for instance, was so badly beaten that after a period in intensive care he was left "in a permanently brain-damaged state, unable to communicate or lead a normal life."[28]

Expulsions or exiling

This was a sanction that victims found particularly hard to bear. For some it was second only to death in the scale of punishments. Separated from family and friends, isolated in a foreign city, often across the sea in Britain, some descended into depression and further trouble. Some were "inadequate people who very often have medical and social problems," according to the human rights campaigner Fr Denis Faul. "They are not made for the society in England."[29] The practice was that the objects of paramilitary and sometimes community displeasure were ordered to leave home and not return to the area, under pain of possible execution. The areas of geographical exclusion might vary. Some were expelled from their neighbourhood to another part of Northern Ireland, either near or far. An unfamiliar area could harbour its own dangers, exposing the refugee to attacks by orange or green gangs, as the case might be. Sometimes a time period was specified. As often as not, the exclusion was open ended. Should the victim reappear in his home area without paramilitary permission, then all bets were off in terms of the possible punishment. Some were told they had to leave Northern Ireland, with many of these finding their way to Britain. The impressionistic evidence is that while some sought refuge in the Republic of Ireland a majority were displaced to England or Scotland.[30]

Thousands were exiled during the course of the Troubles.[31] There are many ironies here, not least from an Irish republican standpoint. The motif of the political exile is inscribed in stories of Ireland, yet within a short space of time republican groups were responsible for more political exiles than the British government had managed during the whole course of the nineteenth century. Incongruously also, the primary place of refuge was Britain, the presumed source of countless Irish ills.

Factionalism within the loyalist paramilitary world led to expulsions and mass movements of Protestant families within Belfast right at the beginning of this century, estates in the Lower Shankill being particularly badly affected. The line of division was between supporters of the UVF and the UDA.[32] But over the time period of the Troubles as a whole, loyalists seem to have been less involved in exiling as a means of controlling so-called antisocial behaviour. However, this is simply an impressionistic view and may need to be revised as fresh evidence becomes available. Suffice it to say here that driving individuals and families out of their loyalist neighbourhoods was also part of the loyalist apparatus of repression.

It may seem counterintuitive but some victims preferred to face a shooting to the leg ("getting it over and done with") in preference to "exiling" which threatened an alienated existence in a foreign environment.[33] The reason that banishment bore heavily on many exiles is that they often came from unemployed backgrounds, suffered from educational disadvantage, might have mental health problems, had few social connections elsewhere, and had few of the personal skills needed to negotiate a strange and often threatening environment. Moreover, if the exiled person was a child or adolescent, as was often the case, the whole family might feel obliged to move. This meant living in emergency accommodation, often hostels. Provision for children was minimal and some of the exiled parents worried that they were sharing living spaces with criminals and alleged paedophiles. On top of that there was the disruption to children's schooling, to social networks, to employment opportunities, and to mental health. Miserable living conditions were likely to exacerbate tensions within the family, with the victim sometimes blamed for the burdens brought on the family. According to care workers, dependence on tranquilisers or even illegal drugs could become part of the downward spiral in which individuals and families were trapped.[34]

Executions

In a number of cases capital punishment, either deliberately intended or the by-product of prolonged group assault, was the ultimate sanction.[35] One well-known instance had a sadosexual element to the killing. David Keys, a member of the Loyalist Volunteer Force, was suspected by his comrades of being an informer. He was raped with a snooker cue, beaten, and then strangled.[36] The Provisional IRA "disappeared" a number of victims during the 1970s, secretly disposing their bodies in the Republic of Ireland. Such revelations prompted the Irish *taoiseach* Enda Kenny, in the course of a Dáil debate, to speak out angrily: "Down here, you buried the dangerous living along with the discarded dead." He also outlined how suspected paedophile volunteers within the IRA were moved from district to district to conceal but not put a stop to their activities.[37] Direct Action Against Drugs (DAAD), a cover name for the Provisional IRA, specialised in the execution of alleged drug dealers in the 1990s, as did other antidrugs vigilante groups. Sometimes, notably in the case of loyalist terror groups, executions were a result of "turf wars" between rival paramilitary gangs seeking a local monopoly of the sale of drugs. Within the republican movement executions were primarily directed against alleged informers, political opponents, drug dealers, and those who had embarrassed a local warlord. Eamon Collins, an IRA intelligence officer responsible for a string of assassinations, was beaten with an iron bar and stabbed to death by his former comrades near Newry in 1999 because he had turned against the organisation.[38] His face was so badly disfigured that his widow agreed to a closed coffin. Andrew Silke, who has a background in forensic psychology and criminology and who has investigated paramilitary-style attacks, reckons that approximately 114 persons were executed in punishment attacks between 1970 and the late 1990s. Since then others have followed them to the grave.[39]

Sometimes beatings that were not intended to be lethal could get out of hand and result in death. One of these was the assault on Paul Quinn, a young Catholic man from Cullyhanna in south Armagh.[40] A dozen or so armed and masked men, believed to be local republicans, were involved in his beating at a farm on the County Monaghan side of the border in 2007.

The chief instruments of punishment were iron bars but nail-studded cud-gels were used on the upper body to puncture and tear skin and tissue. The scene or place of justice was a disused cow house and farmyard. Two of his friends were held down in a neighbouring shed and taunted as the pun-ishment progressed: can you hear your friend squealing for mercy? One said later, "They were beating him, you could hear the bars bouncing off him, maybe four or five bars, he was screaming."[41] This lasted for twenty-five to thirty minutes and continued for some minutes after the young man temporarily lost consciousness. The victim's eighteen-year-old girl friend Emma was summoned on her mobile phone by one of the friends. She found Paul in the byre.

"He was more or less screaming with the pain, he was in a bad way … I thought first that he had got bullet shots in his legs, but it was actually the bone sticking out of his knee. I thought he was just going to have broken arms, broken legs. He had bruises all over his face and his head and there was blood coming out of his arms and legs."[42]

Paul Quinn died on the way to hospital. Every major bone in his body below the neck had been broken. He was just twenty-one years old. No one was ever convicted for the assault. Sinn Féin denied that members of the IRA were involved.[43] Emma emigrated to Australia the following year.[44]

"… A MUCH MORE RATIONAL BASIS"

To sum up, there was a variety of types of punishment techniques available, extending from written or verbal warnings to the extreme of assassination. This suggests a hierarchy of punishments with a degree of calibration as to the level of intervention (bearing in mind that this could be quite arbi-trary). It should also be added that there was variation in the severity of particular sanctions. A few of the beatings, at their most extreme, could take the form of an improvised crucifixion, driving nails or spikes into palms or ankles and then proceeding to beat the "crucified" victim; on the other hand, a shooting could be to a fleshy part of the leg from which re-covery was quite rapid.[45] Bats and cudgels with long nails driven through them could have unexpected consequences: "a number of victims have suf-fered punctured lungs as a result of attacks with spiked bats."[46] In the case of shootings, the calibre of the gun used also determined the seriousness of the wound, which could range from a light revolver to an assault rifle or shotgun. The different punishments were not mutually exclusive. A beating or shooting could precede or accompany an order to leave the country.

Paramilitaries and their spokespersons spoke of established rules and graduated punishments in a stepwise progression of increasing severity. Extreme violence was inflicted with reluctance and then only on recidivists, or so the rhetoric ran. The reality could be very different. The Sinn Féin press officer Richard McAuley freely admitted, "Back four or five years ago, people were getting kneecapped who should not have been kneecapped."[47] Unfortunately physical injuries cannot be undone (unlike penalties in the formal justice system where miscarriages of justice, however egregious, can be rectified and compensation offered). McAuley's statement does, however, underline the point that even by paramilitary standards some of the punishments were disproportionate. Others were admitted to be mistakes. But reform was on its way, "because of the structure of the IRA at that time, decisions could be made at the local level. Now the structure is more controlled, things are done on a much more rational basis."[48]

Andy Tyrie, the leader of the UDA, also had "things" on his mind, though he admitted the counterproductive nature of many of the punishments. In his view, "This is not a normal society. You have to instil fear in those sort of people, but it never works if it occurs over a long period of time. People get used to being threatened. I know someone who has been kneecapped three times and is still doing the same things he was kneecapped for."[49]

These two sets of comments, it is worth noting, were made at the end of the first decade of armed conflict. Few would have imagined that four decades of punishment practices still lay ahead.

SCALE OF THE ATTACKS

The scale and practices of paramilitary repression are almost wholly unknown outside of Northern Ireland. Within Northern Ireland it is imperfectly understood outside of mainly working-class areas. Before discussing issues of magnitude, it is necessary to emphasise again that these are intra-community intimidatory practices. This is important because some outside observers find it well-nigh impossible to believe that so much republican violence was directed against members of its "own" community. It seems

somehow to be less difficult to accept that loyalist paramilitaries perpetrated acts of extreme violence against fellow loyalists and unionists. So, to
be absolutely clear, these were not acts of violence directed against the communal "other"; these were green-on-green and orange-on-orange attacks.
Sectarian, communal, and ethnonational conflicts were another matter,
though inevitably they were all interconnected strands in a larger web of
political violence.

It is impossible to quantify the scale of the lesser forms of intimidation
or to track how these changed over time. There is, however, an unexpected
source that casts some light on threats against young people by paramilitary groups. The Northern Ireland Young Life and Times Survey, 2004,
which interviewed teenagers (sixteen-year-olds), included a number of
questions on the paramilitary presence in the minds of young people.[50] To
the question "Have you ever been threatened by a paramilitary group?"
eight per cent of the sample responded "yes." Roughly one in four (28 per
cent) of the respondents reported that a member of the family or close
friends had been threatened by a paramilitary organisation at some point
in their lives. These are disturbingly high figures, and the proportions varied little as between loyalist and republican communities. The former head
of the Community Relations Council, Duncan Morrow, extrapolating
from the sample findings, concluded, "direct threat by paramilitaries remained a measurable factor for tens of thousands of young people in
2004."[51] This was some years after the Good Friday Agreement, so it would
be a shade on the optimistic side to assume conditions had been much
different during the preceding decades.

We can gain some impression of the scale but not the severity of certain
other types of paramilitary punishments by looking at figure 3.2, bearing
in mind that these represent only the more visible tip of the iceberg of
paramilitary control. Even in relation to the instances represented here,
we are dealing with underestimates. Paramilitary-style shootings were not
categorised separately until 1973 and paramilitary-style assaults were not
counted until as late as 1982.[52] Even then, according to police sources, only
the most severe instances were counted.[53] If the injuries did not require
hospitalisation, they were unlikely to be picked up. Some victims requiring
hospitalisation sought to conceal the circumstances of their injuries from
medical personnel.[54] Rather like rape and domestic violence, the numbers

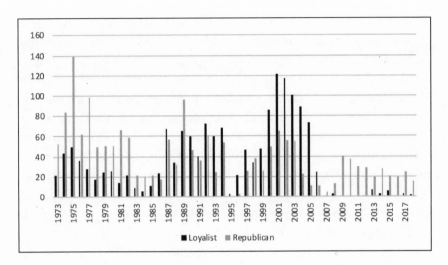

Figure 3.2 The number of paramilitary-style punishment shootings each year, 1973–2018

Source: Statistics branch of the RUC and PSNI.

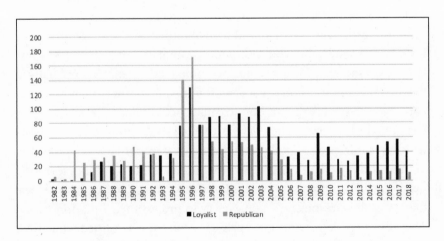

Figure 3.3 The number of paramilitary-style punishment beatings each year, 1982–2018

Source: Statistics branch of the RUC and PSNI.

of *reported* instances fall well below the *actual* numbers. In other words, these are minimum estimates of the extent of paramilitary repression within communities in Northern Ireland.[55] The Youth survey of 2004 reinforces the point: it found that 14 per cent of Protestants and 16 per cent of Catholics knew of a family member or a close friend who had been subjected to a paramilitary beating.[56] Silke's guesstimate is that there were at least 10,000 other beatings of varying degrees of severity between 1970 and 2000.[57] There is every reason to believe that underestimation continued after that date as well. Even without taking these major downward biases into consideration, the official figures paint a picture of frightening levels of gunshot wounds and mutilations. Between 1973 and 2017, according to the statistics compiled by the police, there were 3,401 victims of shootings by paramilitaries and 2,949 victims of vigilante-style beatings, well over 6,000 in total.

EXILING

The practice of exiling individuals and families was present as a largely invisible process throughout the Troubles. Occasionally a family resisted an expulsion order and a flare of publicity illuminated the wider process of intimidation and exiling. But resistance, it should be emphasised, was rare in the extreme. One instance which commanded widespread publicity at the time was an expulsion order against four young Newry men in August 1991. Two accepted their fate, but two others sought sanctuary in the Catholic cathedral in Newry. They were threatened with "direct military action," which was interpreted locally as meaning they would be executed if they did not comply. The threats notwithstanding, the two families formed a neighbourhood organisation, Save Our Sons (sos), and organised a local march on the Drumalane estate, Newry to protest their sons' innocence. They also negotiated with local priests to have the ban lifted while their sons sought refuge in the Catholic cathedral in Newry. One priest, now dead, is alleged to have said to the young men "it's only a bullet you know" (meaning that the punishment, if accepted, would be a minor affair and quickly forgotten).[58] A piece of black humour circulating at the time was that next time round the boys would seek refuge from the Church of Ireland, whose parish church was only a few streets away. The allegation as to taking the bullet, if true, was untypical of the local clergy and Cardinal Cathal Daly during the course of a visit to Newry delivered strong words of condemnation for what he called "gun law": "It is a very serious thing when a society deteriorates, or is brought to that kind of point, when people can be ordered at gunpoint out of their own town without benefit of law, court or legal defence. It is a travesty of any kind of respect for human rights or dignity."59

A compromise deal presented by local priests in consultation with IRA men from Dundalk – exclusion from Newry for a short period of time – was rejected by the young men and their families. While this would have saved paramilitary embarrassment over the spotlight placed on their practices, the families were not prepared to concede the principle of what they perceived to be unjust charges and an unacceptable assumption of authority on the part of paramilitaries. The young men, Liam and Davy, vacated Newry cathedral after a week and went into hiding in Northern Ireland. Eventually, with the help of various peace groups, as well as support from Peter Benenson the founder of Amnesty International and Mary Robinson the president of Ireland, the Provisional IRA rescinded the expulsion order. But this was not until Liam and Davy had spent almost a year in hiding and younger members of the extended family had been subjected to taunts and jibes. For the two families, the strain at times reached almost unbearable proportions during the yearlong campaign, affecting their health and wellbeing. To make the point that resistance carried penalties, irrespective of public opinion, the IRA allowed the other two men who had complied with their orders back into Newry after six months in exile. In effect the writ of the paramilitaries ran despite local opposition, though the expulsion order might well have been permanent, as so many were, had there not been a spirited public campaign on behalf of these young men.60

It may seem strange but the extent of exiling accelerated in the years after the paramilitary ceasefires of 1994. The major agency that dealt with intimidation of this kind, Base 2 (which is a specialised section of the Northern Ireland Association for the Care and Resettlement of Offenders), had an average of 200 cases per year between 1990 and 1994. In 1995 there were 224 referrals to this agency and by the year 2000 this had almost quadrupled to 854. These threats or alleged threats materialised as actual expulsions in more than half the cases noted in 1995 and in almost 40 per cent of cases in 2000. It is widely acknowledged, though, that these numbers are under-estimates.[61] One indication of this is that 19 per cent of the respondents to the youth survey cited earlier had either moved house or had close friends who had been forced to move.[62]

The evidence suggests a surprising level of intimidation and a truly re-markable increase during the early peace process. In part the increase was due to the substitution of the largely invisible practice of exiling for the more visible punishment shootings and beatings. It also reflected the in-creasingly active and repressive role taken by paramilitaries within loyalist and republican communities during the peace process. In the four-year period from 1995 to 1998 a clear majority of the expulsions was attributable to republican groups; as the new century opened, loyalists were responsible for the lion's share of the expulsion orders. Some of the expulsion orders carried the threat of a death penalty. A further perspective on paramilitary intimidation is given by the Northern Ireland Housing Executive. During the period 2006–14 alone there were more than 5,000 cases of people seek-ing rehousing due to intimidation.[63] Though much attention has focused on forced population movements at the beginning of the Troubles, these insidious and largely invisible processes have escaped attention.

Northern Ireland, it is true, has come a long way since the mayhem of the Troubles. Nonetheless, it is a dismal thought that in 2017 (see figures 3.2 and 3.3), paramilitary-style attacks were still taking place at the rate of two per week. Nor had expulsions and other forms of intimidation ended. This chapter could be written in the present tense.[64]

OVERVIEW, 1973–2018

Viewing the period 1973–2018 as a whole, a few summary points may be made. There were 6,463 *recorded* punishment beatings and shootings, that is, instances of physical and psychological torture, and bodily mutilation. The true extent has to be from ten thousand upwards because of nonre-cording and under recording.[65] More than 150 men and women experienced "tarrings."[66] Thousands were "exiled" from their homes and neighbour-hoods.[67] In total for the period 1970–2018, and this may well be an under-estimate, in the region of 20,000 suffered directly at the hands of paramilitaries from within their own communities by virtue of the forms of paramilitary punishment detailed in this chapter, with repercussions not just for the immediate victims but for family and kinfolk as well.

To place this in some kind of context, there were roughly three and a half thousand killings associated with the Troubles, most of them carried out by paramilitary organisations. The two forms of activity are not of course directly comparable but it is clear that the investment in paramilitary punishments was not some incidental aspect of "the struggle," be it for or against the union. It was a systemic part of the paramilitary enterprise.

Over the four decades there was little to choose between loyalist and republican vigilantes in terms of responsibility. Each accounted for roughly one half of the victims of paramilitary-style beatings, with loyalists showing a slightly greater preference for this form of bodily harm.[68] The story was broadly the same for paramilitary-style shootings, though republicans were responsible for a slightly larger share. In the early years, republicans dominated the vigilante stakes; in later years loyalists came increasingly to the fore, in part perhaps emulating republicans, though situational factors were likely to have dominated. In the final years of the period, since the signing of the Good Friday Agreement in 1998, loyalists accounted for a majority of punishment beatings and shootings.

The likelihood is that Catholic communities suffered proportionately more from vigilantism during the period of the Troubles as Catholics formed a minority of the population. Moreover, loyalist paramilitaries were less committed to performing "policing" roles, though they certainly claimed this at times, and many of their punishments were matters of internal paramilitary discipline or of disputes between competing loyalist groupings, thereby limiting to a degree the wider community-wide repercussions. This is particularly true of the post-Agreement period when factionalism proliferated on the loyalist side.

CHRONOLOGICAL PERIODS

The temporal pattern traced out by the grim statistics presented in figures 3.2 and 3.3 gives rise to a number of questions. Are there distinct subperiods within the long time span from 1969 to recent times? Why for instance had 1975 the highest number ever of republican punishment shootings, with 139 reported instances? Did the republican and loyalist paramilitary ceasefires of 1994 or the Good Friday Agreement of 1998 mark sea changes in the incidence of intra-communal violence? What of the more recent years?

Any attempt at periodization (subdividing the full period into discrete segments of time) is bound to be rough, not least as we are attempting to understand the activities of two different sets of paramilitary organisations, each with its own dynamic.[69] Still, it is possible to identify five or so subperiods between 1970 and 2018 that have distinctive elements to them. The first is the chaotic period between the outbreak of serious civil disturbances in 1969 and the shift to sustained armed conflict in the early to mid-1970s. The establishment of "no-go" areas in working-class Catholic areas of Derry and Belfast in August 1969 in the wake of attacks by rampaging Protestant mobs, sometimes assisted by the police, created the conditions for an initial policing vacuum.[70] The origins of paramilitary-style punishments may be traced back to this point. Loyalist areas soon followed suit with their own citizens' defence associations. In these chaotic conditions vigilante justice reigned. The emerging republican and loyalist paramilitary organisations came to monopolise the supply of summary justice, be it tarring and feathering, beatings, or shootings in what were as yet uncharted waters as to how to deal with crime, or alleged crime, in loyalist or proto-republican areas. Viewed in hindsight, the hope and joy that accompanied the creation of "no-go" areas laid the foundations for human rights abuses within these working-class communities on a scale simply unimaginable in the optimistic 1960s.

The extended ceasefire between British security forces and the Provisional IRA in 1975 allowed for the creation of incident centres, manned by republicans, that some see as the beginning of more elaborate systems of community control by the IRA. The year 1975 was also a period of renewed tension between different republican factions. The result was a surge in internecine and intracommunity attacks (something rather similar to the period after the ceasefires of 1994 which is a theme picked up later).

Subsequently the IRA formalised what were called civil administration units (the terms "auxiliary IRA" was also used), and these controlled many aspects of community life, including policing. In time the administration of informal justice became more formal and more centrally controlled. The very high number of vigilante-style shootings in 1977 is probably related to the creation of these civil administration units. The level of intracommunity shootings by loyalists, by comparison, was relatively low in the later 1970s. There was a lull in the frequency of attacks in the early to mid-1980s, as Sinn Féin searched for alternative means of control, but arguably there were no substantial changes to paramilitary practices.

At the end of the 1980s or perhaps the beginning of the 1990s there was increasing resort to exiling by republican paramilitaries, though beatings and shootings continued. This suggests some rethinking within republican ranks. About this time also loyalist punishment attacks were coming increasingly to the fore, though in this case due to rising loyalist militancy and impatience with the restraint – a very relative term – hitherto exercised by an older loyalist leadership.

"... time to look at their own community"

The republican and loyalist ceasefires of 1994 inaugurated a new phase, as both sets of paramilitaries turned their attention more fully to their host communities, demonstrating their continued relevance by meting out punishments, responding to slights to their authority, and maintaining their military structures intact. While the years immediately after 1994 witnessed an explosion in paramilitary-style beatings, there was a sudden and large *decline* in the numbers of loyalist and republican punishment shootings. The explanation for this curious and temporary state of affairs is not hard to find. When the paramilitary organisations called ceasefires in 1994 it was not initially clear if intracommunity shootings might constitute a breach of the ceasefire (though the republican ceasefire in August 1994 was billed as a "total cessation of violence"). Republicans and loyalists kept their guns under wraps for a year or two. In their place they substituted an orgy of punishment beatings and expulsions. The objective was to continue to impose their will on working-class communities. On the republican side the number of beatings quadrupled between 1994 and 1995, up from thirty-two to 141, whereas on the loyalist side it doubled from thirty-eight to seventy-six. Gradually both sets of paramilitaries came to realise that intracommunity violence was of no great concern to either the British or the Irish authorities. Some cynical observers saw it as "enforcing the peace." Loyalist paramilitaries led the way in returning to the use of the gun. A convicted killer and loyalist leader, Billy Hutchinson explained: "Before people were fighting against each other. Now they are on ceasefire it's given them plenty of time to look at their own communities."[71]

Underemployed paramilitaries were given their head. Their expertise was also channelled into fuel laundering, alcohol and cigarette smuggling, illegal dumping of waste, cattle smuggling, protection rackets, some internal feuding, and violent affray. Loyalist groups such as the UVF and the UDA were especially active in the drugs trade, as were splinter republican groups.[72]

It is remarkable that the Good Friday Agreement made little difference. Quite the reverse in fact. Loyalist shootings escalated alarmingly, in part due to feuding between different loyalist groups, and reached an all-time high in 2001. Hundreds were forced from their homes, as loyalist turf wars consumed parts of north and west Belfast. Republican violence within nationalist communities also remained at a high level. Unlike the fragmented world of loyalism, the Provisional IRA enjoyed a monopoly of violence, more or less, within the areas controlled by their members, so the targets came from the civilian nationalist community rather than from rival republican paramilitaries. As well as those deemed to be behaving antisocially, the victims included young men who happened to challenge or offend local IRA volunteers in one way or another.

In the five or so years after the signing of the agreement there was little sign of a letup in paramilitary-style attacks on members of their own community. It seems likely that the decade after the ceasefires of 1994 was qualitatively different from other phases in that paramilitary groups felt a need to flex their muscles and to assert their supremacy locally. It is possible also that a considerably larger share of the punishments involved personal slights and vendettas. It has been suggested that poorer quality but more vicious volunteers were entering paramilitary organisations during the 1990s.[73] Be that as it may (such claims had been made for earlier periods as well), a further phase was apparent from 2005 onwards, as vigilante-style attacks shifted decisively onto a lower plane.

In the context of this lower level of activity (2005–18), and for no discernible reason, wounding by gunshot was preferred by republican vigilantes while loyalists favoured bone-crunching beatings.[74] Indeed it is not clear throughout the whole period of the Troubles and its aftermath why some victims got gunshot wounds and others got disabling beatings.[75] On the republican side, the Provisional IRA increasingly withdrew from vigilante activity – Sinn Féin adopted cooperation with the Police Service of Northern Ireland in 2006 under intense British, Irish, and American pressure – though there were exceptions in some areas, including South Armagh.[76] Continuing loyalist attacks seemed to be tied to disciplinary measures within loyalist paramilitary organisations as well as attacks on alleged antisocial elements.

"that is the way it is …"

The new IRAs, or as the writer Eoghan Harris dubbed them, the "recurring IRA," stepped into some of the space vacated by the Provisional IRA, which is a situation that continues to this day.[77] Many of their volunteers had been schooled in the larger organisation. For example, in late 2008 or 2009 there emerged in the city of Derry a republican grouping – Republican Action Against Drugs (RAAD) – which included former members of the Provisional IRA.[78] Though small in numbers and lacking wide support, RAAD nonetheless succeeded in imposing its will on areas of the Catholic working class.[79] Self-righteous and puritanical, RAAD believed not only in inflicting gunshot wounds on those believed to be drug abusers but in some cases executing them. A feature of the time was the willingness of victims to turn up by appointment and then "take the bullet."[80] An example comes from the father of a 20-year old-victim, Kieran McFadden. The son's name, as it happens, was also Kieran.

Mr McFadden said he went as a father to speak to everyone he could so that his son would not be shot. He even took his son to meet the gunmen. "At the back of my mind, I thought they were not going to do it. It was going to be a scare tactic but it backfired", he said. He was forced to watch as his son was shot. "Kieran said he had done nothing wrong. I am adamant he has done nothing wrong. Even if he did kick someone in the head, that doesn't justify this. They are scary, scary people [RAAD]. Where are the human rights for children?"[81]

One of the finest of an older generation of Irish historians, A.T.Q. Stewart, wrote years ago of the continuity through time of many of the same sites of conflict.[82] He would not have been surprised that the shooting of Kieran took place not far from the historic "Free Derry Corner."

Much has been written of the Irish mother in sentimental ballad and mawkish verse. "A mother's love's a blessing" is one of the most popular, and there is a fine version by the singer Majella.[83] The opening line is "As an Irish boy was leaving ..." In April 2012 another Majella, this time in the city of Derry, was bidding farewell to her teenage son. He had been summoned at his home by a masked man and told to appear at a specified location, to be shot by RAAD. If he did not come straight away, he was warned, "we are going to leave you in a wheelchair." Given little time to reflect, the mother, Majella O'Donnell, persuaded her son that he had to go; she would accompany him to the place of punishment. "I had to let him go because that is the way it is when there is a punishment shooting."

> I shook hands with him and let him walk on down the hill. I knew what he was feeling, I knew how scared he was and I let him go on down and I saw the men coming towards him and I just turned my back. When I heard the two shots I started to run down the lane and my heart kind of went when I saw him lying on the ground. He was white and I said: "Are you all right son?" He said Mammy, I am OK ...
>
> It was something that had to be done to save him. He knows I love him and I will always stand by him, no matter what, and I told him that night but I was powerless to stop it. It might have been brutal but he is not dead, he is not dead. He is alive.[84]

For those who would like to know more about the subsequent effects on the victim, his mother and his troubled younger brother, there is the powerful documentary film *A Mother Brings her Son to be Shot* directed by Sinéad

O'Shea and released in 2018. There are moments of humour but the over-whelming reality is one of tragedy and terror.

CORRELATING ORANGE AND GREEN

Compared to the hot emotion, the hatred, and the cruelty encapsulated in the punishment system, recourse to the statistics of human suffering seems almost irrelevant if not actually blasphemous. Some readers may wish to skip this slightly technical section. Yet statistics have their place, if only as an aid to understanding the enormity of terror and the parallel experiences of nationalist and unionist working-class communities.

The correlation between orange and green paramilitary-style shootings is positive and fairly strong at 0.60.[85] There is a similarly high degree of correlation between orange and green paramilitary-style assaults.[86] This may reflect the overall degree of intensity of the conflict and the malign interaction between orange and green at communal level. There is no clear statistical support from these long-range data for one form of punishment substituting for the other (shootings versus vigilante-style beatings), but it seems likely as indicated earlier that this was the case for the period between 1994 and 2003, that is, in the aftermath of the twin paramilitary ceasefires of 1994.[87] The qualitative evidence also indicates that expelling people from their homes also surged forward in these years, again pointing towards the possibilities of substitution within the repertoire of paramilitary punishments.[88]

Across the forty-year period from 1973 to 2013 it is not clear why there was so much variation in the incidence of paramilitary-style shootings and assaults. The possibilities include changing political circumstances, periodic rethinking within the paramilitary fraternities on the efficacy of their methods,[89] and possibly also variation in the recording methods of the police force.[90] It is likely that some rethinking in terms of the public image of paramilitaries also helps to explain the greater resort to exiling victims from the 1990s onwards, a point which has also been made in relation to the fading out over time of public spectacles such as tarring and feathering or the placarding of victims.[91]

PROFILING THE VICTIMS

Most attacks took place within working-class communities where para-military control was most pronounced. The victims were overwhelmingly of working-class origin. The locations mentioned again and again in news reports were economically and socially disadvantaged areas such as the Shankill and the Falls Road, Ballymurphy, Ballysillan, Ardoyne, Glencairn, Rathcoole, and the larger housing estates in Bangor, Lurgan, and Derry.[92] Though both loyalist and republican groups on occasion espoused left-wing rhetoric, praxis amounted to the maiming rather than the making of the working class.

The age of victims differed significantly as between the two ethno-relig-ious communities. While most victims were in their twenties, the average age of victims of loyalist attacks tended to be older, that of republican vic-tims younger.[93] This is discussed more fully in the next chapter. The gender of the victims was, however, similar in both communities. The casualties were overwhelmingly male. Over the quarter century between 1970 and 1993 three women were subjected to shootings by loyalists, out of a total of hundreds of instances.[94] There were no nonlethal cases of shootings of women by republican paramilitaries, but a number of women who had earned their displeasure were executed. The number of paramilitary-style assaults on women over the same period was by no means negligible: sixty-five were inflicted by loyalists and twenty-seven by republicans. Still, these represent less than 5 per cent of all *recorded* assaults within their respective communities. It is noticeable that loyalists showed a greater propensity to attack women, and this was in part associated with paramilitary feuding within loyalism as between the UVF, the UDA, and the LVF at the beginning of this century.

In the early years of the Troubles (outside of the time period for which we have detailed statistics) young women were subjected to humiliating treatments, and some women were assaulted if they dared to interfere dur-ing the course of a paramilitary operation.[95] One of the most horrific epi-sodes, partly orchestrated by women, was the abduction, torture, and secret burial of a Belfast mother of ten. She was the widow Jean McConville whose body was buried in secret at a lonely stretch of seacoast, Shellinghill Beach in County Louth just south of the border between the Republic of Ireland

and Northern Ireland.[96] This was coming up to Christmas 1972. She left ten young children as orphans. The oldest, Helen, was only fifteen years of age. The family was broken up and the children scattered round different institutional homes.[97]

Still, the general point remains: the victims of loyalist and republican violence were typically male. The cultural restraint or taboo, that women were not considered fair game for shooting and assault during the Troubles, broadly held true, and the fact that it was felt necessary to bury secretly Jean McConville's tortured body is a grisly corroboration of this. There is a qualification that is not immediately apparent. Such inhibitions did not apply to women in police or army uniform nor did bombs discriminate along gender lines.

So far we have been talking about physical attacks on women. If, however, we enlarge the focus to take in threats and warnings, then a still more qualified picture emerges. The youth survey of 2004 makes the surprising point that gender did not make a great deal of difference. Nine per cent of sixteen-year-old males had received threats from paramilitary organisations but remarkably 7 per cent of young females had also been threatened.[98] It is possible of course that this was an untypical cohort of young people but if not it suggests the writ of the paramilitaries was more gender-blind, at least in relation to lesser punishments than many have assumed.

Perhaps the least visible victims were sexual minorities, most notably homosexual men. Well-established traditions of prejudice against sexual "deviants" within Irish nationalism and Ulster unionism meant there was heightened vulnerability during the decades in which violence was widespread and to a degree normalised. As elsewhere in the United Kingdom or the Republic of Ireland, the likelihood is that most attacks were random, perpetrated by homophobic individuals or small, like-minded groups. But it also appears that some paramilitary groups were either involved directly or let it be known that such victimisation was acceptable. A study by Jarman and Tennant in 2003 reported that "in a number of areas the attacks seemed to be more systematic and organised," thereby raising the spectre of "paramilitary organisations that were deliberately and persistently engaging in 'queer bashing.'"[99] Possibly Northern Ireland during the course of the Troubles was a place apart in this respect. Fear of paramilitary reprisal and the danger of leaks from the police back into the victim's community represented, according to one analyst, a key element in "setting homophobic victimisation in Northern Ireland apart from comparable areas of the UK."[100]

EFFECTS ON THE VICTIMS

Severe punishments could result in permanent injury and incapacity. Though it was uncommon, there are instances of amputations following shootings to the leg, as we saw earlier in the case of Andrew Peden. An unemployed Catholic labourer, former republican prisoner, and reputed child abuser, John Collett had to have both legs amputated after a double kneecapping. He died a few days later in hospital.[101] Others were condemned to long periods of pain and reduced opportunities in the labour market. At least as important for many of the victims was the corrosive effect on their mental health and sometimes on the mental health of those close to them.

One of the saddest meetings I recall – this was in the mid-1990s in the public bar of Duke's Hotel in Belfast – was with a young man from the Markets area of Belfast who had refused to hand over the keys of his car to local paramilitaries. He feared his vehicle would be used for a murder attempt. Members of the group returned a few days later and blew off his elbow joint. By his actions, they informed him, he had endangered an active service unit. His one ambition in life had been to become a long-distance lorry driver. That dream was now shattered. One of his arms flopped uselessly by his side.

In addition to the physical damage and resulting disabilities, there is the long-term psychological trauma. The statistics deployed in this chapter cannot convey the crushing effect on the mental health of the victim or of the depression, drug dependence, even suicide that might ensue. The psychologist William Thompson conducted a study of victims of paramilitary punishment attacks in West Belfast and Craigavon and concluded that "those so punished exhibit symptoms of Post-Traumatic Stress Disorder and have CCEI (Crown Crisp Experiential Index which measures psychological distress) scores which are much higher than those of psycho-neurotic outpatients."[102] Difficulties in forming and maintaining relationships, sudden outbursts of uncontrollable anger, and other behavioural problems appear to be part of the longer-term legacy of these attacks. One man, a friend of mine, Brian Ryder (not his real name), was attacked in 1984 when just out of his teens. For years afterwards he experienced flashbacks from the paramilitary-style assault. More than three decades later, as the anniversary of the assault comes round, he experiences a tightening in his stomach; he fills up with hate and a desire for vengeance.[103] As with other victims of torture, the physical and psychological effects can play out over years and even decades.

An unusual subgroup is composed of the sons of fathers who had been active in paramilitary organisations. Many of these fathers had spent lengthy periods in prison, sometimes a marriage disintegrated under these and other strains, and a mother, effectively a single parent, struggled to bring up boisterous youngsters to whom their father was a stranger. New relationships might add further practical and psychological complexities, though this sometimes carried the risk of paramilitary retaliation. For reasons that would repay deeper social and psychological study, some young hell-raisers came from these kinds of backgrounds. The outcome might be a kneecapping or an assault, though some victims complained of unfairness in this regard. Those who had political connections were given lighter punishments or simply given repeated warnings. There was one law for the relatives of republican and loyalist activists and another for the rest.[104]

FAMILIES OF VICTIMS

Victims were not lone persons, though typically a punishment rained down on a single person.[105] The targets of paramilitary ire were bound to family, kinfolk, and friendship networks. Thus other persons were affected and sometimes traumatised. These might include mothers and fathers, brothers, sisters, friends, relatives. For older victims there might be a partner and possibly children. Brian Ryder is again a case in point. When the paramilitaries burst into his parents' house, his father was punched in the face and held captive while his son screamed with pain as his arms and legs were broken on the flagstones in the yard of the house outside. Fortunately his mother was out at a novena in Clonard Monastery. Ten men were involved and seemed to like the task. Brian heard different voices calling out, "Now it's my turn, let me have a go." His father was suffering from cancer at the time and died not long after. Brian believes that his father's life had been shortened by the ordeal. The father seemed to have been possessed of an unspoken guilt that he had not been able to protect his son. A counsellor who worked with family members of other victims in the Newry area made much the same point to me. Some fathers were haunted by an intense sense of inadequacy, perhaps even emasculation, because they had been powerless to prevent or soften the brutalisation of one of their children.[106] The impact on siblings can only be guessed but fear was surely part of the legacy. Some mothers spoke publicly of their pain, but families typically endured their suffering in silence.[107] The victims themselves hardly ever speak out, not then, not after five, ten, twenty, or even thirty years. The fear is too great. These are the silent, or rather the silenced, victims of the Troubles.[108]

On rare occasions, there were instances where family members collaborated in the punishment of another family member. The notorious loyalist Johnny ("Mad Dog") Adair is said to have approved the shooting to the leg of his own eighteen-year-old son, though the circumstances suggest that the shooting was managed so as to inflict a minor flesh wound.[109] The point seems to have been to demonstrate that no one was above local paramilitary rule while also ensuring the injuries were not too serious. For most parents, for most siblings, there was not only the pain of thinking of a loved one who had been violated but also the burden of handling the physical and psychological after-effects. This could include disruption to schooling or work, mental health problems, drug dependence, and physical disability.

PERPETRATORS

Why did they do it? There have been discussions and defences in print of the paramilitary position on "informal justice" practices, though they come mainly from the republican side. Loyalists have been less concerned to elaborate on their motivation, though the loyalist magazine *Combat* and the UDA's *Loyalist*, which were published in the 1990s, offered partial defences.[110] This usually ran along the lines of responding to community needs to deal with antisocial behaviour and other forms of crime that were prevalent in working-class areas. The plight of the little old lady living alone and persecuted by neighbourhood yobs became a stock character for the defence. Sometimes the language scaled grandiloquent heights:

> Acting on requests from the residents of the Lower Shankill area, regarding criminal behaviour (including vandalism, glue-sniffing, intimidation of pensioners and house breaking), a Social Unit of the Ulster Volunteer Force, whilst carrying out a preliminary investigation to ascertain the facts of the matter, was attacked by a relative of one of those involved ... The person instigating the attack has been punished, as will anyone interfering with units of the Ulster Volunteer Force.[111]

There are understandings that come from within the academy. The sociologist Dr Bill Rolston, while acknowledging that the IRA used "rather crude methods" went on to suggest "The community is terrorised by petty criminals: the community has the right to respond. What could be more logical, more democratic than that?"[112] Loyalist as well as republican paramilitaries would have had little difficulty in subscribing to that version of jurisprudence. Invoking the warm-sounding notion of community serves to obscure the difficulty that justice and human rights standards should apply universally and not just in particular pockets of a society. The possibly unintended priority accorded to local sentiment, arbitrary power, and summary "justice" in the passage above would have been understandable to groups as diverse as the Mandela United Club or lynching parties in the southern states of the USA.[113] This line of thought does not address the cruelty of the methods, the lack of provision for rehabilitation, the means whereby the views of the "community" were divined, nor the absence of safeguards for those being accused. The fact that most punishment attacks take place under cover of darkness is hardly reassuring.[114]

Another sociologist, while not advocating "popular justice" as he terms it, tells us that "any insurgent movement must perforce ensure a certain level of 'law and order' in areas under its control." He believes that "the Republican criminal justice," like the state system, took mitigating factors into account. A "careful assessment" of the offender's record is made, in addition to such factors as unemployment, alcoholism, pressures within the home, and a weak educational background. In his view the media tend to ignore the prehistory of an attack and "inevitably focus on the end results – the injured and sometimes dead offender – which are used to generate a 'moral panic' based on the violent nature of IRA justice."[115] Rereading this contribution, I found myself making comparisons with the fate of Jacko (not his real name) as sketched by the independent consultant Paul Smyth.[116] Jacko was brought up by an alcoholic mother who kept him at home from school so he could fetch drink for her, he remembered being beaten with a bat at the age of four or five ("we got beaten all the time"), he was expelled from primary school at the age of ten and from secondary school a few years later, and his career as a petty criminal saw him becoming heavily dependent on drink and drugs. He spent some time in prison under the state system of justice. In 2016 one of the new IRAs ordered him to turn up for an appointment. He was told he would get flesh wounds. They shot him through the kneecaps and anklebones and left him with permanent injuries. He often can't sleep because of the pain and craves drugs to deaden the suffering.

Danny Morrison, a leading member of Sinn Féin and a former editor of its paper, *An Phoblhacht*, has presented arguments from within the republican movement. In his view, for decades there had been a policing vacuum in nationalist areas. The RUC was unacceptable because of its sectarian composition and practices. So, the nationalist community turned to the republican movement and "put pressure on the IRA to fill the policing vacuum."[117] But republican vigilantism was rough and imperfect argues Morrison, especially when the IRA was fighting an armed struggle and had little time for niceties. Moreover, these practices were a propaganda gift to anti-republicans (if so, the obvious implication was not drawn). In fact, according to Morrison the IRA viewed community policing as a major distraction from its chief purpose and suspected that the RUC indulged criminals in order to tie down IRA resources, demoralise the nationalist community, and recruit informers.

There is a patina of plausibility to these arguments. In the late 1960s the Northern Ireland state was denied legitimacy by increasing numbers of northern nationalists, though the policing of crime was much the same as in neighbouring jurisdictions before the descent into large-scale violence. During the era of the civil rights movement in the later 1960s one of the slogans was "British rights for British citizens." And there is no doubt nationalist alienation from the state became increasingly widespread during the 1970s, as the offensive of the Provisional IRA and the repressive response of the state plunged the region into ever deeper political conflict. The RUC was the most visible coercive arm of the state and found it difficult to gain acceptance in some but by no means all nationalist areas. (There is a tendency in some writings on Northern Ireland to generalise too easily about nationalist areas and also to assume a constant relationship of antagonism between nationalists and the police through time.)

But it needs to be recalled that the Provisional IRA, and to some extent its loyalist counterparts, did everything possible to create and sustain a policing vacuum. The vacuum theory is also overstated. The police operated, albeit with varying degrees of effectiveness, in most parts of Northern Ireland – south Armagh is perhaps the big exception. Many of those "punished" by paramilitaries were also being prosecuted by the state. In effect, they received double punishment. Brian Ryder, for example, was severely roughed up by policemen on a number of occasions and eventually given a substantial prison sentence for car theft and so-called "joy riding." This was on top of his paramilitary beatings. His experiences indicate that there was an alternative, however ponderous, but the IRA and loyalists preferred to substitute their quick-fire "rough justice" in place of the policing and judicial services provided by the state.

The reasons for this are not hard to locate but some further problems with the Morrison argument may be mentioned. At the time this article was published, the IRA's "total cessation" of violence of August 1994 was more than ten years old. The "armed struggle" had been suspended, so the republican movement (and loyalist paramilitaries) had ample time for "niceties." The IRA not only stuck to the pathway of internal repression but it enlarged the scale of its operations. So, paradoxically, in the years when the IRA was less "distracted" from its main mission, paramilitary-style attacks on Catholics and nationalists were increasing. This contradiction is evident from figures 3.2 and 3.3.

No doubt the RUC sought to recruit informers among disaffected youths, though how widespread this was is open to doubt. The information the typical victim might possess must have been low grade by comparison with the high quality intelligence coming from informants *within* paramilitary organisations. As we now know, loyalist and republican organisations were heavily penetrated by the security forces at the very highest levels from the earliest years of the Troubles. Loyalist informers within the UVF such as Mark Haddock or republican informers such as Denis Donaldson are cases in point.[118]

The leadership of Sinn Féin presented the view publicly that paramilitary-style shootings and beatings were wrong and counterproductive – hence the Morrison aside in parentheses above on these practices being a boon to critics – but in their heartlands in north and west Belfast, in Derry, Strabane, and south Armagh members of Sinn Féin and the IRA were actively prosecuting their "war" on antisocial elements. The Sinn Féin headquarters in West Belfast, Connolly House, was the centre for information gathering and files on members of the local community who had come to the attention of the paramilitaries.[119] Interrogations sometimes took place there, as in other Sinn Féin advice centres or in "safe houses" but "kangaroo courts" seem to have been the exception rather than the rule.[120] More typically there was no court, no right to protest innocence or mitigating circumstances, no advocate, and guilt was decided in secret by one or more paramilitaries. "Summary justice" followed. Curiously, during the peace process and at precisely the same time as leaders of Sinn Féin were protesting their public opposition to such practices, rank and file members were busily increasing the frequency of battering and shooting. This was a bilingual world in which much was lost in translation between the two wings of the movement and hardly by accident.

The usual assumption is that perpetrators were exclusively male but this belief needs to be examined more critically. Indeed we cannot presume that women associated with loyalist or republican groups held views that were very different from those of men on the merits of the punishment system.[121] More research is needed on the role of women associated with the UDA, the UVF, and other loyalist organisations.[122] Though this is not the public perception, there appear to have been female units in the UDA, and women had an active role within the ranks of the UVF. It has been claimed that in addition to such activities as ferrying weapons, engaging in surveillance, and supplying medical services, some participated in punishment attacks on other women.

The most horrific case known to the public is that of Ann Ogilby whose body was found discarded near the M1 motorway in 1974. She was a single parent who was beaten to death in the loyalist stronghold of the Sandy Row by a group of ten women from a women's unit of the UDA because she was deemed to have transgressed certain moral and political codes. Her assailants were aged between seventeen and fifty years of age and included a mother and daughter duo.[123] The orders were given by a female commander. At one stage, it was claimed, some of the women stopped for a smoke before resuming the beating.[124] Ann Ogilby's six-year-old daughter was outside the door in an adjacent room, screaming for her mother, during the course of the frenzied attacks.[125]

This case was both extreme and untypical, but it certainly challenges easy assumptions about gender and violence, including links between female identity and nonviolence. It also poses problems for those who see the induction of women into paramilitary organisations as a marker of female empowerment.[126] The problems are even greater for those who see bonds of female identity as necessarily transcending divisions of social class, ethnicity, and national identity.

Within nationalism, women in the IRA and in Sinn Féin appear to have had a role in maintaining punishment practices, among other activities. As with the case of loyalist women, it is not easy to be specific as these forms of "community activity" tended not to be written into press statements or election manifestoes.[127] Nonetheless, photographs of women holding Armalites or providing guards of honour were a staple of propagandist publications.[128] A mother from Ballymurphy told me how she had observed a woman accomplice transferring a gun to a paramilitary figure just before a punishment shooting. The activity of ferrying and concealing weapons can hardly have been exceptional, as was confirmed to me by a former prominent member of the IRA. "Women were much less likely to be searched," he believed and were often used to carry guns to and from punishment attacks.[129] As we have seen, women undoubtedly participated in the cropping of hair, and the tarring and feathering of other women. And despite the sexualised nature of these particular assaults, feminists in Northern Ireland were, if anything, conspicuous by their absence, casting "stones of silence."[130] Much as political labour perished on the rocks of intercommunal violence in the 1970s, feminism in the north seems to have been similarly stranded. There were a few brave exceptions. Two Derry-based feminists, Avila Kilmurray and Cathy Harkin, deserve to be written more fully into history, as these remarkable women led resistance to "tar-ring" and may well have been responsible for reducing the incidence of these assaults. The timing would suggest so, as these particular violations faded out in Derry in the later 1970s.[131]

Sinn Féin women representatives are known to have called personally on parents informing them as to where their children were to be taken to receive a punishment.[132] Mairia Cahill, the grandniece of Joe Cahill, one of the founders of the Provisional IRA, recounted how at the age of sixteen she was raped by an IRA volunteer. When she complained, she was sub-jected to a "kangaroo court" where she was obliged to confront the alleged rapist. She states that women participated in her interrogation.[133] This is how she described her terrified reaction to the summons she received:

> In the beginning, I walked around in a complete daze. I was frightened. I knew that I had no option but to meet them, and I was running scen-arios in my head. I thought I was going to my own execution. I had seen stories of people over the years on the news who had been beaten and tortured and dumped by the roadside. I thought I was going to join them.[134]

We may recall that the republican volunteer Dolours Price admitted publicly that she had driven a number of people, including the widow Jean McConville, to their execution following IRA interrogations of alleged trai-tors.[135] Possibly afflicted by her own demons, Dolours Price became an alcoholic and died of a toxic mix of sedative and antidepressant medi-cation in 2013. Mrs McConville, we may recall, had been initially seized by a group of women. One might also argue that women who brought com-plaints of antisocial behaviour to loyalist or republican organisations, knowing the likely consequences, were to a degree complicit. The con-clusion must be that women could be victims, bystanders, advocates, or perpetrators of paramilitary aggression. That said, the administration of "popular justice" or (more grandiosely) "people's justice" lay primarily in the hands of men. The more general point, viewed through the prism of gender, is that during the Troubles the dominant pattern was of men kill-ing and being killed by men. The burden of the consequences was borne disproportionately by women.

PERPETRATOR GUILT?

Some may find it difficult to think of perpetrators as in any sense victims, though there is a discourse surrounding the Troubles that sees all participants as victims, that is, that all were equally victimised, whether killer or killed, whether vigilante or other. The shorthand for this, in which the distinction between perpetrator and victim is flattened out, is contained in the Orwellian sound bite, "there is no hierarchy of victims." But, going beyond Northern Ireland for a moment, would many seek to fudge differences between coloniser and colonised, torturers and those they tortured, racists and those they abused racially? I suspect most detached observers would find no moral equivalence in these polar opposites.[136]

Still, it may be admitted that some perpetrators later came to see themselves as victims, however confusing the claim. Might some sympathy be extended, without compromising fundamental values? Perhaps so. Many were very young when entering paramilitary organisations; there was local peer group pressure; some at least spoke of their "lost years" in prison and how much they had missed in their personal lives.[137] Less controversially, it may be acknowledged that perpetrators were brutalised by their own experiences. After all, this has been observed in other conflicts where torture was rife, so there is no reason to believe that Irish or Ulster volunteers were immune to these psychological aftereffects.[138] Apart from the small numbers of psychopaths and committed sadists within the loyalist and republican movements, it is difficult to see how ordinary volunteers exposed to the screams of victims and witnessing the effects of iron bars and nail-studded cudgels on defenceless bodies can have been other than brutalised.[139] Some may well have participated under duress. It is possible also that there were different experiences as between members of kneecapping squads and those involved in "batterings" but this would require detailed psychological research. One hypothesis might be that the gunman accomplished his task swiftly, was quickly removed from the scene, whereas teams of "batterers" might be at it for extended periods of time, seeing and smelling the blood, the urine, the excrement, the body changes.

A member of Sinn Féin and former member of the IRA, who by his own admission was active in the game of punishments, told me, almost casually, "But when you have young criminals breaking into some poor old lady's home, you have to do something. I shot several of them myself. We had no prisons to put them into. You had to do it."[140] Others were not so insouciant. A special edition of the BBC Talkback program in 2014 was told, "For many years I was a perpetrator. I was a member of the Provisionals and my life was in a mess ... There is not a day goes by that I don't regret it. My life was destroyed by it. We are all victims."[141] It is difficult not to feel some sympathy (but then I am writing as someone whose son was never a victim of paramilitary violence).

There is also evidence of loyalist and republican perpetrators who are said to have died of alcohol or other drug-related problems and of others, still alive, who suffer from various forms of addiction.[142] For whatever motive, but presumably for stress-related reasons, some former volunteers committed suicide in later life. Once again, these are subjects worthy of further exploration but these few instances point to something of signal importance. It is this: there was a ragged struggle, of a kind, within communities (albeit overwhelmingly one-sided in favour of those with the guns); there was another conflict, a more personal one troubling the hearts of at least some of the perpetrators.

Another aspect to the role of participants in punishment attacks is also not so obvious. It is that we are dealing with very large numbers of perpetrators. If we take the most conservative estimate, that of the recorded numbers of beatings and shootings, not to mention exiling, then we are dealing with more than 6,400 events. If we assume, for the sake of argument, that an average of five volunteers were involved directly or indirectly in each incident (and this is surely a conservative estimate), this amounts to 32,000 volunteer actions, as viewed from the side of the perpetrators. (A more realistic figure of 10 to 15,000 attacks, on the same assumption would imply 50 to 75,000 incidents.[143]) Of course some of the same individuals were involved over and over again, while others may have been "blooded" or inducted into loyalist and republican circles with only limited participation in punishments thereafter. Others again were involved in other forms of intimidation including "exiling." These crude estimates suggests that the pool of perpetrators was large and almost certainly embraced not hundreds but thousands of the foot soldiers of paramilitarism. Furthermore, if only a small minority of volunteers was directly engaged in major operations such as ambushes, assassinations, and bombings during the Troubles, the paradoxical implication seems to be that the typical volunteer exerted violence primarily through the medium of punishment attacks and community control. Even more paradoxical, these attacks were directed exclusively against members of the volunteer's own community.

OPERATIVES AND "SCUMBAGS"

But were the active service units within the IRA (cells engaged in high-prestige operations fighting the police and British army) separate from those of the civil administration units? The latter were responsible for enforcing "informal justice" at community level, along with other forms of community control. Loyalist paramilitaries seem not to have had such a division of functions. Silke's view is that the civil administration units of the IRA were composed of low-grade volunteers, volunteers seeking to improve their standing within the organisation, and including also new volunteers who were being "blooded."[144] Others have suggested that the lines of division were more blurred and as some of the punishments arose from personal disputes that may well be the case.[145] Still, the weight of evidence, meagre as it is, is in favour of some division of functions.

It seems also that members of punishment squads were held in low repute even within the broad republican movement ("low lifes," "cowards," "scumbags" being some of the terms floated about). An IRA squad in the Markets area of Belfast earned the epithet of the "hallions' battalion," which is Belfast vernacular for lazy, good-for-nothings.[146] One former senior member of the IRA told me of a conversation with a fellow IRA man, Bill (not his real name), who had served a long prison sentence and was released in the mid-1980s.[147] Bill felt insulted when on his release he was given responsibility for civil administration. In his view (as recalled by my informant) those were the units "that attracted the real scumbags." Bill favoured exiling people suspected of criminal acts because

> we don't have to look at them every day and maybe have to do them again. After all, the Brits created the problem and they should deal with it and pay for it. Much cleaner and satisfactory all round.[148]

These recollections also suggest internal debates and changes of attitude on the part of some members of the IRA and Sinn Féin.[149] Fanciful notions of "community courts," "people's justice," and the "people's army" emerged periodically, cresting at the beginning of the Troubles and again at the beginning of the 1980s. Ultraleft rhetoric served to cloak the ugliness of the implications. But the constant is that the beatings, shootings, and expulsions continued, though as the medical columnist manqué of *An Phobhlacht* reassured its readers and perhaps practitioners as well, "very few of those kneecapped suffer serious consequences from this injury."[150]

EXPLAINING PARAMILITARY "POLICING"

There are many interlocking reasons why the practice of "informal" justice became deeply embedded in urban working-class areas of Northern Ireland and in some rural localities such as south Armagh. The first was the military or security imperative: paramilitaries needed to exercise control over certain territories and peoples so as to have relatively safe havens within which to operate (be it racketeering, carrying out attacks on the army and police, bombing public buildings and workplaces, or assassinating civilians).[151] Unpredictable and uncontrollable antisocial elements within the community endangered these activities by drawing police attention. Paramilitaries had the power – it really did come out of the barrel of a gun – and so could exercise control over the communities from which they emerged. In time, given the longevity of the Troubles, given the cumulative brutalisation of populations, and given the narrowing of options facing local people, this control congealed as authority.

Sometimes the consolidation of authority needed the iron fist, as often as not taking the form of iron bars and guns. Authoritarian regimes, in a sense understandably so, tend to be intolerant of political competition from within the polity. Thus SDLP councillors such as James Fee of Crossmaglen in south Armagh or Hugh Lewsley in west Belfast were given severe beatings for criticising paramilitary activity. Lewsley was assured by his attackers that "the beating would end his television appearances."[152] We have already seen the fate of leading politicians such as Fitt and Devlin who criticised the IRA and loyalist paramilitaries from a nationalist and labour position, but there can be little doubt that less prominent public representatives were subjected to threatening behaviour. To varying degrees these were punishments but punishments of a political kind. Similar type intimidation or worse was deployed against witnesses prepared to give evidence in the formal court system.[153] Attacks on politicians and expulsions seem to have been more characteristic of republican groups and their supporters than of loyalist organisations but both made free use of intimidation.

Second, there was the struggle for legitimacy and again this relates more to republican than to loyalist paramilitaries. The institutions of the British state were deemed illegitimate, hence the desirability of creating alternative institutions in nationalist areas, as happened in parts of Ireland in 1919–21. This included a military organisation (the IRA), a policing and sometimes judicial system (run by Sinn Féin and the IRA), and various cultural and Irish-language enterprises. The enforcers of punishments, as we have seen, were sometimes referred to as civil administration units, the formal language serving to legitimise uncivil actions.[154]

Third, there was the satisfaction of wielding power, of being acknowledged as "big men" or as "hard men" in the community. These distorted performances of masculinity may have been a more pronounced feature of loyalist paramilitarism, as the division between political activity, criminality, and self-gain seems to have been more blurred.[155] But there is no doubt that local paramilitary leaders, of whatever colour, took it as an affront to their prestige and status that some others – perhaps wild, culturally deviant, defiant, sometimes criminally minded – did not fully acknowledge their standing. Insecure egos and male pride required that these local warriors should impose their authority, even if that meant inflicting life-changing injuries on others. Power meant prestige in working-class communities where inevitably status was in short supply. Maintaining personal standing meshed with the political and security imperatives of loyalist and republican organisations.

Before, more often perhaps after they had been inducted into underground organisations,[156] volunteers felt a sense of ideological purpose allied to the fellow feeling of being part of a group and a movement. Conforming to peer group pressure might be a conscious or unconscious part of the process. For some it was an opportunity to release the hero within. There was the thrill of active service and what it might entail. Some spoke of newly inducted volunteers developing a swagger, which signalled their newfound

status. Though the material rewards were meagre, these were not incon-
siderable benefits for young volunteers who typically were unemployed
and had limited prospects in life. "'RA men were celebrities, especially in
the 1970s."[157] The anthropologist Elena Bergia speaks of the unexpected rewards (for some) of paramilitary service, in particular the acquisition of
what she terms "seductive capital." Seductive capital, which she distin-
guishes from "erotic capital" – a sociological concept developed by Catherine Harkin – granted some ex-prisoners ... access to local and foreign
women for sexual encounters or long-term relationships.[158] One of Bergia's
interviewees referred to the first IRA man to refuse to wear prison clothes
in the Maze Prison in these terms: "I can remember when Kieran Nugent
got brought out ... the first Blanket man. I mean ... all these women
throwing themselves at this man! The ugliest man [you've ever seen]!" In-
triguingly, and for complex reasons relating to history and gender stereo-
typing, this paramilitary bonus – enhanced sexual attractiveness by virtue
of engagement in heroic struggle – applied to male ex-prisoners but not
female ex-prisoners. As ever, double standards ruled; patriarchy had its way
and its play. On the loyalist side a prominent feminist and working-class
unionist told me of "women throwing themselves at loyalist paramilitary
'hard men.'"[159]

Inevitably there was for young men a sense of power by virtue of being
a member of the brotherhood.[160] This power was used by loyalists and republicans to combat ideological enemies within and without, but it could
also be used to settle personal vendettas or presumed slights or as a cloak
for sadistic and sexually deviant behaviour (see later on the Shankill
Butchers). McDonald and Cusack speak of the "brutish male culture" of
both republican and loyalist volunteers.[161] At least a minority of punishments had the hallmarks of uncontrolled aggression, with no obvious connection to paramilitary objectives and conceivably such visceral explosions
became more common after the paramilitary ceasefires of 1994. A tragic
case is that of Robert McCartney of the Short Strand in Belfast, whose efforts to assist a friend who was badly beaten by paramilitaries led to his
death. He was jumped on by a group of men outside Magennis' bar in the
Markets area of Belfast, beaten with iron bars, stabbed with a kitchen knife,
kicked on the head, and left for dead. As he lay wounded by the roadside,

the paramilitaries involved cleaned the crime scene of any forensic evidence.[162] He died the following morning in a Belfast city hospital.

An equally tragic case was that of twenty-two-year-old Raymond McCord Jr who was abducted in November 1997 by members of the Mount Vernon UVF. He was a low-ranking volunteer of this notorious unit. He fell foul of the local "commander." His comrades used concrete blocks to beat him to death at Ballyduff quarry outside Belfast for reasons that had nothing to do with the cause of the UVF.[163] His father, Raymond McCord Sr, worked tirelessly to bring his son's murderers to justice, at least one of whom was believed to have been an agent of the security forces.

A variation on this is that violent, occasionally psychopathic individuals were drawn towards paramilitary organisations – Lenny Murphy's fearsome Shankill Butchers were a case in point – and these in turn found outlets for personal, sadistic gratification through the medium of punishment attacks.[164] The unnecessarily large numbers involved in paramilitary-style beatings give some indirect credence to this suggestion. A victim once asked me rhetorically, did they really need ten men to overpower an under-sized teenager?[165]

A fourth motive was the self-created need to discipline members within the organisation or to discipline members of rival organisations within one's community. The intrarepublican feud between the Official IRA and the Provisional IRA in 1974 began with a series of assaults and kneecappings.[166] The Provisional IRA's pogrom against the IPLO in November 1992 (the "Night of the Long Knives" as some term it), when one was shot dead, ten others received gunshot wounds, and many others were exiled, is but one of the more extreme examples.[167] Loyalist gunmen devoted considerable energy to kneecapping or wounding gang members, and the massive feud between the UDA and the UVF in 2000 led to deaths, woundings, and a large-scale displacement of population in the Upper and Lower Shankill.[168]

Finally of course paramilitary organisations claimed they were protecting their communities by fighting antisocial elements within. This justification presents some problems not least the admission by some paramilitary spokespersons that the punishment attacks simply did not work in relation to determined wrong doers. Deviant behaviour, including late-night parties, assault, robbery, housebreaking, drug dealing and drug taking, car crime, and murder did not fall away in the wake of the "rough justice" of the paramilitaries. The fact that the enforcers were engaged in many similar type activities but on a larger scale – the absolving effects of ideology helped minimise cognitive dissonance – further undermines these claims of "community defence." Moreover, some punishments were directed against "political crime," that is, impeding or opposing the work of the paramilitaries or not showing sufficient respect, and these had little or nothing to do with community demands. As one former IRA commander bluntly told me, and this could be generalised to loyalist attacks as well, "The IRA doesn't *have* to do anything. It acts as it *wishes* to act."[169]

There was a problem of crime, as conventionally understood, in areas where the paramilitaries drew support, just as there was in the wider society. But there is no reason to believe Northern Ireland was especially prone to criminal activity; if anything, conventional crime levels were below those of many regions of the United Kingdom.[170] But given that conventional policing was not possible in the midst of armed revolt, there was, for a variety of reasons, popular support for vigilantism. There was anger, fear, and a primitive urge for vengeance against local rowdies, petty criminals, and sexual deviants. A detective constable told a court in Derry in 2014, for instance, that paramilitaries and members of the public "were baying for the blood" of a man accused of a particularly violent rape in the city. Such surges of emotion were no doubt characteristic of neighbourhood responses during the Troubles, particularly on the part of those habituated to the gratification of instant, informal justice.[171]

An important question is how this localised and patchwork support for informal justice, with virtually no safeguards, came to be engendered. In January 1969 a banned People's Democracy march from Belfast to Derry was ambushed at Burntollet Bridge by loyalists, including off-duty members of the Special Constabulary. Bottles and stones were thrown at the marchers and some were attacked with cudgels and chased across fields. The scenes were shocking and media photographers radiated images of the injured marchers round the world. Yet within a few short years far more serious assaults had become routine in working-class areas of Northern Ireland, though images of the injured and the injuries rarely circulated beyond the province and in most instances were not made public at all. What was once viewed as beyond the pale had become normalised within some neighbourhoods.

How did this come about? We have little detailed evidence of the erosion of standards, but a small survey undertaken on the Ardowen housing estate in Craigavon in 1999 in the wake of a particularly cruel attack may offer a pointer or two. The attack itself is detailed at the beginning of the next chapter but the salient point here is that a door-to-door survey conducted a week or so after the incident found that local people overwhelmingly disowned the brutalisation of the youngster.[172] It seems that local people were genuinely shocked. Some of the residents on the Ardowen estate were vehement in their expressions of disgust. This was a relatively new estate that did not have a tradition of paramilitary "policing." These were normal reactions, what might have been expected anywhere in Ireland or elsewhere in Western Europe.

Drawing on the Ardowen experience, a speculative set of stages as to what happened might be as follows. When punishment shootings and beatings were introduced into a neighbourhood, the initial reaction was one of revulsion, at least on the part of many families. Over time, as paramilitaries become more active locally, speaking on behalf of "the people" (who would dare say otherwise?), there was a transition to a second or mixed phase in which there was grudging and partial acceptance of some punishment attacks and not of others. Changing conditions generated pressure for attitudinal change. Police attention to conventional crime was intermittent as the level of the paramilitary threat rose. Ambushes of the police when investigating crime become more frequent, further delaying or deterring police intervention. In this partial policing vacuum, antisocial behaviour such as car crime, break-ins, public drunkenness became less restrained, and demands for vigilante action became more insistent.

Finally, out of fear, respect, need, or varying combinations of these, a process of normalisation of extreme forms of punishment took hold. These psychological adaptations took place against a backdrop of powerlessness in the face of not only paramilitary power but of antisocial elements as well. In a world of stark choices some came to identify closely with the primary wielders of force, that is, the paramilitaries. This may have had its psychological as well as its pragmatic compensations. Moral scruples and, for some, a humiliating sense of subservience to paramilitary norms could be assuaged by embracing the new power realities.

The abnormal became the normal, as local opinion formers and some outside ideologues extolled the value of paramilitary "policing." In national ist areas the role of Sinn Féin was crucial. To adapt Gramsci's somewhat ill-fitting terminology, the task of the "party of the masses" is to promote critical awareness and overthrow the inherited and apparently naturalistic order of things.[173] This the republican movement managed to do – loyalist militant organisations were much less effective in this respect – in part because it could tap into a tradition of alienation from the Northern Ireland state. It could attack the state and the agents of the state at public meetings, demonstrations, and in local papers, magazines, murals, and graffiti. Ideological power flowed in parallel with military power and succeeded in conferring local, sometimes supralocal, legitimacy on acts of extreme violence.

If one thing is clear from the breakup of another European society, that of Bosnia, it is that decivilizing processes can be quickly set in motion once intercommunal relations come under strain. A major but largely neglected aspect of the Troubles was the progress of decivilizing processes in parts of the body politic in Northern Ireland. Once again, the sheer longevity of the Troubles was a powerful factor in stripping away conventional restraints. Acts of mutilation, maiming, and torture that characterised life in working-class communities in loyalist and republican areas since 1970 become not only imaginable but acceptable. In some areas the hegemony of paramilitary groups was maintained for four decades, so generations of children were socialised into small, claustrophobic worlds in which extreme violence against children, against men, and sometimes women was taken for granted. The high degree of ethnoreligious segregation in Northern Ireland facilitated these processes: according to the 2011 census almost four out of every ten local government wards were "single identity" wards (that is more than 80 per cent of the residents belonged to one of the two main ethnic groups).[174] Only one in twenty of the 582 wards was fully mixed, in the sense that no one group had an absolute majority. Needless to say, paramilitaries played a dynamic rather than a passive role in forming and deforming social life within these monocultural segments of civil society.[175]

Let me add a twist that in a perverse way is understandable. Some of the enforcers of punishments, from both loyalist and republican backgrounds, had themselves been kneecapped as youngsters or young men. Bryan Ryder listed for me a number of fellow joyriders from his area in Lenadoon in Belfast who had later joined the IRA.[176] But why? A former paramilitary leader, who had himself been shot in the leg for a minor robbery, explained to me that joining up was a means of regaining respect in the community. This he did and rose through the ranks to a senior position in the IRA.

Paramilitary punishments might be sometimes popular but the point is easily overstated. What people in disadvantaged areas desperately wanted was policing, and some were indifferent as to what the agency was. After all, the RUC, however much anger was directed against the force because of its ill discipline at the outbreak of the Troubles, had policed ordinary crime relatively effectively in the 1960s and earlier. A voluntary youth worker and stepfather of a young joyrider from Twinbrook in West Belfast told me in 1997 that he didn't care who policed the area, be it the RUC, the Garda, or any policing force.[177] He and others simply wanted an effective police presence. This was of course impossible as the RUC had been largely and deliberately excluded from normal policing work in the west of the city. How representative this view was it is hard to say. A partial indicator was the response to the reconstituted RUC – the police service of Northern Ireland – in the early 2000s. Contrary to some predictions, support for the republican movement increased rather than diminished as the IRA withdrew from its self-appointed policing role, though of course other factors were at play. Still, even in hardline nationalist areas there were only the faintest tremors of disquiet as Sinn Féin backed the new policing dispensation. The outcome was that electoral support for Sinn Féin, the political wing of the IRA, was consolidated, which suggests more complicated attitudes to the police and policing than some academic (never mind partisan) accounts have assumed.

It is important also to remind ourselves that despite much propagandist rhetoric about the "people's army," community service, and the like, the fact remains that most areas of Northern Ireland did not adopt the darker attitudes portrayed above. Most did not want justice, paramilitary-style. The due process of law might be slow, cumbersome, and sometimes biased, but it clearly specified what the charges were, it presumed innocence on the part of the accused, it did not admit rumours, it allowed evidence and challenges to evidence, it allowed legal defence, it allowed the right of appeal, and it did not inflict cruel or degrading treatment on those convicted.[178] On all of these counts vigilante-style justice constituted not simply "rough justice": it was a system of torture as defined by the United Nations Convention against Torture.[179] The UVF, the UDA, the PUP, other loyalist paramilitary organisations, the IRA, the INLA, and Sinn Féin were deeply implicated in these human rights abuses, not as exceptional or reprehensible actions but as routine procedures. Finally, it cannot be maintained that controlling crime was the primary motive behind vigilante activity. Control of communal territories, and their inhabitants, was the overriding objective. The paramilitary agenda was self-serving and the organisations helped to exacerbate the problems they presumed to remedy. Had paramilitaries been responsive to the demands of northern Irish society, they would have disbanded within a few years of the outbreak of the Troubles, at the latest. But they were on another journey. Some still are.

"HOODS" AND OTHER ANTIHEROES

In view of the severity of the punishments handed out by paramilitary organisations, it is not easy to understand why a small number of people, mainly youths and young men, did engage in activities such as car theft, joyriding, drug dealing, house breaking, and the like.[180] No doubt some were deterred but others were not. Thompson and Mulholland concluded in 2005, "The informal criminal justice system has exerted some degree of superficial control over the delinquent young people of West Belfast but it has not stopped the rising tide of drugs, nor made a significant impact on levels of car crime among West Belfast young people."[181]

It is widely accepted that the methods of the paramilitaries were ineffective and sometimes counterproductive. This is what one former joyrider – or "death-rider" as some label it – told me in relation to his activities in the mid-1980s. "I wasn't really stealing cars before this [his punishment beating]. I ran with a crowd who were into joyriding. I wasn't a big joyrider. What I got, for what I was doing, wasn't in line with their Taliban law. It wasn't expected."[182] He was so angry because of what he regarded as unfair treatment that he became a committed car thief and joyrider. He claims to have stolen hundreds of cars for purely joyriding purposes. He was happy to admit that he and his mates "tortured" the IRA in West Belfast with their nightly escapades of roaring engines, screeching tyres, and daredevil driving round the estates. Excited audiences of young people cheered them on. There were high-speed car chases with RUC Land Rovers in hot pursuit. Crashed cars were abandoned and new ones stolen, often in the same night. The narrative reads like a masculinity contest in which the Provos, the police, and these out-of-control youngsters were all playing much the same game. The police eventually put him away for several years in prison, thus ending years of mayhem. Significantly, it was the formal justice system that induced a change of heart. He is now a caring father and homemaker but still holds the paramilitaries in utter contempt. They are simply "scumbags" in his mind, responsible for far greater crimes than those they punished. In his words, they were the really big criminals attacking minor offenders. He no longer lives in West Belfast.[183]

These kinds of countercultural activities have been traced in detail by the social scientist Heather Hamill in a brilliant study entitled *The Hoods: Crime and Punishment in Belfast*.[184] The "hoods" are defined as young people aged ten to twenty years of age who were habitually, almost compulsively, involved in antisocial activities and in particular in joyriding. Hamill draws on game theory to explain the high-risk behaviour of the hoods. In her view these social outcasts were engaged in a competitive quest for status and respect among their peer groups. (Not unlike some of their paramilitary tormentors, one might add.) Thus a punishment attack had little effect. In fact, it signalled to other members of the group the toughness, bravery, indifference to pain of the individual gang member. Scar tissue was displayed with pride and bravado. Broken limbs were badges of honour, not deterrents. So the antisocial behaviour continued. These were alienated rebels without a cause or at least without a cause that polite society would recognise. They were not polite and some were dangerous. The outcomes were horrific. There is a poignant description of the regular "assembly" of these refugee-rebels, by the journalist Jim Cusack:

They gather at the corner of Castle Street and King Street, at the bottom of the Falls Road in Belfast almost every day. Two or three or four youths in wheelchairs, usually a couple on crutches and their friends, most of them bearing scars of vicious beatings and gunshot wounds. The daily gathering at the corner of the run-down street is one of the most pathetic sights in the city … The youths, known locally as "hoods", display their injuries with a grim defiance. They are like a dishevelled, handicapped brotherhood saying: "Look at us. Look at what the Provos did. We don't care".[185]

Creative writers, among others, have sought to capture the cruel interplay between youths and paramilitaries. Anna Burns' award-winning novel *Milkman*, set in north Belfast (or a conflict zone anywhere), reveals how coercion and sexual exploitation can be the lot of young women on claustrophobic housing estates dominated by armed groups.[186] Jenny McCartney, the daughter of a prominent Northern Ireland politician, places a punishment attack in a loyalist neighbourhood in the 1990s at the centre of her debut novel of friendship, violence, and revenge.[187] At one point the protagonist, Jacky, reflects, "No one ever really believes in something bad until it happens. Not even the one who predicts it." This may help explain why some victims of loyalist and republican paramilitary violence do not make the imaginative leap when under threat and fail to get the hell out of Northern Ireland or at the very least out of their own neighbourhood.

LOYALISTS AND REPUBLICANS

Was there much difference between the punishment methods operated by loyalist and republican paramilitaries? Differences there certainly were. Loyalists targeted older individuals, many of their victims were members of paramilitary groups, they invested fewer resources in elaborating justifications for their actions, and they inhabited a more conflicted ideological space in that they sought to preserve the existing institutions of the state while also attacking agents and agencies of that state. Because much of their violence was directed at fellow paramilitaries, within their own or rival loyalist organisations, their punishments were less invasive of the wider loyalist and unionist communities.

By contrast republicans aspired to wider ambitions of community control; they targeted younger victims, particularly children (as discussed more fully in the next chapter); the injuries inflicted were more serious, at least in the subperiod for which we have a detailed assessment;[188] and vigilante-style justice was directed not only against alleged criminals and juvenile delinquents but also against perceived enemies of the IRA or other republican groups within nationalist communities. During the period of intense conflict, from 1970 to 1994, a majority of recorded punishment shootings (60 per cent) and beatings (60 per cent also) were carried out by republicans.[189] This indicated a deeper commitment to "policing" nationalist areas and to excluding the police and security forces. The result was that Catholics were *almost twice as likely* to be subjected to shootings or beating as compared to Protestants, which is surely one of the lesser-known ratios relating to the Troubles.[190] This in turn reflected a different perception of the state and its institutions and a desire to create alternative institutions in "liberated" spaces within the British state, a strategy that had its precedents in the early twentieth century in Ireland when Sinn Féin sought to create "a polity within a polity."[191] Republicans, particularly Sinn Féin and the Provisional IRA, invested more resources in vigilante-type activity and devoted more energy to ideological justifications of their actions as compared to loyalists. This sometimes involved using or exploiting state agencies, including the social services and probation services as well as Catholic clergy, in its web of measures.[192] During the course of the peace process from the mid-1990s onwards the republican movement also took more interest in denying involvement in some of the more flagrant abuses of human rights, bringing the art of dissembling – in plain language lying for the cause – to a new level of sophistication. Loyalists, on the whole, didn't bother.

But there were similarities as well and perhaps in the end these counted for more. Each set of paramilitaries inflicted cruel and degrading forms of terror on their captives. These were denied the safeguards that could be found in conventional justice systems in western democracies. Moreover, the latent objective, whatever the rationalisation, was to demonstrate and consolidate the power of the paramilitary organisation. Paradoxically perhaps, with the exception of a small minority of psychopaths and committed sadists within the paramilitary ranks, the perpetrators were acting within moral frameworks shared by a good many people. These also set limits to what could be done, at least openly. *Killing Rage* is a remarkable memoir of life inside the IRA, written by the former IRA intelligence officer Eamon

Collins. With clinical precision he records his own changing moral and psychological states. His view, nonetheless, was that an IRA commander ought to show exemplary behaviour in his professional and private life (though he details deviations from the ideal).[193] As Silke also argues, republicans had a sense of community responsibility and dealing with antisocial elements locally could be seen in this light. The same may well be true of loyalists and it is worth recalling that loyalist groups brought forward some progressive documents such as *Common Sense*, which advocated power-sharing long before it became acceptable within the unionist family.[194] Following the loyalist ceasefire of 1994 it was also possible to discern progressive as well as reactionary voices within paramilitary loyalism.[195]

These arguments need to be teased out a little further. Moral boundaries certainly existed at each and every moment of the Troubles but these varied and in any case should not be conceived in largely static terms. Moral concerns proved flexible enough to accommodate radical change over time. The imperatives of organisational survival, dignified by reference to that most elastic of concepts – "the community" – led to adjustments to moral frameworks and the embedding of acts of extreme violence in local cultures. Thus the evolution of both loyalist and republican torture rooms, and what the human rights campaigner the late Fr Denis Faul called "death houses," might well have been barely thinkable at the birth of the Provisional IRA or the UDA.[196] Similarly the use of civilians as "human bombs" in the later stages of the Troubles represented a further twist to the steep downward spiral into inhumanity and states of decivilization. Like history, morality was also in a state of flux.

THE POLITICS OF PUNISHMENTS AND THE COMPROMISES OF THE PEACE PROCESS

The problem of punishments swam into the public consciousness after the paramilitary ceasefires of 1994. For most of the period of the Troubles they were in the shadows of the conflict, of limited concern to politicians, the police, and the army. As attacks on the security forces ceased, the spectre of paramilitary repression within communities came into sharper relief. With the signing of the Good Friday Agreement in 1998 the expectation might have been that vigilante-style attacks would also subside. The remarkable fact is that shootings more than doubled between 1999 and 2000 and reached their high-water mark for the whole period of the Troubles in 2001 (see figure 3.2). Assaults oscillated from year to year but at a high level. A clear downward trend did not emerge until the middle of the first decade of the twenty-first century and that was only clear in retrospect. It seems that London, Dublin, and the Northern Ireland Office were prepared to turn a blind eye to paramilitary rule within working-class communities on the understanding that attacks were directed inwards rather than outwards towards members of the police and the British army. The realpolitik was that the victims of the punishments – alleged criminals and political opponents – had to be sacrificed on the altar of the peace process.

It is also apparent that paramilitary organisations, and in particular the political wing of republicanism, were seeking alternatives to "rough justice," including restorative justice schemes under the control of paramilitaries. Gerry Adams, speaking as the leader of Sinn Féin, stated unequivocally during the general election campaign of 1997 that paramilitary-style attacks were unacceptable.[197] Nonetheless, for whatever reason, it took another ten years for the pronouncement to be translated into practice.

Some argue that the IRA wished to discontinue punishment attacks but were prevented from doing so by popular pressure in their heartlands.[198] The dynamic interrelationship between the IRA and its host communities, it is argued, precluded anything but a slow disengagement. My own view is a more sceptical one, while acknowledging the embeddedness of the IRA in some areas through networks of kinfolk, friends, and neighbours. The IRA still had an interest in controlling local communities: this was against competing political groups, against dissident republicans, against hoods, and against other out-of-control elements (including drug dealers). Prestige and status were also at stake, as the murder of Paul Quinn graphically illustrated.[199] There may well have been conflicting priorities between members of Sinn Féin and the IRA from time to time but at leadership level the same people called the shots in what were ostensibly two separate organisations. Moreover, the surge in beatings during the early peace process seems at odds with the reluctance hypothesis and fits more readily with the image of paramilitaries adjusting awkwardly to a post-ceasefire world.

There were volunteers to be kept busy, sadistic impulses to be indulged, potential threats from other individuals and groups to contend with, as well as neighbourhood pressures in some localities.

The Independent Monitoring Commission, set up to track paramilitary activity during the peace process, summed up the situation for loyalist and republican paramilitary organisations in 2004 along the following lines: "To maintain their positions paramilitaries have developed methods of community control, all too many examples of which involve extreme violence, and virtually all of which involve the exertion of influence through fear."[200]

The case of Patrick Doherty illustrates how the effects of a paramilitary attack might extend into the community. Set upon by a group of vigilantes, his nose and jaw were broken, and one eye closed in the assault. There were almost immediate ramifications for family and friends.[201] The following morning, one of his brothers on his way to Sunday Mass was involved in angry exchanges with a local Provisional IRA man who may have been one of the attackers. At lunchtime a group of paramilitaries, wielding iron bars, attacked the home of the parents of the Dohertys. "My mom was very, very ill at the time and one of my brothers was badly beaten. And that has never been recorded, never been reported." A neighbour, two doors down the street, came to the assistance of the Dohertys and was badly beaten as well. There was further overspill from the original assault. Patrick Doherty's family home in Twinbrook was subjected to attack. He was warned he would no longer be allowed to live in his community. "So it wasn't a [pause] a very nice way to live. And the house was attacked several times after that again. So I decided it was time for me – not for me but for my children, not to have to live in that sort of environment." The family left Belfast. So the initial incident rippled outwards to produce assaults on at least three other people, though only one punishment incident would appear in police statistics. At least half a dozen family members, including two young children, experienced trauma as a result of the original attack and presumably this was true to varying degrees for many of the incidents represented in mute figures in the statistical tables produced here. The broad pattern applies as much to loyalist as to republican communities.

By the early twenty-first century a trade-off between running patchy "informal justice" practices and the electoral ambitions of Sinn Féin was increasingly apparent. Punishments might be viscerally gratifying in some areas, for perpetrators and host neighbourhoods alike, but they were not acceptable to many, perhaps most, nationalists. Electoral advance was incompatible with brutal manifestations of paramilitary aggression, and increasingly there were constituencies in the Republic of Ireland that had to be taken into account. It was also the case that Washington, London, and Dublin were taking a less tolerant attitude to paramilitary extracurricular activity from 2004 or 2005 onwards.[202] The macropolitical context was changing. American nerves were jangled by the September 11 (2001) attacks in the United States; attitudes towards terror were hardening in the western world. The Provisional IRA had to find its place in the new order. It did, and further electoral advances by Sinn Féin ensued. Significantly, when the IRA and Sinn Féin phased out vigilante attacks in the early twenty-first century there was no loss of electoral support (quite the reverse) in constituencies like north or west Belfast where support for vigilante activity had been highly developed.

Like their republican counterparts, loyalist paramilitary groups showed no great wish to leave the stage after 1994 or indeed 1998. Popular support for a "policing" role for paramilitaries was much less apparent in unionist areas of Northern Ireland and the police were that bit more acceptable.[203] As Monaghan and Shirlow have argued, pro-state paramilitaries have a more difficult relationship with their community of origin as compared to antistate armed groups.[204] If one held to the view that loyalists had reluctantly adopted a policing role then one might have expected loyalist vigilante activity to have faded even more rapidly than in the case of republicans. The evidence points in the opposite direction. Since the Good Friday Agreement loyalist shootings exceeded those of republicans in every year between 1998 and 2005. The same was true of beatings. It was not until 2005 or so that loyalist vigilantism shifted onto a lower plane. The dynamic seems to have been different from that in nationalist Northern Ireland. Between 2000 and 2005 the UDA, the UVF, and the LVF engaged in intermittent, internecine warfare involving murder, woundings, and beatings.[205] Elements within the UDA and the LVF were critical of the peace process, and in that sense there was a link to the larger political context. But organisational rivalries, involvement in criminality, and the role of bizarre paramilitary leaders such as Billy Wright and Johnny Adair provided the main motive force for mayhem within loyalism.[206] From 2005 onwards the need for disciplining members of own or competing loyalist groups slackened. But the fractious nature of loyalism and the involvement of breakaway loyalist paramilitary groups in the drugs trade and other criminal activity meant that upsurges of vigilante activity were still possible.

CONCLUSION

The "black" criminal justice system, administering the kinds of unaccountable terror detailed here, has been explained in various ways. Some have dignified the practices with the heading "popular justice" or using other ideologically loaded designations. This chapter has looked afresh at the totality of these practices and their functions. Their systemic nature is apparent. It is also possible to venture a model of paramilitary activity that recognises these practices as one of three subsystems that were fundamental to the world of paramilitary political violence.

The three great spheres of paramilitary activity during the Troubles, it is suggested here, were attacks on the security forces and "representative others," intracommunity repression, and fund raising. These fulfilled the military, the security, and the economic functions of the organisations. Contrary to popular misconception, there was little direct confrontation between republican and loyalist paramilitarism. Neither could protect its host community but both were capable of vengeance raids across the communal divide. The focus of this chapter is the second of the three spheres, the system of vigilante "justice" and neighbourhood control. This in fact outlived the quarter century of "armed struggle" and should be viewed as one of the major arenas of the Troubles.[207] It extended through the period of the "peace process" and exists in attenuated form to the present day. The sheer longevity of punishment practices testifies to their importance in the recent history of Northern Ireland and may well hold lessons for postconflict societies elsewhere. Powering the system of "informal justice" – ramshackle, arbitrary, and patchy as it was – occupied far more volunteers and volunteer time and was a higher priority than is often acknowledged. That said, the use of the terms system or subsystem is to overstate the degree of consistency of judgements, penalties, and even the motives involved.

The focal points of paramilitary concern shifted through time. In the 1980s so-called joyriding was a prime target of paramilitary outrage in republican areas, but in the 1990s and the 2000s the focus switched to drug dealers. However, loyalists were more indulgent of drug dealing, not least because it helped fill their coffers. Both loyalist and republican paramilitaries engaged in periodic rethinks and the mix of punishments varied. Expulsions for instance came to the fore during the 1990s. But paramilitary organisations were conservative organisms: the crudity of the methods, and the justificatory discourses offered, showed more continuity than change.

Shootings, beatings, and exiling, as well as the less frequent tarrings and killings, come under the heading of paramilitary-inflicted punishments. The term itself is objectionable. In the case of serious vigilante-style attacks, torture, disfigurement, mutilation would be more appropriate terms. But the label has gained currency and is used here without losing sight of the darker reality. The social visibility of these attacks was, however, deliberately obscured from outside viewing. (It was of course visible locally and from within and intended to be so.) An imposition of silence, under threat of savage retaliation, was part of the punishment regime. The indications are that there were in excess of twenty thousand instances of shootings, assaults, and exilings within nationalist and unionist communities since 1970. Few of the victims ever spoke out or even achieved a form of collective identity. They and their kinfolk bore their pain in private.

Because of its local character and its relative invisibility, the centrality of the punishments to paramilitarism and armed conflict is insufficiently realised in the wider society and possibly not even amongst paramilitaries themselves. To acknowledge its importance to the paramilitary enterprise would be unhelpful in terms of heroic narratives of resistance and struggle, be it of the orange or green variety. This chapter has drawn attention to the brutalising effects of paramilitary control, that is, the progressive erosion of civilized values and norms as individuals and neighbourhoods came under the grip of hooded vigilantes. Perpetrators and victims inhabited microterritories in which feelings of anger, hurt, fear, contempt, vengeance, and sadism were acted out. Paramilitaries called the shots and relentless propaganda at a local level served to harden attitudes against perceived wrongdoers, particularly within nationalist communities. In such areas the partial policing vacuum meant the range of alternatives for dealing with crime was artificially constricted. These were among the hidden costs of the Troubles that are slowly being remedied through the disbanding of the paramilitary organisations and the efforts of a reorganised, renamed, and reconstituted police service in Northern Ireland.

Having ranged widely, it is time to return to the start, to the centre of the narrative as it were. There is the victim, the hero, the antihero, the scumbag. Often isolated and outcast, he nonetheless has his poet. Ciaran Carson was brought up in west Belfast and was once interrogated by republican paramilitaries because he was seen riding his bicycle from the direction of the Protestant Shankill. He knew the world of the paramilitary presence. A poem of his, starkly titled "The Knee" introduces us to the hood, or so it was said, who kept on doing what he was not supposed to do. A bullet. His knee. Vengeance fulfilled.

Ciaran died in 2019. I hope he doesn't mind my borrowing the final verse, which is set in the sanctuary of the hospital ward – the destination of many of the kneecapped, where they took their first clumsy steps into a pain-filled future.[208]

> Visiting time: he takes his thirteen-month-old-son on his
> other knee.
> Learning to walk, he suddenly throws himself into the
> Staggering
> Distance between his father and his father's father, hands
> held up high,
> His legs like the hands of a clock, one trying to catch up on
> the other.

4

They Shoot Children, Don't They?

They never said what he had done wrong. They just dragged Eamon from the
bed, threw him all the way down the stairs, lay him on his back and beat him
with sticks embedded with huge nails while my parents pleaded with them
to leave him alone because of his age. He only turned 14 in July.[1]

This is the voice of Eamon's sister who dared to speak about the ordeal of
her younger brother. Five masked men from the North Armagh Brigade of
the Provisional IRA burst into the O'Hanlon home, late at night, threatening the parents at gunpoint. The mother and father were obliged to stand
by and listen helplessly to the screams of their son. After the ordeal the child
was taken to the Royal Victoria Hospital for Sick Children, some thirty
miles away in Belfast. His parents did not speak openly or publicly. To do
so would have invited further retaliation, possibly against the whole family.
The attack took place in the year following the signing of the Good Friday
Agreement of 1998.

Dr Lawrence Rocke, senior consultant surgeon in the accident and
emergency department of the Royal Victoria Hospital in Belfast says that
the youngest victim of a punishment beating he treated was just fourteen
years old. But many others were only a year or two older. "It beggars belief
how people can set out to cause pain and hurt of the terrible type we see
in here so often."[2]

One of the major revelations in the history of Irish society in the late
twentieth century was the extent of institutional child abuse, often carried
out by Irish Catholic priests, brothers, and nuns. This was on a scale that
was both shocking and hitherto unrealised.[3] At the same time as these
abuses were being uncovered, the systematic abuse of children by paramilitary organisations was widespread. As in the case of Catholic religious organisations in the past, the strictures to remain silent ensured little publicity
or none. This was pain endured in private by isolated individuals. But when

Figure 4.1 Children of the Troubles

the ecclesiastical power structures cracked and the walls of silence began to crumble towards the end of the twentieth century, the acts of child abuse perpetrated by parents, relatives, siblings, and clergy emerged as a huge public concern within Irish society. Perversely, this was the period when paramilitary child abuse was becoming more widespread. Moreover, unlike the case of the Catholic church, which used legal agreements to bind their victims, loyalist and republican paramilitaries enforced silence with the threat of a return of the men armed with guns, cudgels, and iron bars.

IRON DISCIPLINE

"One of them pulled an iron bar from inside a jacket and hit him across the face." This was the opening blow of a punishment attack on a fifteen-year-old child. The intruders did not spare the rod. The beating, which involved a number of masked men believed to be members of the Provisional IRA, took place in a home in the strongly nationalist New Lodge area of north Belfast on Sunday, 11 March 2001. The boy, who had special needs and admitted to juvenile delinquency, was taken to the bedroom where he was struck with iron bars for twenty minutes. The blows were mainly to his head and upper body. His jaw was fractured during the attack. Traumatised, disfigured, and barely able to speak, he was taken to hospital. Because his mother, a single parent, voiced her outrage and despair, the name of the boy, George McWilliams, flickered momentarily in the columns of the nationalist *Irish News*.[4]

In January of the same year up to ten masked men, carrying guns and batons, forced their way into a home on a housing estate in Belfast. Their target was a sixteen-year-old boy with a reported IQ of 45. Gerard had a troubled history, including severe depression since he had been raped as a child by a relative. When his mother tried to protect him from the intruders, she was also struck and called a "fucking bitch." The administration of justice then took a more violent turn. Gerard was pulled upstairs to the bathroom. In the words of his mother, "I could hear him screaming from in there. After that they dragged him outside to the alleyway. I went into the bathroom and saw blood everywhere; after that I passed out."[5]

Master of Punishment

Freddie Scappaticci, an Irish republican of Italian descent, was head of the IRA's internal security unit (the "Nutting Squad") during the 1980s. But he was also in charge of the Civil Administration Units that "policed" nationalist areas. Described as having an interest in pornography and preteen girls, he has been connected to at least eighteen killings. At some stage in his long IRA career he became an agent for the British intelligence services.

In the words of John Ware, the award-winning, former BBC investigative reporter, Scappaticci exercised "a kind of psychological control, if not terror, over the general population of west Belfast which went beyond the strict limits of the IRA itself."[6] Ware presented a special BBC Panorama program on the *The Spy in the IRA*, aired 11 April 2017. What follows is part of Ware's account of Scappaticci's role in the punishment system, as published a few days later in the *Irish Times*, 15 April 2017:

> He [Scappaticci] ran the IRA's "Civil Administration," which policed parts of Belfast under IRA control. Ordinary "decent" crime (as it was known) was rife. Criminality gave Gerry Adams the opportunity to create "an alternative government."[7]
>
> Scappaticci ran the Civil Administration "with a heavy fist," a former IRA man who had dealings with him told me. Joyriders and drug dealers were routinely kneecapped. Civil Administration put the fear of God into locals in order to enforce collaboration with the IRA.
>
> In Belfast, kneecapping became a weapon. A licence for an ordinary decent hood to continue living in the community was to ensure their future was spent limping up and down the street on crutches. Equally, they had to limit their statements to the police after the shooting to say only that "two masked men held me down and then shot me in the back of the legs, but I don't know their names and I can't remember their descriptions."
>
> But, of course, the victim usually did know the perpetrator. The (usually) teenage culprit had actually turned up to Civil Administration HQ – better known as Sinn Féin's HQ – at Connolly House by appointment with a parent.

There, the parent would have pleaded with the gunman not to shoot his child "here" pointing away from the joint, but "there, please" to minimise lasting damage. Repeat offenders risked a "six pack" – six shots, one for each knee, elbow and ankle. One mother vividly described her meeting with Scappaticci after he had demanded that she bring her errant son to see him.

Scappaticci told her: "The next time we hear he's been at it or of any complaints against him, I will personally blow the head off him." Adams, she says, sat beside him, saying nothing. Some years later her son was shot dead.

AGE AND PUNISHMENT

Children are at one extreme of the age range of victims of paramilitary punishments. Andrew Silke in a powerful article, "The Lords of Discipline," quotes a youth worker to the effect that "the rule is that the Provos don't punish – that is, don't shoot or severely beat – kids under sixteen."[8] This might be the theory but the evidence points in a different direction.

Detailed statistics on the age breakdown of victims are only available from 1990 onwards, which misses out most of the period of the Troubles. Still, this gives a time span of almost a quarter century and covers the period of the early peace process and its aftermath. The information is from the files of the Central Statistics Unit of the RUC and later the PSNI Statistics Branch.[9] As always, it needs to be borne in mind that these are the *reported* cases only.

Tables 4.1 and 4.2 present the *proportion* of victims falling into the different age groups. (Because of rounding, the figures do not necessarily add to one hundred.) The age profiles of the casualties from shootings and beatings appear broadly similar, with the exception of the upper and lower age bands. Men in their twenties – the great majority of victims were male – account for almost half of the casualties, be it punishment shootings or beatings. The proportions taper away on either side of this modal age group. A simple majority of the victims were in the age range eighteen to twenty-nine years. A small minority were much older, aged fifty years or above, and these were more likely to be subjected to beatings rather than shootings. The age range across the punishment spectrum was wide. The oldest man shot by loyalists was aged fifty-eight years, while the oldest shot by republicans was sixty-eight years and a pensioner. The oldest age for an assault victim was seventy-five years. He was punished by loyalist paramilitaries in the year 2000. Republicans had given a paramilitary-style beating to their oldest victim, a seventy-three-year-old man, a few years earlier in 1997.

CHILDREN AND PUNISHMENT

The United Nations Convention on the Rights of the Child came into force on the 2nd of September 1990. Article 1 defined a child as "every human below the age of 18 years" (unless there was specific national legislation that conferred adulthood earlier).[10] This is the definition of a child adopted here, though a more detailed age classification is also used. Just how young were some of the victims? This information is presented in tables 4.3 and 4.4. The sheer scale of these attacks on children comes as a shock to many, even to well-informed commentators on Northern Ireland.

More than 500 children were subjected to vigilante-style shootings or beatings during the quarter century 1990–2013, and the practice continues.[11] The fate of Charley Valliday, the leader of a joyriding gang, underlines how unrestrained the shooting of children could be. The seventeen-year-old was taken away by masked men on New Year's Eve, 1988, shot in the knees, ankles, and elbows, in all receiving ten shots, in what was evidently an attempt not just to "punish" him severely but to cripple him for life.[12] Even very young children – fifteen-year-olds – could be subjected to a shooting.

In terms of beatings by vigilantes, the youngest victims were very young indeed. Loyalist paramilitaries attacked a nine-year-old child in 2009, while republicans gave paramilitary-style beatings to three twelve-year-olds in 2001. One of the youngest victims of paramilitary-style justice is not included in the official statistics because his plight predated the collection of such data. It is a paradigmatic case because it involved child abuse at so many levels. The boy was eleven-year-old Michael McConville, one of the ten children of Jean McConville (mentioned in the previous chapter) who was abducted by the IRA in 1972, interrogated, and murdered in the Republic of Ireland. According to Michael McConville, "The IRA came to the

Table 4.1
The Age of Victims of Loyalist Punishment Attacks: the *proportion* (%)
in each age category for the period 1990–2013

Age groups	14–15	16–17	18–19	20–29	30–39	40–49	50 +	%
Shootings	1	8	14	48	21	6	1	100
Beatings	4	8	11	42	21	10	4	100

Source: Calculated from data supplied by the statistics branch of the PSNI.
Note: The actual number of shootings was 1,077 and the number of beatings was 1,413

Table 4.2
The Age of Victims of Republican Punishment Attacks: the *proportion* (%)
in each age category for the period 1990–2013

Age groups	14–15	16–17	18–19	20–29	30–39	40–49	50 +	%
Shootings	1	9	18	50	14	6	1	100
Beatings	3	14	14	46	14	5	3	100

Source: Calculated from data supplied by the statistics branch of the PSNI.
Note: The actual number of shootings was 759 and the number of beatings was 1,022.

door and took our mother, we were all crying, my mother was crying, she had cuts and bruises on her face from the night before when the IRA had taken her out of the bingo hall … We were all clinging on to her. We were holding on to her. It took five to ten minutes for them to take her away."

Michael was eleven years old at the time, but this did not save him from further terror. A week later the IRA abducted him as well, put a hood over his head, and took him to a strange house. "They tied me to a chair and they beat me with sticks and put a gun to my head. They said they would kill me if I gave any information about the IRA. This went on for about three hours. At the end of it, they said they were going to shoot me and they fired a cap gun."

Even though Michael recognised some of the IRA members and still saw some of them in his locality he was not prepared to name them to the police. Forty years after the event, he still feared for his life and that of his family.[13]

Moving from the particular to the general, during the period 1990–2013 most shootings of children were carried out by loyalists (ninety-four cases); most vigilante-style beatings of children, or "batterings" as one IRA man graphically put it,[14] were carried out by republicans (178 cases). Making allowance for differences in population share, nationalist children were more likely to be the victims of paramilitary violence and particularly so of paramilitary-style beatings. This was probably also the case for the two decades of the Troubles prior to 1990 (for which we do not have child data), in view of the attitude to "policing" adopted by the Provisional IRA. Nonetheless, little should be made of these differences. All too often in debates on the Troubles small differences are highlighted so as to deflect attention onto secondary considerations. Of far greater significance is the bloody common denominator, which is that both sets of paramilitaries terrorised large numbers of children and young people, using broadly similar techniques, over long periods of time.

CHILDREN OF THE PEACE?

Peace came dropping slowly for the children of Northern Ireland, as figures 4.2 and 4.3 demonstrate. So, looking at change over time, both loyalist and republican paramilitaries increased the level of repression against children in the decade after the paramilitary ceasefires of 1994. The point is underlined further if we take into account the large numbers of young people exiled in these years, for whom no precise figures exist. Vigilante-style beatings roughly doubled as compared to the years immediately preceding the ceasefires. In a belated improvement they then tapered off steeply after 2004, in part it would seem due to political pressure and persuasion. This was particularly true of the Provisional IRA, the organisation which historically had been responsible for most shootings and mutilations and which withdrew into the shadows in these later years. Between 2004 and 2013 most beatings were due to loyalist paramilitaries, while in those years responsibility for shootings was roughly equally shared between loyalist and republican groups. This was also a period of murderous attacks on al-

Table 4.3
The *Number* of Children Attacked by Loyalist Paramilitaries During the Period
1990–2013, by age group

Age groups	Under 14	14–15	16–17	Total
Shootings	0	12	82	94
Beatings	8	48	110	166

Source: Statistics branch of the PSNI.

Table 4.4
The *Number* of Children Attacked by Republican Paramilitaries During the Period
1990–2013, by age group

Age groups	Under 14	14–15	16–17	Total
Shootings	0	7	66	73
Beatings	3	32	143	178

Source: Statistics branch of the PSNI.

leged drug dealers by republican paramilitaries, particularly but not exclusively in Derry.[15] Moving closer to the present (but not the endgame in the child abuse stakes), three children were shot by republican vigilantes in 2016 and a further three in 2017. Loyalist vigilantes did not shoot any children in this subperiod, but they "battered" one fourteen-year-old and two sixteen-year-olds.

GENDER AND PUNISHMENT

It is overwhelmingly the case that males from working-class backgrounds were the targets of the paramilitary punishment system. This was because young males were more likely than young women to be involved in antisocial behaviour as perceived both by paramilitaries and members of local communities. But gender mattered in its own right and the line was not easily crossed. One IRA operative for instance claimed that the IRA was

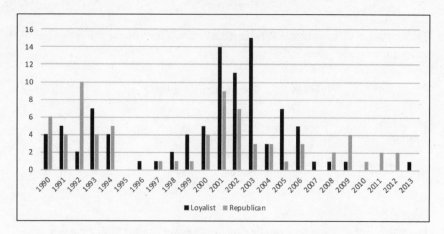

Figure 4.2 Punishment shootings of children by loyalists and republicans, 1990–2013
Source: Statistics branch of the RUC and PSNI.

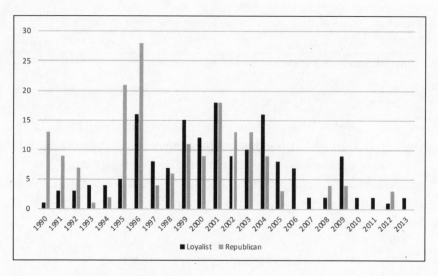

Figure 4.3 Punishment beatings of children by loyalists and republicans, 1990–2013
Source: Statistics branch of the RUC and PSNI.

Table 4.5
The Number of Paramilitary-style Assaults on Females, by age group, 1990–2013

Age groups	14–15	16–17	18–19	20–29	30–39	40–49	50 +
Loyalist	4	1	5	22	25	4	4
Republican	0	4	0	10	7	4	2

Source: Statistics branch of the PSNI.

"operating within a sophisticated set of informal restrictions on their be-haviour, no less powerful for being largely unspoken."[16] There were limits no doubt but a claim of this kind is too timeless to capture the arbitrary nature of paramilitary control and retaliation. The informal codes them-selves evolved over time under pressure of circumstances. Gender alone was not a safeguard against attack. This was particularly evident on the loyalist side, where loyalist paramilitary assaults on women (of all ages) were much more frequent than in republican-controlled areas.[17]

Most of the women attacked by loyalists and republicans were in their twenties or in their thirties, but young girls were not exempted either. Fif-teen per cent of the female victims of loyalism and republicanism were aged nineteen years or less. In the case of loyalist attacks four of the victims were very young indeed. It is also striking that older women were enmeshed in the punishment system. More than a tenth of loyalist victims were older women; the corresponding ratio for female victims of the republican move-ment was higher still at one-fifth, though of course the absolute number of older women attacked by loyalist gangs was higher. Further research is needed to tease out the motivations, circumstances, and practices that lay behind the bare statistics, but it is evident that the reluctance to punish women was by no means absolute. The point still stands, though, that fe-males were much less likely than males to be the victims of vigilante-style justice. Confining the comparison to punishment assaults alone, females accounted for 3.8 per cent of all such victims, though the proportion may well have been higher in the opening years of the Troubles when "tarring" was a more frequent occurrence (see chapter 3).

There is a contrast in the time pattern of loyalist and republican assaults on women. The peak year for republican beatings was 1995, the year after

the Provisional IRA's ceasefire, when seven women in the nationalist community were assaulted. Such attacks virtually ceased after 2000. Loyalist assaults on women within the unionist community were more evenly spread
across the two decades, but there was a distinct clustering of attacks in the
period 2000–03, which coincided with the years of intense conflict between
different loyalist paramilitary organisations. Nineteen (29 per cent) of the
sixty-five attacks took place during these years. There were no reported assaults by loyalists or republicans on women after 2010, which suggests that
a gender taboo was reasserting itself, though there is always the problem
of underreporting.

WOMEN UNDER THREAT

These official statistics do not of course capture the full extent of suffering by women. Far more were driven from their homes, and even larger
numbers were subjected to threats and intimidation of one kind or another.
As indicated in chapter 3, the Young Life and Times Survey (2004) reported
that 7 per cent of young women (sixteen-year-olds) were threatened by
paramilitaries and 16 per cent knew of a family member or close friend
who had been subjected to a paramilitary-style beating.[18] Mothers, wives,
partners, sisters, daughters had their homes invaded by hooded men; they
were threatened verbally, sometimes physically; they were sometimes
obliged to witness the beating of a male family member or listen to the
screams from an adjoining room or yard; women were in the frontline in
terms of caring for the traumatised and broken bodies of their loved ones;
and women had to pick up the pieces in relation to interruptions to education and health care.[19] Hardly surprisingly, in view of the prevailing
gender roles and the large numbers of single mothers, women bore a disproportionate share of the worry for children and adolescents who had
been expelled from their homes and neighbourhoods by the IRA, the UVF,
the UFF and other strong-arm associations. Even in the case of nuclear
families, and in line with conventional gender roles, mothers frequently assumed the major burden of worry for the welfare of the children.[20] Very
occasionally a case came before the public because a relative felt he or she
had the authority to challenge a particular punishment. Thus Donna Maguire, a convicted IRA bomber, demanded a top-level inquiry into an attack

on her brother Malachy Maguire. Malachy was pulled from his car in south Armagh and taken to a nearby children's play area. He was first beaten with iron bars. He was then held down and shot with a handgun in both his wrists and his ankles.[21] The Maguire family were said to be furious, not least presumably because of past service to the republican movement. Somewhat unusually in this attack, extensive gunshot wounds were preceded by a severe beating.

"... TO SEND HER SON OUT TO GET SHOT"

Acting collectively, women sometimes campaigned against the paramilitary punishment system or against political violence more generally. An important example was the mass women's peace movement of the mid-1970s, and a few years earlier there had been a mobilisation by women from Andersonstown in west Belfast calling for peace. In more recent times there was a spontaneous "uprising" of local women in Creggan, Derry, against the vigilante group Republican Action Against Drugs. This was in 2012, after several families on the estate were visited by members of RAAD and ordered to bring their sons to a certain location to be shot in the leg. Some of the leading figures in the subsequent campaign of public meetings were women.[22] As one woman put it, "No mother should have to send her son out to get shot."[23] There were other demonstrations during the Troubles, though relatively few given the scale of the problem. In 2007 some fifty women from Tiger's Bay, a loyalist stronghold in the north inner city of Belfast, held a protest meeting close to a UDA mural. They carried placards proclaiming "Drug Dealers Out" and "Get off our Backs." This was a stinging rebuke to an organisation – the UDA – which claimed to defend the loyalist people but was itself mired in drug dealing and the exploitation of young loyalists.[24] There were also individual women who took brave public stands, despite the risks involved. These included Carmel Donnelly from Coleraine, whose son was abducted and beaten by a paramilitary group and who later lost his life while joyriding, and Nancy Gracey from Downpatrick, whose son Paddy was subjected to a paramilitary-style shooting.[25]

Equally remarkable was the campaigning grandmother Bridie McCloskey from Derry. The McCloskey case demonstrates how a crisis initially relating to one person could quickly envelop several generations and a wider kin network. Bridie's son Joseph McCloskey, from Shantallow in the city, was threatened because he intervened in a pub brawl involving two local IRA "hard men," one of whom, lacking more than a sense of self-caricature, warned, "Listen, big fella. Do you know who I am?"[26] Some days later a punishment squad of up to fourteen republicans armed with guns and sledgehammers, surrounded their home and tried to break in. Using a legally held firearm, Joseph McCloskey and his uncle Danny McBrearty fought off the vigilantes, wounding one of them in the engagement. Quickly afterwards, and with little choice, Joseph and his wife Rosie fled to England.[27] They had six children. A year on, Joseph and part of his family had been re-housed on an impoverished estate in the north of England, one of a number of moves. Because of their peripatetic state, Joseph had found it difficult to make friends and get work. His wife found their isolated circumstances so depressing that she was on tranquilisers. Joseph summed up their plight: "This is not a life. The kids really miss home – all they talk about is Derry. We don't belong here and it is really hard to settle but what can we do? Who knows when we will be able to stop hiding and have a normal life again?"[28]

In fact the story had a satisfactory ending of sorts for the McCloskeys, if one discounts the fear and pain of more than a year in exile, the financial costs this involved, and the disruption to the children's schooling and socialisation.[29] Embarrassed by the relentless public campaign conducted by grandmother Bridie McCloskey – "I am not stopping until my whole family is back at home with me in Derry where they belong"[30] – republicans in Derry eventually allowed the family back. The secret deal was concluded in the weeks leading up to Christmas 2002 and followed numerous visits to Sinn Féin offices in Derry to intercede with Sinn Féin and IRA representatives. The eventual agreement with a senior Provisional IRA operative was witnessed and guaranteed by a priest from the greater Derry area. The family was not allowed any representative to accompany them to the meeting, though they had asked if the Human Rights Commissioner for Northern Ireland and the Clonard priest Father Reid might be present.[31] The family entered alone. The McCloskeys were ordered not to give any further interviews or make contact with the press. They agreed.

THE UNITED NATIONS CONVENTION ON THE
RIGHTS OF THE CHILD

Northern Ireland has probably the best resourced human rights sector of virtually any place on the globe. The recent tradition has been to highlight human rights abuses by the state but not by nonstate actors, as if the far more frequent paramilitary violations took place in a parallel universe. By way of redress, albeit of a very belated kind, we might look at paramilitary child abuse through the lens of the UN Convention on the Rights of the Child. The reluctance of human rights groups within Northern Ireland to do so, which is an issue taken up in more detail later, suggests that the exercise might have both a historical and a contemporary policy relevance.

One of the key articles in the convention has a chilling relevance in the context of Northern Ireland. This is Article 37, which reads in part, "No child shall be subjected to torture or other cruel, inhuman or degrading treatment or punishment." Or as the pithy version produced by the charity Save the Children puts it, "You have the right not to be punished in a cruel or hurtful way."[32] It is difficult to square such standards with the characteristic activities of paramilitary organisations when dealing with children, including those allegedly involved in antisocial behaviour.

It is abundantly clear that during the Troubles children were subjected to beatings, mutilations, and shootings by organised groups of volunteers from the ultranationalist and loyalist traditions of a kind that constituted torture and inhuman treatment.[33] One might object that corporal punishment has been a cultural feature of Irish families and schools for generations. Without in any way wishing to excuse the excesses of parents, teachers, and religious authorities in the past, the actions of the IRA, the INLA, the UVF, the UDA, and other republican and loyalist organisations were qualitatively different, with consequences of the most brutal and far-reaching kind. It is also troubling that these human rights abuses are not part of the past, not part of the world before the paramilitary ceasefires, or even the time before the Good Friday Agreement. They still persist and look set to continue into the indefinite future.

ARDOYNE, BELFAST

To abduct a child is outlawed under Article 9. One of the less remarked aspects of the paramilitary punishment system is that children were sometimes taken from their parents, transported in a car, and held against their will in a strange house before being interrogated and physically brutalised.[34] The consequences of such terrifying ordeals could be far reaching. The fate of seventeen-year-old Anthony O'Neill was edged with tragedy. He was abducted from his own bedroom, bound with electric cable, beaten about the head, and thrown down a manhole by the self-styled Irish National Liberation Army.[35] This was in Ardoyne in north Belfast, a few years after the Good Friday Agreement of 1998. He was accused of joyriding, which the family denied. Trapped in darkness underground, he must have experienced intense terror. He managed to chew his way through the cable and after seven hours emerged covered in blood. He then found refuge at his older sister's home. He was a changed boy. His sister Patricia said he never recovered from the punishment and was tormented with extreme feelings of anxiety and paranoia: "He felt he was worthless, he thought he was scum … Because there is no longer a war on, these groups are turning on their own. They need to find something worthwhile to do."[36] Anthony committed suicide a year later.

The sequel was macabre. His friend Barney Cairns was sixteen years old when he insulted a member of the INLA in Ardoyne. Perhaps he should have been more sensitive to the fragility of the paramilitary ego. Revenge was swift. He received a shooting to both legs. Depression and paranoia followed. He became mentally unstable. Later on the day of his friend Anthony's funeral, perhaps overcome by grief and hopelessness, he was found hanging from the scaffolding placed round the spire of Holy Cross church in north Belfast.[37] The local priest, Father Troy, had to climb up to administer the last rites. Barney was the thirteenth teenager in six weeks to take his own life. The apparently interlinked wave of suicides in Ardoyne was no doubt related to a number of personal and societal factors, but it also seems clear that paramilitary intimidation was a pervasive force in the community. Appealing to the INLA to release the almost unbearable pressure on young people in Ardoyne, Father Troy stated, "If they were to make a statement saying to any young person in north Belfast under threat from us [the INLA] of any sort, that we abandon interrogation, sentencing, punishment attacks and harassment, that would instantly relieve the pressure."[38]

At the height of the INLA power trip in Ardoyne, the mother of a thirteen-year-old boy reported that INLA members would approach young boys in the park and ask their age. "It won't be long before you're getting shot" was their avuncular parting shot.[39]

EXILES

Articles 9 and 10 of the convention are especially relevant to children who have been exiled, with their emphasis on the right of children to live with their parents. The McCloskey case illustrates the role of members of the IRA in ensuring that these rights were not respected. The larger picture is that hundreds of children were driven from their homes and deprived of the right to live with their parents during the course of the Troubles. It is extremely difficult to get at reliable estimates, but evidence supplied to a British parliamentary committee of inquiry in 2001 indicates that the numbers were large and that many went uncounted.[40] Members of the Maranatha Christian church in the north of England, among others, were especially active in opening refugee trails and providing accommodation and support for these reluctant migrants.[41] While the major destination outside of Northern Ireland was Britain, some found their way southwards to the Republic of Ireland.

For a variety of reasons, both historical and practical, it was difficult for the British state to apprehend republicans and loyalists involved in human rights abuses directed against children. These were virtually risk-free activities. But both the United Kingdom and the Republic of Ireland (where vigilante-type activity spread along republican channels on a small scale from the 1990s) had a responsibility to try to ensure that children were protected from "all forms of physical or mental violence, injury or abuse" (Article 19). There was also an obligation under Article 20 to ensure special protection and help for children forced to live apart from their parents. The period of negotiations leading up the Good Friday Agreement and beyond offered an opportunity through Sinn Féin's involvement in the peace process. There is little to suggest that the two guarantors of the Good Friday Agreement, the London and Dublin governments, or the higher tiers of the Northern Ireland administration, used this leverage to any effect. This was, admittedly, less easy in relation to loyalist paramilitaries because their political representatives had such limited success in the electoral arena and their politicians were incidental to the final settlement. It is at least arguable, in view of the evidence on escalating punishment attacks from the later 1990s, that British and Irish policy makers turned a blind eye to paramilitary repression within loyalist and nationalist communities prior to and after the signing of the Good Friday Agreement.[42] If so, they were not the only ones.

NELSONIAN BLIND EYE

Northern Ireland was a black spot for the abuse of children in a form that had no parallel elsewhere in Western Europe. Why so little public discourse focused on the problem is itself a puzzle. After all, the conditions would seem to have been excellent. Northern Ireland was a highly politicised society; the language of rights permeated public discourse; and, at an institutional level, there was an active Equality Commission, a Human Rights Commission, a Children's Commissioner, a Children's Law Centre, and a range of other state-funded initiatives. The community sector was said, somewhat self-regardingly, to have a vibrancy that was unmatched in most other civil societies. More specifically, there were several well-funded voluntary organisations, principally the Committee on the Administration of Justice, which dealt explicitly with human rights issues. Yet the silence was resounding.[43]

A number of social processes helped produce this anomalous state of affairs. The longer-term context was the brutalisation of individuals and communities over three decades or more as a result of violence emanating from paramilitary organisations and the British state. These interactions lowered the threshold of acceptable behaviour in relation to people generally and children in particular. Some individuals in civil society, for a variety of motives, came to acquiesce in the activities of paramilitary organisations, either averting their gaze from the systematic brutalisation of children or supporting such abuses or offering justification for such abuses. Some politicians associated with the UVF and the UDA offered tacit support for loyalist paramilitary "policing," though members of the main unionist parties did not. The former convicted loyalist volunteer and leader of the Progressive Unionist Party David Irvine spoke of the "populist" nature of "punishment attacks."[44] The position of Sinn Féin was at least as ambivalent. At leadership level it publicly dissociated itself from punishment attacks, while at ground level Sinn Féin members (some of whom had overlapping IRA membership) helped operate and justify punishment practices. Breakaway factions from mainstream republicanism in the new century were at least as brutal in their "policing" methods as earlier groups such as the Provisional IRA, the INLA, and their loyalist counterparts, the UDA and the UVF.

During the 1990s the conduct of politics changed radically in Northern Ireland. There was the realpolitik of the peace process and some policy makers seemed to be of the view that for a transitional period paramilitary organisations had to be treated with special sensitivity (a sensitivity these same organisations conspicuously failed to accord their child victims). It was never explained satisfactorily, however, how the blighting of young lives was a means of consolidating a peace process founded on principles of nonviolence and respect for human rights.

The indifference of human rights groups in Northern Ireland was, if anything, more difficult to understand. After all, the politicians were seeking to advance the "imperfect peace" of the later 1990s and this process involved many compromises, including dual standards that indulged paramilitary leaders. The burden on politicians of competing demands and priorities, of short- and long-term considerations, must have weighed heavily. But human rights groups suffered no such inhibitions. The Committee on the Administration of Justice (CAJ) is an especially interesting case in point. Founded in Belfast in 1981, it began by focusing on issues of civil liberties. It did good work in its time, particularly in relation to policing, ethnic, and sexual minorities. It is still in existence. But it resisted any attempts down the years to extend its remit to cover paramilitary or nonstate violations, despite the fact that two of its founding members, the first Human Rights Commissioner for Northern Ireland Professor Brice

Dickson and the academic lawyer Professor Tom Hadden, both argued for change.[45] In 2019 Dickson restated his conviction that it was "perfectly proper to describe what nonstate armed groups do as violations of human rights."[46]

This resistance was not dictated by resource limitations: the CAJ was comfortably funded by Atlantic Philanthropies among other funding agencies. The motives of individuals within the organisation for turning a Nelsonian blind eye to human rights violations in Northern Ireland were presumably varied, ranging from adherence to conservative legal principle to politically motivated concerns not to embarrass particular political parties. Both points were made to me by members and former members.[47] A minority of members had political sympathies that made it difficult for them to oppose publicly the punishment system, as this would have meant criticising Irish republican actions. The unintended result was that the prevailing paradigm of human rights in Northern Ireland became an artificially partitioned one: violations by the state were highlighted, and rightly so, but violations by paramilitary organisations – far more widespread and severe – were ignored. This studied indifference was all the more curious in that international human rights organisations such as Amnesty International and Helsinki Human Rights Watch encountered no insuperable difficulties in attending both to state and paramilitary abuses in Northern Ireland.[48] A Helsinki Watch mission to Northern Ireland examined the question of the use of force by paramilitary groups and concluded that "the use of such force is in violation of customary international humanitarian law."[49] In April 1993 Amnesty International issued the first of its statements, condemning "IRA practices of torturing, maiming and deliberately killing civilians."[50] By contrast, the CAJ and other locally based organisations subsisted for many years on a thin gruel of "celebrity" cases involving state violence.

This failure of concern was present in other organisations. The Children's Law Centre, Belfast, again surprisingly, seemed to find great difficulty in developing a public position on paramilitary child abuse.[51] The reasons for this are obscure. When Northern Ireland was given a Human Rights Commission, as part of the outworking of the Good Friday Agreement, the expectation was that this body would take a prominent role in highlighting and opposing paramilitary abuses of children and adults. The commission was a troubled body from its inception, with ideological and possibly personality clashes limiting its effectiveness.[52] For whatever reasons, some members seemed reluctant to draw attention to abuses of human rights by paramilitaries.

Save the Children, an internationally reputable body, had a presence in Northern Ireland. As with the Children's Law Centre, child welfare was its primary concern. I might mention one experience of mine. I was invited in 2004 to contribute to a seminar series, "Righting the Wrongs," arranged by Save the Children (Northern Ireland) in conjunction with the Institute of Irish Studies, Queen's University, Belfast. The intention, I was told beforehand, was to publish the papers from the seminar series, including my contribution on punishment attacks.[53] It was suggested that a human rights perspective would be particularly welcome. On the day of the seminar a lone news reporter from the *Belfast Newsletter* was somewhat perplexed to be told that the organisers did not favour publicity and so would not speak to her. The seminar benefited from the participation of two victims of paramilitary attacks, who turned up unexpectedly and had their say. Strangely, the proceedings seemed to embarrass Save the Children (Northern Ireland). Not wholly to my surprise, my paper was never published.[54] This nonaction – was it censorship? – was not without precedent. Sometime before this, Save the Children (Northern Ireland) had commissioned research into the rights and needs of young people forced into exile by paramilitary groups. The researcher submitted a draft of his findings in December 2004. This paper, of which I have a copy, was suppressed on the grounds (I was told informally) that its findings might destabilise the peace process.[55]

COMMUNITY AND ALL THAT

In May 2015 a full-page advertisement was taken out in the *Irish News*, the leading nationalist newspaper in Northern Ireland. What was unusual about this was that it was a eulogy to a community worker named Gerard "Jock" Davison who worked in the Markets area of Belfast. No such notice was placed with any of the other Belfast daily newspapers. The message, it seems, was for nationalist readers. "Jock is renowned in his area and across the city and country," the notice stated in the course of gushing tributes to the man. Jock, as he was known, had been murdered by a lone gunman a few days earlier. Contrary to the image presented in the notice, Jock's community work had something of the dark about it. He and his associates were feared by many in south Belfast.[56] Mr Davison was widely believed to be a senior member of the IRA, one who was mainly but not exclusively involved in the killing of drug dealers and the orchestration of punishment beatings. He is also believed to have been the "commander" who ordered the slaying of Robert McCartney and the subsequent cover-up in 2005. Catherine McCartney, one of Robert's five sisters, described him as "a so-called community worker who put people in early graves."[57]

What makes this episode all the more curious is that no fewer than sixty-three community associations, at short notice, had rushed to affix their signatures to an advertisement celebrating the life of a serial killer. These included residents' associations, women's groups, youth projects, and a GAA club.[58] Did this suggest that swathes of community activity in the city were under the control of a political movement identified with "armed struggle"? Or was it simply coincidence?

One might also wonder about the funding of certain community groups and the basis on which some community workers were appointed. Some politicians and political commentators were of the view that British and European Union funds were being distributed in ways designed to "buy off" loyalist and republican paramilitaries as part of the peace process. A controversy surrounding the employment of the loyalist Dee Stitt in 2016 brought concerns into the open. In 2016 Stormont's Social Investment Fund allocated £1.7 million to a community group called Charter NI, based in loyalist east Belfast. The highly paid chief executive was Dee Stitt, whom some claimed was commander of the UDA in North Down.[59] The BBC described him as "a leading UDA member."[60] An embarrassed police spokesman admitted during the course of a radio interview on BBC Northern Ireland that "people connected to the controversial Charter NI project have recently been involved in paramilitary activity."[61]

THE POLITICS OF HUMAN RIGHTS

Almost inevitably in a highly politicised society, the human rights agenda also came to be politicised, like virtually every other public issue in Northern Ireland.[62] There was a view in some quarters that human rights concerns were the preserve of the nationalist community. This view could only be sustained by turning a blind eye to paramilitary violations of human rights. But rather like bowdlerised versions of history, a selective human rights posture could serve as a useful standpoint for militant nationalists seeking to challenge the legitimacy of the state. And, in an equally reprehensible way, unionist politicians and ideologues, by contrast, tended to ignore human rights abuses by the state, fearing to criticise state institutions, particularly the police, in case this might lend succour to their political opponents. Both stances were in fact highly selective, though in different ways. Staunch unionists saw little merit in investigating abuses of power by the British state or in the promotion of a human rights culture, while republican ideologues sought to keep paramilitary punishments off the human rights agenda. The universalistic principles that underpinned the idea of human rights got lost somewhere along the line, as provincial and communalist mind-sets prevailed.

Other voluntary organisations with more diffuse briefs in terms of children's welfare or human rights concerns in a broad sense were, on the whole, silent as well. The much-vaunted voluntary sector was the dog that didn't bark.[63] This again seemed to be due to a variety of motives and circumstances: some were wary of stepping into controversial areas of public life; others were fearful of endangering their existing relationships with paramilitary organisations and their political representatives; others again were controlled directly or indirectly by paramilitary organisations and so were unlikely to speak up for children's rights or voice criticism of the perpetrators of abuse, that is, unless the abusers were agents of the state.[64] The mid- and later-1970s saw a heavier investment by the Provisional IRA and Sinn Féin in creating or infiltrating community, housing, transport, youth, and sporting organisations. By the 1990s a lattice work of community and residents' associations, funded in the main by the British state and the European Union but often controlled by members of Sinn Féin or its auxiliaries, criss-crossed working-class Catholic areas.[65] Symptomatic of these invisible processes, some of the early initiatives in community restorative justice employed former paramilitaries. Gaelic Athletic Association grounds hosted hunger strike commemorations. Certain taxi firms employed former volunteers who had been imprisoned for political violence. In Belfast Irish language groups and publications became closely associated with the republican movement.[66] There were reflections of these developments on the loyalist side but to a lesser extent, it would seem.[67]

Open and truthful discussion of paramilitary violence – orange-on-orange and green- on-green violence – might have found a place under the power-sharing arrangements in Northern Ireland. But here, as elsewhere, there were complicating considerations: two of the political parties, Sinn Féin and the Progressive Unionist Party, had historic links to paramilitary organisations and child abuse. The Alliance Party, Northern Ireland and the Social Democratic and Labour Party took consistently principled positions in public against paramilitary-style punishments, as did some but not all trade unions. David Trimble's Ulster Unionist Party was instrumental in the setting up of the Independent Monitoring Commission, which fixed its gaze firmly on paramilitary deviations from their ceasefire promises.[68] The Democratic Unionist Party also opposed paramilitary punishments but some might question its sense of urgency and its sense of priorities on the matter.

Perhaps the media bore some responsibility for the restricted public discourse? A resort to blaming the messenger is a little too convenient. Media coverage is predicated on the existence of the oxygen of factual detail, as well as interviews and comment that go into the construction of news stories. To attract and sustain media interest there had to be child victims and families prepared to break the silence. They had to be willing to describe how and why a particular attack took place, sharing their feelings of hurt, terror, and injury with a wider audience. In a world where Mafia-style *omerta* prevailed this was asking the near impossible.

In addition, the media needed to be able to talk to medical practitioners about the injuries and to social workers and community workers, teachers, police, and others about the knock-on effects in terms of the welfare of the child. This rarely happened, which brings us to the most important reason of all for the neglect of the paramilitary abuse of children. As with clerical child abuse, it came down to differences in power and the willingness to use power ruthlessly.[69] If victims, or their families, took a stand and brought their plight into the public arena or sought to give evidence against suspected perpetrators, then they were inviting ever more violent abuse at the hands of the UVF, the UDA, the IRA, and related organisations. The simple and fundamental truth was that fear ruled, often reinforced by rumour and further vilification.[70] In this closed world, *the punishment system generated its own automatic cover-up.* Being silenced was not the least part of the punishment.

ORGANISED AND VIOLENT CHILD ABUSE

The extension of human rights obligations to nonstate actors is complex, as the academic lawyer Andrew Clapham acknowledges.[71] His conclusion, which is a challenge to conservative lawyers and human rights activists, not only in Ireland, is as follows: "The message is that international human rights obligations can fall on states, individuals, and non-state actors."[72] If this position on human rights is accepted, then the UVF, the UDA, the IRA, and Sinn Féin (as a collaborator with and an apologist for the main armed group) have much to answer for. The same may be said of the PUP, which has links to the UVF. A commitment to compensation for victims is implied, and in principle the extensive black-economy revenues of paramilitary organisations would permit this, but it is hard to see this happening. It is hardly in the nature of nonstate abusers of human rights.

In a world of small mercies it may be noted that loyalist and republican paramilitaries did not use gunshot wounding for children less than fourteen years of age, though on occasion a victim was already being eyed up for future attention by the gunmen.[73] This modest show of restraint did not extend to fourteen- and fifteen-year-olds. Wayward children from deprived social backgrounds, it appears, could not be allowed to become a burden on the cause of Ireland or Ulster. As far as the military establishments within loyalism and republicanism were concerned, vigilante-style beatings of children using a range of everyday instruments, from cudgels and baseball bats to iron bars and lump hammers, were acceptable. Shootings and exiling were further options.

Attacks on children intensified following the paramilitary ceasefires of 1994. Even the signing of the Good Friday Agreement in 1998 did not mark a turning point. The authorities in London and Dublin seemed relatively unperturbed. Many of those under threat were children; others were children of adults under threat. Sometimes, as we have seen, the attacks on children were by arrangement, rather like a dental appointment or a job interview, with an already-stretched National Health Service obliged to pick up the pieces. Exiling progressed apace from the 1990s. It was only in 2004, a full decade after the paramilitary ceasefires that a significant decline in vigilante-style attacks became apparent.

There are many ironic twists to the story of the children of the working classes during the course of the Troubles and its slowly cooling embers. As the era of the abuse of unmarried mothers and children within Irish society was drawing to a close in the 1980s, some of the most vicious and systematic forms of child abuse were gaining momentum in Northern Ireland. This was the heyday of the rule of paramilitary organisations in disadvantaged communities. Human Rights groups and community associations in Northern Ireland doubtless did many good things.[74] But with eyes wide shut they failed to address the dominant human rights problems of the day.[75] A case of *trahison des clercs* some might say. The failure of children's advocacy groups is especially striking. To their immense credit, Amnesty International and Helsinki Human Rights Watch kept an occasional eye on paramilitary violations of human rights during the 1990s but understandably their main concerns lay elsewhere in the globe.

In the late twentieth century Northern Ireland was home to waves of organised and violent child abuse, of a kind that had no exact precedents in the history of the Irish or British states. The closest parallels may be abuses within the Magdalene asylums, mother and child homes, reformatories, and clergy-controlled schools. Even in these institutions there was no general policy of organised and systematic physical abuse of children. Rather it was the case that perverted individuals took advantage of existing power structures for their own personal gratification.

A dual standard of rights pertained in some neighbourhoods in Belfast, Derry, Lurgan, Newry, Strabane, and elsewhere. The abnormality of it all may be illuminated by a simple thought experiment. Let us imagine that a gang of policemen and women ordered a child to appear at an alleyway or at a barracks at a specified time, and had one of them then coldly and deliberately shot a child in any part of his or her body there would have been a public outcry. Had rogue police cornered and overpowered a child and smashed his limbs or joints, while the parents were held powerless within earshot, the public would have been shocked beyond belief. Had this gone on, week in and week out, the international community would have been outraged. Every human rights group in the western world would have been alerted. Not so in the demimonde of paramilitary control in Northern Ireland. Paramilitaries enjoyed and enforced silence and compliance, even though the signs of abuse – welts, bruising, bandaging, swellings, crutches, wheelchairs – were highly visible. For once, and yet again, the old Heaney line proves best: Whatever you say, say nothing.[76] The silence is only beginning to be broken, but for many – already broken in spirit as well as body – the stories, with their manifold ramifications, are unlikely ever to see the light of day.

Figure 5.1 Ireland's Holy Mountain

5

Guilt, Shame, Ideological Evasion
(and Even Atonement)

*After the Nazi era, Germans had to face their past: not just the genocide,
but also the violent, undemocratic nationalism. They did it, despite the
emotional anguish associated with challenging the tribal gods, and telling
one's parents that they were wrong.*
Fr Séamus Murphy, S.J., *Irish Times*, 12 May 2009

INTRODUCTION

Can there be collective guilt and responsibility, as acknowledged by a community or a people with respect to the violent actions of members who
come from within that community? If the militants are a tiny minority
who wrap themselves in ideological garb and claim to be speaking for the
"people," the answer must surely be in the negative. The Baader-Meinhof
terrorist network in Germany, the Red Brigades in Italy, or some Islamist
jihadists are cases in point. To take the last example, Muslims generally are
not responsible for individuals and small groups within their ranks who
indulge in terror in the name of Allah. But if speaking of a large minority
of the population, who regularly reaffirm their tolerance of violence in
various tests of public opinion, then there are indeed grounds for enter-
taining some notion of wider guilt.

Postwar German society is the supreme case of a successful acknowledgement of past wrongs. Many Germans – by no means all – came to recognise the enormity of the terror inflicted on the world by an appalling
regime in the hallucinatory grip of machismo, militarism, and racism. But
there are also the great failures, neighbouring Austria being a particularly
salutary case in point. Many Austrians, including leading Catholic clergy-
men, turned out to be enthusiastic supporters of the Nazi vision at the time

of Anschluss, the unification of Germany and Austria in 1938, but later con-
trived a self-image in which they were victims of German expansionism.
This failure of memory, history, and conscience may help explain the continuing strength of ultranationalist political forces within Austrian society.[1]
Without an acknowledgement of at least partial complicity, there was no
atonement and hence no deep questioning of Austrian responsibility for
atrocities committed during the period of ultranationalist ascendancy.
Similar observations might be made in relation to modern day ultranationalism in Poland and Hungary where histories of collaboration during World War II are fiercely contested. Closer in time to us, many will recall
the Bosnian war of the 1990s when the Serbs held a huge military advantage
and were practising ethnic cleansing on a large scale – culminating in the
massacre of eight thousand Bosnian Muslims at Srebrenica in July 1995 –
ordinary Serbs still complained bitterly about the West's indifference to the
historical sufferings of the Serbs.[2] There is little to suggest that Serbian
society has faced up to the enormity of the war crimes committed both by
its troops and by Serb irregulars. As in Austria, Poland, and Hungary, the
effect is to open up space for right-wing, nationalistic parties.

There may of course be moments of private guilt on the part of former
killers. I think of my friend of many years, the former IRA commander and
later Garda informant Sean O'Callaghan. He renounced the use of violence
and my distinct impression is that his earlier experiences haunted him, thus
testifying to the role of conscience and self-reflection.[3] He bore his responsibilities seriously, working behind the scenes to help restore peace in Ireland.[4] Shane Paul O'Doherty is another, also a teenage recruit who later
used his formidable intellectual abilities to excoriate his former Provisional
associates.[5] I know of comparable cases of remorse on the loyalist side.
Another friend, once a notorious car thief (see earlier), spent some years
in prison and struck up an unlikely friendship with one of the Shankill
Butchers, "Basher" Bates. Though from a nationalist background, he was
impressed by Bates' embrace of Christianity and his desire for forgiveness.
As it happens, Bates was murdered by a fellow loyalist in 1997, between the
paramilitary ceasefires of 1994 and the signing of the Good Friday Agreement in 1998. My friend is a deeply committed Christian who also regrets
the actions of his earlier self.

The "Shankill Butchers"

The most notorious paramilitary and criminal gang to emerge during the 1970s was known as the Shankill Butchers. The leader was a sadistic, serial killer named Lenny Murphy, assisted by his lieutenant Robert "Basher" Bates and a string of associates. Both had been involved in conventional crime before the Troubles erupted. For people like Murphy the emergence of paramilitary groups such as the UDA and UVF provided new opportunities for personal gain, heavy drinking, womanising, and, above all, giving unrestrained expression to their violent fantasies.

Figure 5.2 The Shankill Road, Belfast, in the 1970s.

Their modus operandi, which brought terror to the streets of Belfast, was to abduct a lone Catholic, force him into a car, head back to a club or safe house in the Shankill, torture their victim using knives, and hours later cut the throat of the victim and discard the body on a piece of waste ground. This UVF gang of serial killers was responsible for the deaths of at least nineteen victims, including a number of Protestants.

But why, other than blind sectarian hatred? Martin Dillon writes, "There is plenty of evidence to suggest that Lenny Murphy committed the crimes firstly for pleasure and secondly for extracting information. The amount of time spent in torturing Madden [Thomas Madden, a Catholic and an early victim] supports the thesis that his killing was for pleasure."[6] Murphy was assassinated in 1982 by the IRA, probably involving collusion with higher levels of the UVF who regarded Murphy's gang as out of control. Most of the members were eventually arrested by the RUC and given lengthy prison sentences. Reflecting on these horrors, the Irish writer and politician Conor Cruise O'Brien expressed himself puzzled "both by the phenomenon of the Butchers, and the absence of an exact parallel among the Catholic murderers." In his view, part of the explanation was the lack of centralised control on the Protestant side as compared to the tight hierarchical structure of the IRA. In addition, he suggested the IRA was "much more interested in its public 'image' than the Protestant paramilitaries have been in theirs."[7]

Then there are those former combatants who have been consumed by alcohol and even suicide.[8] The disintegration of their lives and relationships, in some cases at least, suggests arrows of remorse, even if only subliminally. Still, there is little in the wider public sphere to indicate critical reflection on the part of most paramilitaries, their supporters, and bystanders. My friends Ruth and Lionel may well have been correct in their dismissal (described in the opening chapter of this volume) of signs of guilt, either consciously or subliminally.

Does this mean that large sections of the nationalist community were, perhaps still are, largely immune to the sufferings of the Protestant "other," even when under murderous attack? Might the same be true of swathes of unionism that appear to show little concern for the sufferings of the

Catholic "other"? At times it seems as if each political community has been culturally programmed to amplify emotions of anger, fear, resentment, self-righteousness. What the two neighbouring circuits do not conduct easily are positive emotions such as understanding, empathy, and fellow feeling. Such failures, if such they be, evolved over time and are an ethnic and nationalistic rather than an intrinsically Irish reaction, best thought of as responses to circumstances of hurt and alienation.

DEFENCE MECHANISMS

Rather than look for signs of collective guilt within strands of northern Irish nationalism at this stage of its historical evolution (I reflect on Ulster unionism later), it may be more profitable to try to identify some of the defence mechanisms that hold at bay the awkward reality that for the period 1970–97 most killings, most bombings, most maimings were due to republicans from within the nationalist community.[9] For the two subsequent decades, up to the present, republicans of one variety or another have dominated the armed-violence stakes. As remarked earlier, the *consistent, purposeful*, and *enduring* impetus towards violence came from one part of Northern Irish society and one part only. This is not to deny that loyalist killers have also been responsible for heinous acts.

So, what might the defence mechanisms be? Here are some suggestions, beginning with the long view.

There is the *historical legacy* of a divided society in which economic and political power was identified with Protestants and unionists, in turn producing hurt and anger within the Catholic and nationalist population. Protestants might well retort that they should not be penalised for high levels of entrepreneurship and economic performance, while Catholics might point to land dispossessions in the seventeenth century and discriminatory practices subsequently.[10] In any case, remembrances and perceptions of disadvantage and status deprivation served to insulate minds against feelings of empathy, even when a Protestant of the meanest social status was gunned down in his or her everyday life. Many UDR men were small farmers or tradesmen, supplementing their meagre incomes with part-time military service. They were particularly easy targets for assassination by the IRA, as they went about their ordinary business in isolated local communities, be it working on a farm, having a drink in a local pub, or visiting a sick relative.

County Fermanagh is the extreme case. The Troubles there claimed 116 lives.[11] Of these, the British Army was responsible for five deaths, one was due to the RUC, one was due to the UDR, and five were due to loyalist paramilitaries. The remaining deaths, 104 or 90 per cent of the total, were due to the IRA.[12] Many of the IRA victims were part-time, off-duty, or former members of the security forces. A third were civilians. Eight members of the IRA lost their lives: five were shot dead, one died from a premature bomb explosion, another drowned while on active service, and a third was executed by his comrades as an informer. It is a striking disproportion that 90 per cent of the Fermanagh deaths were due to the IRA. Six murders were attributed to the security forces or loyalists. In three of these cases prosecutions for unlawful killings followed. Virtually all of the killings by the IRA remain unresolved. The pain could be distributed very unevenly. Jimmy Graham, a part-time member of the UDR and bus driver, assassinated in 1985, was the third of three Graham brothers to be killed. He was shot dead while waiting to pick up schoolchildren at St Mary's primary school in Derrylin, County Fermanagh. By contrast with Belfast and north Armagh, there was little loyalist retaliation. One can almost visualise the shadow of death moving across the beautiful landscapes of County Fermanagh or West Tyrone as another, usually defenceless Protestant was taken out. Who might be next, they must have wondered, as they sat round the family table, turned the lights out late at night, or journeyed down backroads to church or school. There were expressions of outrage from the other community but these tended to be episodic and short-lived.

Self-segregation

Different histories aren't of course the only empathy blockers: voluntary or self-segregation in education, housing and cultural life, and other more subtle practices built social and psychological walls round Catholic and Protestant families and neighbourhoods. Selective recollection and the compartmentalisation of awkward realities are a common way of reducing cognitive dissonance or the psychological discomfort arising from holding contradictory propositions. One or two examples may serve to illustrate this. The hunger strikes of the early 1980s for example have an iconic significance in the nationalist imagination. Yet there were more killings outside the prisons during this period than deaths by self-starvation within the prisons.[13] The murder of prison staff during the strikes, to take one subcategory of noncombatant victims, barely merits a mention, as if their lives and the feelings of their families, kinfolk, and friends could be set at nought. In terms of republican ideology these were "legitimate targets," agents of the state no less, but the more striking point is the wider indifference within nationalism. Over the years I have had many conversations on Bobby Sands, the prison protests more generally, and the climactic hunger strikes. Rarely if ever have nationalist friends paused to mention the other victims of those strife-torn months and years.

Yet there were people like Mabel Hempton, a twenty-six-year-old County Armagh woman and prison officer. Going about the ordinary business of having lunch with three friends in Armagh, the women were subjected to a grenade and gun attack by gunmen from one of the more fanatical strains of Irish republicanism, the self-styled Irish National Liberation Army. One woman was killed and Mabel was left wheelchair bound. She lived for a further thirty-one pain-filled years.[14]

I recall organising a conference on victims of the Troubles in Belfast in the early 1990s, to which we invited Emma Groves, a Belfast woman and mother of a large family.[15] She had been blinded by a plastic bullet fired by a soldier at close range through her kitchen window during a British Army search in nationalist West Belfast. This was in the early years of the Troubles when the army was much less disciplined as well as being ill suited to policing roles. When I met her, some twenty years later in the Europa Hotel, wearing (if I remember correctly) dark glasses and being guided by a nurse-friend, it was impossible not to be struck by her dignity and her refusal to be blinded or silenced by her traumatic past. Lest this appear ignorant of the dilemmas involved, I should also say I am not for a moment implying that police or military should respond passively as rocks and petrol bombs rained down on them during the intense, sometimes murderous rioting that characterised loyalist and republican working-class areas of Northern Ireland between the 1970s and the 1990s. Even policemen and policewomen are not for burning. Police lives matter. But I felt this particular instance had been an abuse of power by the forces of the state. More generally, there can be little doubt that some of the killings and wounding by the security forces were unlawful, with rubber and plastic bullets being fired more out of vindictiveness and fear than rational calculations of risk. Yet my unionist friends rarely if ever questioned these disputed shootings. Ethnic autism ruled, on both sides of the communal divide.

"Whataboutery"

Then there is that coarse art form known as whataboutery, which usually takes a verbal form. Anyone who has lived in Northern Ireland for any length will have encountered the response, well-practised on both sides of the divide, of avoiding dealing directly with an atrocity perpetrated by those on one's own side of the communal divide. So,

> "Bloody Sunday in Derry was an appalling massacre of innocent people."
> "What about the La Mon massacre in Belfast?"
> "Hah! What about the Monaghan bombings?"

And so it goes, round and round in circles of bitter exchange. Some day we may all acknowledge *both* the massacre at the La Mon Hotel and the Monaghan-Dublin bombings. We may also come to hold in our heads in the same moment not only the massive injustice done to the Birmingham Six but also the murder of twenty-one Birmingham residents, including two Irishmen, in 1974 that precipitated the subsequent abuse of judicial processes.

There is, incidentally, some interesting psychological research that touches on this. Sullivan et al. found that one way of maintaining a group's positive self-image was to engage in what they describe as "competitive victimhood." They ask why should social groups compete with each other "for the right to claim victimhood?" It seems a curious position to adopt. The answer seems to be that this can be a useful strategy for deflecting awkward questions about the group's own behaviour and may even legitimise extreme actions that might otherwise appear unjustified.[16] By way of illustration, the authors allude to Arabs and Israelis in the process of negotiation and quote Vamik Volkan, an expert in conflict resolution: "They began by citing past injuries ... as if competing to see who had suffered more."[17]

Denial

A further defence mechanism is *denial*. Indeed this occupies a prime place in warding off uncomfortable realities and maintaining ideological and psychological equilibrium. So far as I know, the murder of Joanne Mathers, a young married woman collecting census forms in Derry during the course of the 1981 census of Northern Ireland,[18] was never acknowledged by the Provisional IRA and certainly not at the time. I recall the news of the killing vividly. I was sitting with a group of students in a café in Magee University College in Derry, a few miles from the murder spot, when the news came in over the radio. My nationalist students, shocked by such violence towards a young woman with no connection whatsoever to the security forces could not bring themselves to believe that republicans were responsible.

Yet as we sat drinking tea or coffee we all knew that republicans were conducting a public campaign of opposition to the census, seizing and destroying census documents. Who else could it have been, unless it was the armed wing of the Legion of Mary (a Catholic devotional organisation), I wondered to myself? After a few days it was impossible to sustain the fiction of noninvolvement, though the IRA remained silent on the murder, but events had moved on and the sense of personal shock and of collective responsibility had drained away. The point is that the suspension of belief, even for a short time interval, served to take the sting out of the original outrage.

More usually, though, denial operates within a longer time frame, with an outright denial of incidents that might reflect badly on the republican movement or the deflection of responsibility onto other agencies, usually the British security forces. Where this is impossible, then various rationalisations may be invoked. War is a messy business; mistakes happen; the nobility of the cause absolves all who hunger and thirst for the nation. Individual acts may sometimes appear squalid, sectarian, or even psychopathic. So what? Look what they've done to us down the years.

"Confirmation bias"

Interwoven with and reinforcing many of these cognitive tendencies is what social psychologists call confirmation bias.[19] In its broadest sense this encompasses much of what has been said already. Advocates of "armed struggle," as well as their ideological fellow-travellers, tend to be resistant to information that might undermine their heartfelt convictions and, conversely, will be eager to embrace ideas and experiences that serve to confirm their preexisting beliefs. Attitudinal change of a fundamental kind is not easily brought about.

These various feints and ruses are defence mechanisms at the individual level. But the individual is also part of a social whole, in this context the republican movement. The party has been a powerful source of political interpretations long before we began to use phrases such as a post-truth politics. The old-fashioned term propaganda has much to commend it. On the nationalist side,this is largely orchestrated by Sinn Féin with smaller republican factions making their contribution. The network of republican offices, conferences, commemorations, graveside orations, press statements, social media messages, ballads and wall murals, newspapers, and other publications ensure that the republican view of the conflict is articulated over and over again. The propaganda offensive is on an enormous scale. This is made possible because by working within the interstices of a liberal, democratic state paramilitary organisations have been successful in extracting tens of millions of pounds through racketeering of various kinds, from extortion schemes to bank robberies, from counterfeiting to cross-border smuggling. The kingpins in these Mafia-style operations have been the Provisional IRA, hence, some suggest, the substantial funds available to Sinn Féin for an infrastructure of party offices, party workers, publications, and election campaigns. The raid on the Northern Bank in central Belfast – IRA involvement was of course denied – in the run up to Christmas 2004 alone netted in excess of £28 million, but this was only the most spectacular among a wide range of illegal activities extending over three decades or more. This may help explain the paradox of how a largely working-class party, with little or no corporate or trade union backing, ranks among the best resourced parties in Europe.[20] Not all operations were

illegal. Republican, and indeed loyalist-controlled community organisations, have also been adept at channelling funds from the British and Irish
states, and from the European Union, into the grey areas of republican and
loyalist activity.[21] In any case, it needs to be appreciated that the scale of the
propaganda offensive, both within and without republican-controlled
communities, was enormous and, in many respects, quite effective. Moreover, within tight, working-class areas there was little room for competing
or questioning narratives.

Not responsible

Formal denial was a common response. Among the various organisational
lies were the following: the IRA was not responsible for a bomb placed in
the small village of Claudy in 1972 that killed eight people, including
children; the bomb that exploded in Anderson Street, Short Strand, Belfast
in the same year, killing IRA men and local people, was a British "dirty
tricks" effort rather than a bungled IRA operation; the IRA did not cause
the explosion in the Abercorn restaurant in central Belfast in March 1972
in which two young women were killed and 130 people were maimed; Jean
McConville was not abducted and killed by the IRA, nor were several others
now referred to collectively as the "disappeared"; the IRA had nothing to
do with the Kingsmill massacre, in which ten Protestant workmen were
singled out and executed in cold blood by the side of the road as this was
due to agents unknown; Robert McCartney, beaten and stabbed to death
outside a centre-city bar in Belfast was murdered by men unknown and the
subsequent forensic cleaning of the bar by republicans had nothing to do
with the IRA; the South Armagh man Paul Quinn was beaten to death with
iron bars, not by the IRA but by local criminals; Martin McGuinness (testifying under oath to the Bloody Sunday Inquiry) had left the IRA in 1974.[22]

Most of these claims of noninvolvement have now been decisively rejected, as fresh evidence has come to light. The scale of lying, particularly
to the nationalist community itself, was on such a scale as to leave one
aghast that so many could have been persuaded, even persuaded to lie to
themselves, for so long. The writer and political commentator, Malachi
O'Doherty captures this well:

The lies and the manipulation speak of a devious ruthless leadership. For the IRA was lying more to the Catholic community and its own members than to the British ... It is time old republicans asked themselves why they were so pliable and gullible.[23]

Forcing the truth

Perhaps part of the answer lies in the systematic crushing of critical comment from within nationalist, working-class areas. Brute force may be the final, or the first, resort. When the Peace People, encouraged by Mairead Corrigan and Betty Williams, organised a joint march for peace, thereby bringing together real, living Catholics and Protestants, unionists and nationalists, on the Falls Road in 1977 they were attacked by republicans. The irony of the use of the term "republican" in this context will be obvious. Rocks and stones rained down on the peace demonstrators and "republican" women invaded the platform. This is at the mild end of repression, however. Like many people who have lived in Northern Ireland for any length of time, I have met individuals who have been threatened with beatings or death should they dare to speak out.

Writing from personal experience within the IRA could be a problem. Eamon Collins was put to death in a gruesome manner by his former comrades for publishing *Killing Rage*, which presented an unflattering picture of life within the conspiratorial movement. Anthony McIntyre, once a leading member of the IRA who spent eighteen years in prison for the cause but later disagreed with the direction of Sinn Féin politics, when asked if he ever felt under threat, responded, "I certainly have felt fear. My wife Carrie and I and our two children have had Sinn Féin mobs picketing our homes – our previous one in Belfast and our current one in Drogheda – and members of the IRA leadership came to our home to intimidate us."[24]

Ricky O'Rawe, the public relations officer for republicans during the hunger strike of 1981, contemplated writing an account of the negotiations, which had been conducted via intermediaries with the British government but was warned, "I could be shot for opening my mouth."[25] The problem was his recollections deviated from the authorised version of the faith. There were others.

Social control

There are less visible forms of social control. Local critics, should they be foolish enough to "mouth off," could be stigmatised as touts (informers), perverts, drug dealers, or antisocial deviants Such deliberately propagated messages – gossip being a hugely effective, low-cost, largely invisible communal resource – left the victim vulnerable to intimidation, physical assault, or expulsion from the area.[26] In these many ways, responsibility was shifted, evaded, or minimized.

Concealment

If the tactics of deflection, denial, or intimidation were insufficient, concealment had a role to play. This is encapsulated in the tragic life and death of Jean McConville. For years Sinn Féin and the IRA concealed the fact that republicans had abducted, murdered, and secretly buried this Protestant widow, once living in the Falls area of Belfast.[27] To compound the tragedy, her bewildered children had to be taken into institutional care. Because of the lies they were fed by republicans – it is entirely acceptable to lie for the cause and rank-and-file members were generally happy to swallow the "official line" however implausible – it was many years before the children finally realised their mother would not be coming back. Difficult questions and potential criticisms of the conduct of the Provisionals' self-declared war were buried for many years with the corpse of Jean McConville and of more than a dozen others.[28]

Rewriting the past

Sanitising the past is especially important for those who were "on active service" and who experienced the brutal side to conflict. An outsider's glance at the republican paper *An Phobhlacht* shows up a dreary litany of commemorations and obituaries for fallen comrades. Adult men and women traipsing round graveyards, marching in formation with flags, listening to formulaic speeches in all weathers, may seem about as absorbing as collecting used bingo tickets but this is to miss the vital reassurance these ceremonies provide. The cause was noble, wasn't it? All that suffering, all those killings, all those maimings must have been worthwhile? Commemorations serve to ward off self-corrosive thoughts. Doubts and remorse of conscience, or what James Joyce in a coruscating word-image called the "agenbite of inwit," are not helpful to the political struggle (and possibly not to the personal psychological one either).[29]

Capturing the human rights agenda

There is one further recourse that has proved important in revisioning the past. As discussed already, efforts to capture and distort the humanitarian record of the conflict have proved to be a productive area of "struggle" for republican activists. Local self-styled human rights organisations, by turning a blind eye to the torture, mutilation, and degrading treatment of thousands of citizens have served (some would say unwittingly) to cloud understandings of the present and past.

The more partisan of these specialise in investigating abuses by the security forces, though most killings and maimings were by nonstate, armed groups.[30] The policing and justice system generated an extensive paper trail, much though not all of which is open to discovery. By contrast, conspiratorial organisations, both loyalist and republican, leave few documents in their wake, so a structural bias exists which favours inquiries that disproportionately target the fraction of killings by the police and army, leaving responsibility for most killings beyond effective scrutiny. Were there unlawful killings by the security forces, particularly the army? Certainly so. But few would suggest that a large proportion were of that nature in view of the lethal attacks to which the army and police were exposed. Inevitably and understandably the popular media focus on the emerging revelations of disputed cases that contain the kind of documentary detail that is essential to making a news story. Of the much more common violations by nonstate actors, the rule of omerta, backed up by threats, creates silences which do not make for good copy. Thus the smokescreen across the past thickens with the passing of time.[31]

PROTESTANT DEFENCE MECHANISMS

Protestants and unionists have also of course practised selective recollection and amnesia in relation to abuses of power in the past. The mechanisms of defence are much the same as those just outlined. The burden of responsibility for policies and practices pursued by the Northern Ireland parliament and the Unionist Party during the first fifty years of devolved government must lie with unionists. The grievances created or reinforced should be acknowledged much more fully than has been the case so far. It is absurd for some unionist politicians to take refuge in the form of words that runs along the lines of accepting the "nationalist *perception* of grievances." There were perceptions and they were founded in real grievances, *tout court.*

Sometimes the issue is one of bad history or at least a limited knowledge of Irish history. At the Thomas D'Arcy McGee summer school in Carlingford in August 2014, to give an example, there were several sessions on the Great Famine of the 1840s. One session was composed exclusively of a panel of politicians. A backbench unionist MLA and soon-to-be minister at Stormont, Jim Wells, admitted candidly that he had never thought about how the famine might have affected Ulster. I pressed him on this afterwards, and he reiterated that it just wasn't part of his community's sense of history. In fairness, he said he now looked forward to finding out more about what for him was part of the "lost history" of Ulster.

By and large, apologists for loyalist violence put little energy into articulating a defence of their actions (which is a problem for historians seeking to be even handed) other than to claim they were resisting republican attacks on the union. Some rejoiced in the belief, though the evidence was scarce, that they were fighting for "God and Ulster." In the eyes of these zealots the role of the RUC and the British army in countering political terror was not enough and needed to be supplemented. Some it is fair to say later saw the contradictions in the loyalist position: loyal to Queen and country but also prepared to bear arms against the Queen's representatives or burn RUC members out of their homes (as in the aftermath of the Anglo-Irish Agreement of 1985). Perhaps only a minority but some ex-combatants absorbed the perverse logic that all were victims of the Troubles. Without human agency there is no responsibility, so this was nothing if not convenient. Self-delusion may well be a necessary attribute of the paramilitary mindset.

FACING THE MOUNTAIN

> It seems to me very strange that people can move from the violence of the past to assuming power without ever acknowledging their past."
> Eoin O'Callaghan, *Belfast Telegraph*, 25 February 2016

I believe in the possibilities of redemptive change. This chapter touches on issues of guilt, reparation, and the deep foundations for a society at ease with itself. Each of these themes might be developed at length, a task best left to thinkers and writers more skilled than the present author. It makes chronological sense to begin with the Protestants of "Ulster." There is no doubt the Protestant and unionist community of Northern Ireland has its weight of guilt to expiate. The Nobel Laureate and former leader of the Ulster Unionist Party David Trimble acknowledged that Northern Ireland had been a "cold house" for Northern Catholics (even if some wanted to burn the house down).[32] But I have to confess this study comes from within my own national community, so the emphasis is on *our* burdens and re-sponsibilities, on *our* responsibilities to reach out to the unionist "other."[33] In my estimation, we bear the major weight of responsibility for the mod-ern Troubles. I have suggested the existence of layers of evasion and re-pressed feelings. If so, it might be helpful to consider also the notion of "moral injury." This is a relatively new concept and so is best treated with some caution until empirical studies are more fully developed. It has emerged from the study of war, the insight being that war combatants suffer "emotional, spiritual, and psychological wounds" that arise when a com-batant's moral and ethical standards are compromised during the course of violent conflict. Thus Drescher et al. use the term "moral injury" to de-scribe "the impact of various acts of omission or commission in war that produce inner conflict."[34] In a sense, some of the earlier discussion is close to this meaning, but the concept helps highlight the relevance of the inner conflicts of combatants and bystanders. So there may be a case for ar-guing that republican activists and possibly wider swathes of the Catholic community of Northern Ireland have suffered "moral injury" that may take another generation to acknowledge and make right. The condition, if valid, surely applies to loyalist paramilitaries and their cheerleaders as well.

At this point I want to shift to a more purely normative form of analysis. There seems not to be an appropriate word within the English language for what I have in mind, surprisingly so as the idea is simple enough. It is the need to render the individual conscience more receptive to the gross wrongs that have been visited on neighbours and fellow citizens. It is a cry for reflective conscience making. Atonement is a concomitant. Perhaps the word *conscientisation* will do, though a similar word has been used in a rather different sense by Paulo Freire the Brazilian educationalist.[35] The onus is on all of us to face up to the central realities of the conflict and the contradictions that cluster beneath the surface rhetoric. Irish nationalists were responsible for maintaining, year in and year out, the longest-running conflict in postwar Europe. It is time to understand the seriousness of the charge – I hesitate even as I write – and seek to undo some of the harm. To use a colloquial term, the blackguarding of the Protestants of the north over three decades, as with the blackguarding of northern Catholics and southern Protestants during the shorter interval of 1920–23, cries out for public recognition.

How might we help? For one thing, those of us who are Irish citizens might listen more attentively to our British neighbours on this island, the British Irish if you will, in the northern part of the island of Ireland.[36] If they say they are British – some also claim to be Irish (or Northern Irish) as a secondary identification – then respect for the principle of self-determination, not to mention a bit of common sense, would suggest that we accept this characterisation. After all, a majority of Ulster Protestants have been saying so publicly and consistently since at least the first Home Rule debates of the 1880s.[37] Uncomfortable pennies, it seems, take a century or more to drop. Sometimes they fail. In the early 1990s I first met Roy Johnston who had exercised such a major influence on the direction of Sinn Féin and the IRA in the 1960s.[38] We both shared a commitment to promoting agricultural and worker cooperatives but our views on "the North" diverged sharply. This is a rough rendition of what I recall:

"We must show the Protestant working class that their interests are best served in an Irish socialist republic."

Bono on the Revolution

And let me tell you something
I've had enough of Irish Americans
Who haven't been back to their country in 20 or 30 years
Come up to me, and talk about the resistance
The revolution back home
And the glory of the revolution
And the glory of dying for the revolution
Fuck the revolution!
They don't talk about the glory of killing for the revolution
What's the glory in taking a man from his bed
And gunning him down in front of his wife and children
Where's the glory in that?
Where's the glory in bombing a Remembrance Day parade
Of old age pensioners, their medals taken out and polished up
   for the day
Where's the glory in that?
To leave them dying, or crippled for life, or dead
Under the rubble of the revolution
That the majority of the people in my country
Don't want.
Bono, of the band U2

This passionate condemnation of the Enniskillen Remembrance Day massacre was made as U2 were holding a concert in Denver, Colorado on the day of the bombing, 8 November 1987. Eleven were killed and sixty-four injured in this attack. One of these was Marie Wilson. She and her father were both trapped under rubble from a collapsing building. As they lay there, holding hands, the last words he ever heard her say were, "Daddy, I love you very much." His offer of forgiveness for her killers carries the wisdom of ages.

I bear no ill-will. I bear no grudge … I will pray for these men to-night and every night.
Gordon Wilson (1927–95)

We are proud of our history; proud of our freedom fighters.
Michelle O'Neill, Sinn Féin leader, 2018

Austria: the suppressed past

Many Austrians see themselves or purport to see themselves as victims of Nazi aggression. In fact, when German troops marched into Vienna in March 1938 they were widely welcomed and the unification of the two states was popular. Hardly coincidentally, in view of this selective recall and the reluctance to face up to its ugly past, levels of support for extreme right-wing nationalist groups have been high in Austria. In 1986 Austria knowingly elected a former Nazi, Kurt Waldheim, as its president, while the extreme right gained more than 25 per cent of the vote in the general election of 1999. In elections in 2008, the two far-right parties, the Freedom Party and the Movement for Austria's Future, together polled almost 30 per cent of the vote.[41] As one alarmed commentator observed, "Thirty percent for people who portray national socialism as innocuous; who crawl around in forests with neo-Nazi mates; who are surrounded by skinheads; who campaign against foreigners; make common cause with the European extreme right; toy with anti-Semitism; campaign against Muslims, and develop contacts with the Serbian Radical party whose leader, Vojislav Seselj, is in the dock at the war crimes tribunal in The Hague."[42]

By 2016 the extremists had made further ground. The candidate of the Freedom Party of Austria Norbert Hofer received the largest number of votes in the first round of the Presidential election of that year. In the head-to-head contest in the second round he secured 46 per cent of the vote, a massive indication of ultraright sentiment.[43]

Why the easy resort to ultranationalist politics? The Austrian political scientist Professor Anton Pelinka puts this down to the fact that "In comparison to the Germans, the Austrians were late and reluctant to accept any responsibility for their role in World War II, seeing themselves as victims of Anschluss rather than willing participants."[44]

"But they don't want to be part of an Irish republic."

"That is because they don't realise where their true interests lie, their true identity."

"Do you mean that *deep* down Ulster unionists realise they really are part of the Irish nation?"

"Yes. Yes, that's it!"

"What would you suggest then? That we get one million psychiatric couches and psycho-analyse each unionist until he or she gets in touch with the *true* self?"

It was intended as a mischievous retort. But at this point, the exchange ended abruptly.[39] Just before he turned away, Johnston raised his voice and in agitated tones remonstrated, "I don't want to talk to people like you." Had I had the wit or presence of mind I might have invoked the words of one of my favourite singer-songwriters, Joni Mitchell: writing of an earlier lover, she advised him to accept her as she was, "strung out on another man." I guess it has to be much the same with our relationship to Ulster unionism and its love affair, conflicted and all as it is, with Britain.

If the central thesis of this book is correct, that this has been an asymmetrical conflict, that sections of the Catholic and nationalist population have waged a deliberate and prolonged "war," not only against the British state but against their Protestant neighbours as well, then certain "good neighbourly" recommendations follow. There is a case for a communal apology, as the Provisionals' self-declared war is a matter for shame and regret on the part of all nationalists, north and south.[40] This presupposes a radical revision of nationalist consciousness in relation to the Troubles, a point all the more pressing in view of the overwhelming dominance within northern nationalism of the party that advocated the "long war" and all that entailed. Progressive politics in Northern Ireland is unlikely to be built on twisted folk histories and rationalisations of past atrocity. Pleasing if delusional interpretations of past struggles are likely to foster a politics of war-by-other-means. At worst, we could be sleepwalking into deeper communal divisions.

A failure to interrogate the past has its consequences, as suggested earlier. There are many instances from European history playing out in the present: residues of anti-Semitism in modern day Poland and Austria; strains of ultranationalism in Hungary, Serbia, and the Russian Federation; issues of repressed memory in post-Francoist Spain. A much closer example, though, may be read off from twentieth-century Irish history. When the north went up in flames in 1969, most of the cherished stereotypes of 700 years of heroic struggle, unionist bigots, and the perfidy of Albion were still in place, at least at a popular level. The celebration of the 50th anniversary of the Easter Rising of 1916 might have been an occasion for some critical reflection, but the opportunity was missed. All this hadn't mattered greatly before the 1960s and in time the deconstruction of these apparently harmless narratives would have taken place. In those days we were all off to Dublin in the green, in song and drink. But time was not on the side of the progressive forces within Irish nationalism, including in particular those within the three major political parties, Fianna Fáil, Fine Gael, and Labour.

As stones and petrol bombs flew in 1969 and bloodied faces appeared on our black-and-white television screens, the Irish nation was still in the grip of outmoded ideologies. Irish troops were moved to the border, some Irish government ministers began plotting to arm northern Catholics, and large numbers in the Republic of Ireland were left confused and ambivalent about political violence. Fortunately, at an elite level, Irish politicians and civil servants resisted a descent into visceral nationalism, but in many parts of Irish society the reaction was different. A failure to revisit critically the Irish past and dispel some of the self-delusional mythmaking left southern society vulnerable to the rise of unaccountable armed groups and the associated civil strife.

The same was true on the other side of the border. There was little evidence of creative rethinking within Ulster unionism, least of all in relation to the malign legacy of Edward Carson, James Craig, and the Ulster Volunteer Force.[45] Stormont, even more so than Dáil Éireann, found itself ill prepared to handle the emerging crisis. So did its unionist rank and file, guided by folk histories stuffed with ideological imaginings.

For democrats the lesson is clear: without going head-to-head with the past and facing it honestly there is at least a raised probability of a repeat of earlier miscalculations. It is clear that following Bloody Sunday the British state and the security forces learned much, and this is not to deny there were some later unjustified killings. Loyalist paramilitaries have learned little, other than the fruits of criminality, though it is notice-worthy that they have not responded to the provocations of the new IRAs. The dynamic force in the Troubles – the Provisional IRA and Sinn Féin – if anything, have learned even less. Self-induced wishful thinking, a deliberate myth-ologising of the past, and the creation of self-justificatory discourses have served to insulate the principal actors from acknowledging either guilt or responsibility. One by-product of this is the opening up of political and military spaces within which "dissident" republicans can operate, both now and in the future.[46] More importantly, a bendy, flexible understanding of the past makes reconciliation between the two communities less likely in the long run. The necessary trust must rest on understandings of history that are based on rigorous scholarship rather than self-comforting ideo-logical make-belief.

REPAIRING DEEP HURT

This is not the place to suggest in detail how collective apologies might be orchestrated and given effect. Others, including the churches, are probably better placed to outline an architecture of acknowledgement and atone-ment. The centrepiece has to be an apology to the unionists of Northern Ireland by the latter-day representatives of armed republicanism. A wider northern nationalist apology might be in order also, as indicated in the discussion in chapter 2 of the "arc of responsibility." But republican rep-resentatives also need to acknowledge their further responsibilities in re-lation to the northern nationalist community. Of the death risk facing the two communities, that for Catholics was the higher.[47] Defending Catholics turned out to be a mere fiction, while the conduct of an insurgency on the back of a largely helpless Catholic population exposed those same Cath-olics to attacks by loyalists and by the IRA itself. The latter included the mutilation of thousands of working-class Catholics and nationalists, many of them from deprived social backgrounds. The agony visited on piggy-in-the-middle Catholics and nationalists should be acknowledged. The loyalist situation, embodying the same perverse logic, is the mirror image of the republican case. Thousands of working-class Protestants were also maimed and shot by loyalist paramilitaries. Thus the form and content of any apology from loyalist and republican paramilitaries are complicated in that a sincere apology for past actions would necessarily have to be two-directional, involving not only an apology to the "other" but also to the communities they claimed to be defending. As with other authoritarian movements, as often as not repression was inward directed as well as outward oriented.

Incense-laden words cannot make fragrant the national and transnational tragedy that was the "Provisionals' war." An honest opening of hearts and minds to history and truth (however elusive both concepts may be) is called for, not only on the part of ex-combatants but within the ranks of those giving support to an unreconstructed Sinn Féin movement. The task is a mammoth one, as two-thirds of northern nationalists currently give their vote to a party that is in denial of its own abusive past. Loyalist paramilitaries enjoyed little political support within unionism but its representatives also bear responsibility and need to be called to account.[48]

There may also be a case for other communal or national apologies. Ulster unionism, though far less repressive than its enemies claimed or pretended, has its own ghosts to exorcise. A unionist appreciation of the fearful dilemmas facing northern nationalists during the Troubles is long overdue. The Irish state, if it is really serious about "cherishing all the children of the nation equally," has cause for regret, as does the British state. But, it bears repeating, the primary responsibility for a collective apology rests with the Irish republican movement, as it supplied the dynamic force that drove the Northern Ireland conflict beyond 1970 and into the 2000s. This might take a variety of forms but the key point is acceptance of the *principle* rather than the mechanisms as to how such an apology might be delivered. We have of course precedents: Dr Robin Eames, head of the Church of Ireland, apologised for the activities of proselytisers during the Great Famine; the Methodist Church in Ireland apologised for its uncritical support for the Ulster Covenant of 1912; Cardinal Cathal Daly and other ecclesiastics apologised for the sexual abuse of children by Catholic clergy; Taoiseach Enda Kenny apologised for the callous failures of the Irish state in relation to the Magdalene Asylums and their unfortunate female inhabitants; Prime Minister David Cameron apologised for the slaughter of Bloody Sunday, Derry, 1972. There are international precedents as well which might be fruitfully explored. Australian Prime Minister Kevin Rudd, for instance, apologised in 2008 for the "past mistreatment" of the indigenous population.[49] In the same year Canadian Prime Minister Stephen Harper apologised and asked for forgiveness for the treatment of children under the Indian Residential

Schools system whereby more than 150,000 Aboriginal children were separated from their families and communities as part of a century-long policy of forced assimilation. He concluded, "The Government of Canada sincerely apologizes and asks the forgiveness of the Aboriginal peoples of this country for failing them so profoundly."[50]

The international arena also offers some ethical guidelines as to the construction and delivery of public expressions of remorse or regret. The United Nations has produced a special report that defines a public apology and that explores the conditions that would make it meaningful.[51] These include a truthful admission, a victim-centred approach, and a guarantee of nonrecurrence. A public apology for past actions is itself a form of reparation, though of course other forms of reparation are not only possible but desirable.

MORAL OUTRAGE AS AN EXPRESSION OF INDIVIDUAL AND COLLECTIVE GUILT

There is a strand of psychological research that may shed some light on the *problématique* with which this book opened. It will be recalled that what struck me that evening at the Whiterock Centre in West Belfast was an almost frightening intensity of feeling and self-righteousness. Might part of the explanation be as follows? In an article headed "A Cleansing Fire," published in the journal *Motivation and Reason*, the authors Rothschild and Keefer suggest that the expression of moral outrage "is sometimes a means of reducing guilt over *one's own* moral failings and restoring a moral identity."[52] It is generally accepted in the psychological literature that guilt is a *social* emotion. We, and that includes this writer, want to believe that we act in line with moral principles. To violate these principles, either individually or collectively, is painful. After all, the moral worth of our community – its moral integrity – is at stake.

Hence the need for action, possibly of an evasive kind, with a view to reducing guilt feelings and repairing the moral damage being experienced. Strategies of this kind might take a variety of forms, as discussed earlier. When I read "A Cleansing Fire," my earlier, inchoate intuitions regarding the drama, both on and off stage at the West Belfast Festival all those years ago, became charged with meaning. What better way to reduce feelings of discomfort, even guilt, than to ransack history for instances of the cruelty of the other and stack these up, case on top of selective case, in the imaginative space that is the theatre. This is Aristotelian catharsis in the sense of purgation (but maybe not in the other senses of purification or an opening to wonderment).[53]

A related contribution from the literature of psychology underlines the point about the use (and abuse) of history, bearing in mind that the play *Forced Upon Us* was a historical play, of sorts. Two American-based psychologists Michael Wohl and Nyla Branscombe argue that one way of "lessening feelings of collective guilt for current harm to another group" is by citing earlier episodes of victimisation at the hands of their adversaries (in our case, Protestants and unionists).[54]

We need to be cautious of course. The effects found by these investigators were under laboratory conditions. The results of experimental research may translate more powerfully, more weakly, or not at all into real-world emotions and behaviour. Historians do not typically include laboratory-style experiments in their toolbox of methods. So, I may well be wrong, particularly as the results produced by Rothschild and Keefer for instance, statistically speaking, are not that strong. But the cap does seem to fit. Thus, they argue, a way of maintaining "a positive moral identity" is to divert attention on to a blame-worthy other party "in order to exculpate perceived personal or collective responsibility."[55] In certain circumstances, and this is quite counterintuitive, collective outpourings of moral outrage serve this function. My tentative conclusion is that this was what was going on in the sweaty intimacy of the drama barn in the Whiterock way back in 1999. The backdrop was that of a war-torn society emerging from conflict. In this largely republican audience some may have had blood on their hands. All would have been acutely aware of recent instances of atrocity, some perpetrated by republicans, others due to loyalist paramilitaries.[56] Confronting one's own communal responsibility would have meant grappling with cognitive dissonance of a painful kind. Far better to avoid the pain and be reassured of the infamy of the "other." Only the brave, or possibly the foolhardy, could look directly into the flames of the past and acknowledge that the Troubles, in their intensity and longevity, were largely the creation of the Provisional IRA and its republican-supporting community.

EPILOGUE

I saw another play. It was in 2015, well after I had completed this book, as I thought. It was called *Those You Pass on the Street* and was put on at the Brian Friel Theatre, Queen's University, Belfast.[57] The playwright was a former IRA man, Laurence McKeown, and the play was a fine, multiangled appraisal of the trauma and the hurt inflicted by the Troubles. Much of the action centred on the widow of an RUC man and a sympathetic Sinn Féin activist whose older brother had been executed as a "tout" (informer) by the IRA. It succeeded in evoking emotions of sympathy, even identification with the principal characters, and it aired difficult questions about the burdens of the past.

The discussion afterwards was revealing but again for reasons that did not bear directly on the play. The playwright introduced himself as a former republican prisoner. The facilitator of the after-show talk, a loyalist, also described himself as a former prisoner. But why as ex-prisoners, I wondered? They had each been in a death-dealing business. I recognised their sincerity but wondered why they (and so many other ex-combatants) found themselves assuming identities that were incidental to their main purpose in life, identities that seemed like a negation of their activist roles.[58] When recollecting their early ambitions in life did they recall thinking, "no, I don't want to be a fireman or a footballer, I want to be an ex-prisoner"?

The years before the ceasefires of 1994 were especially violent. Scrutinising the two harmless looking, middle-aged men sitting on folding chairs at the front of the audience, almost within touching distance, I questioned mentally: Was this a hero of the battlefield? Was the other an executioner? Was this an expert bomb-maker? Was that man skilled in kneecapping? Perhaps they were both simply "soldiers," believing they were only defending their own community and neighbourhood? These, and variations thereon, were identities that were open to the two interlocutors. But perhaps the remembrances were too troubling within a culture that has not wholly lost sight of the moral sentiments of personal responsibility, guilt, repentance, and atonement. Perhaps it was that in prison virtually all agency had been withdrawn. This was a segment of their lives that could be safely presented to the audience without fear of guilt or shame. More importantly maybe, it was one it was safe to present to themselves.

Notes

PREFACE

1 Edwards, *The Sins of Our Fathers*, vii.
2 Ibid., vii.
3 I develop these arguments more fully in "Making History in Ireland," *Dublin Review of Books*, May 2017.
4 Fay, Morrisey, and Smyth, *Northern Ireland's Troubles: The Human Cost*, 4.
5 Ibid., 5.
6 McKittrick et al., *Lost Lives*, 310.
7 Hammersley, *What's Wrong with Ethnography?*, 16.
8 O'Ferrall, *Daniel O'Connell*, 132.

INTRODUCTION

1 My intention was to write a short article, possibly for a current affairs magazine such as *Fortnight Magazine*.
2 This NGram (figure 0.1) shows the frequency of references to the "IRA" and to "Irish Studies" in the vast digitised repository of Google Books. It is apparent that both series follow an upward trajectory and that each tracks the other through time. There is a short time lag in the Irish studies response that suggests the line of causation runs from political violence to scholarship. My colleague and friend Richard English says a similar pattern is apparent in international terrorism studies. The rising incidence of terrorist incidents, most notably Islamist attacks in the late twentieth and early twenty-first century, gave rise to a surge in studies and publications on political terror.
3 The documentary, *I Dolours* (2018), directed by Maurice Sweeney, is a fascinating insight into the fanatical mindset of a woman who ferried alleged informers across the border from Northern Ireland into the Republic of Ireland to meet their execution. Possibly Dolours Price also acted as an executioner, as some accounts suggest.

4   Bergia, "Women and War: A Complex Matter," 22–3.
5   Ibid., 23.
6   Duggan, *Queering Conflict,* 14–16.
7   Jarman and Tennant, *An Acceptable Prejudice?,* 42–8.

CHAPTER ONE

1   According to its promoters, they were the victims of political discrimination
    at the hands of the Arts Council – a circumstance of some symmetry as the
    play itself was about victimhood. The council's view was that it had already
    invested heavily in the play but was withholding further payments because
    of problems of an artistic rather than a political kind. Ironically, a short
    while before this the festival organisers had prevented the internationally
    renowned singer Sinéad O'Connor from speaking out against punishment
    attacks – a paramilitary speciality in West Belfast – during her scheduled
    performance. Faced with such political censorship, she withdrew from
    the program. See *Irish Times,* 29 July 1999 and on the controversy round
    the play, the *Andersonstown News,* 7 August 1999.
2   This is actually the title of an interesting critique of contemporary Irish
    society, including views on the conflict in Northern Ireland, by Rosita
    Sweetman. See *On Our Knees: Ireland 1972.*
3   The notion of the Irish as akin to American blacks in terms of a history of
    slavery and oppression has been pressed into service not only in extremist
    Irish political circles but also by white supremacist and neo-Nazi groups in
    the USA. Versions of this ahistorical claim have gone viral on social media.
    See the interview with Liam Hogan, "How the Myth of the 'Irish Slaves'
    Became a Favourite Meme Online," Southern Poverty Law Centre, 19 April
    2016, https://www.splcenter.org/hatewatch/2016/04/19/how-myth-irish-
    slaves-became-favorite-meme-racists-online. See also Hogan et al., "Why
    We Need to Confront the 'Irish Slave Myth,' 18–22. The former president
    of Sinn Féin Mr Gerry Adams has spoken of himself as "A Ballymurphy
    Nigger," followed by "Nationalists in Nth were treated like African Ameri-
    cans." See the *Guardian* newspaper, among other accounts, 2 May 2016. He
    later apologised for the use of the term but felt the context for the compari-
    son was appropriate. See also the critique by Donald Clarke in the *Irish
    Times,* 30 July 2016.
4   That is my recollection from the live performance. The script, which may be
    found in the Linen Hall Library, Belfast, has this line: "But as soon as I could
    I voted for republicans, and I will do till I die."
5   The text of the IRA statement on its cessation of violence, 31 August 1994,
    may be found on the authoritative CAIN website at http://cain.ulst.ac.uk/
    events/peace/docs/ira31894.htm.

6 The political scientist Frank Wright has written about apparently random
killings as forms of representative violence. In a conflict where each side is
clearly defined, victims may be selected independently of any personal characteristics and simply because they are perceived as representing the other
side, be he or she nationalist or unionist. "Very few people in Northern
Ireland today would try to claim that the victims of violence are chosen because of their individual characteristics: they are attacked because they are
identified as representing groups of people." Wright, *Northern Ireland*, 11.
There are perceptive comments on this aspect of Wright's work in Wilson,
"Frank Wright Revisited," 277–82. It might not be expected but some republicans took this view as well.

7 *Disturbances in Northern Ireland: Report of the Commission appointed by the
Governor of Northern Ireland* (Belfast, September 1969), 11. Known as the
Cameron Report after its chairman, Lord Cameron.

8 Ruane and Todd, *The Dynamics of Conflict in Northern Ireland*; Ruane and
Todd, *After the Good Friday Agreement*; Kennedy, *Unhappy the Land*, 76–7.

9 McCann, *War and an Irish Town*, 91.

10 Bardon, *A History of Ulster*, 670.

11 *Violence and Civil Disturbances in Northern Ireland: Report of Tribunal
of Inquiry*, 71–6.

12 Following disturbances linked to the Apprentice Boys parade in Derry in
August 1969 the RUC might have pursued a very different strategy that
would not have required army support. It might have cordoned off the ap-
proaches to the Bogside, kept loyalists at bay, and simply sat out the trouble.
Instead an aggressive policing approach was adopted involving baton
charges and tear gas on one side, and stones and petrol bombs on the other.
The subsequent mayhem was quickly dubbed the "Battle of the Bogside,"
frightening for some but exhilarating for many of the younger participants.
I am grateful to Dennis Kennedy, who was a young reporter at the time, for
his reflections on this seminal episode and its sequel.

13 Bloody Sunday: soldiers of the British Parachute Regiment shot dead thirteen civilians at a civil rights demonstration in Derry (Londonderry) on
that Sunday. Another victim later died of his wounds.

14 Bloody Friday: on the 21 July 1972 the IRA placed a series of bombs in
Belfast city centre, resulting in the deaths of nine people and injuries to
130 civilians.

15 One example in particular highlights this political restraint: armed sentries
at the Maze Prison near Belfast did not have the right to fire on prisoners,
even in the event of a mass breakout (as happened in 1983). This has only
come to light much later, with the release of state papers by the Public
Record Office in Belfast. See the *Irish Times*, 2 January 2010.

16 McKittrick et al., *Lost Lives*, 1478–9.

17 That is, including members of the Royal Irish Rangers. One of my mature students at Magee University College, Derry, in 1980 was a *former* part-time UDR man seeking a new career through the education system. At a party in the college he confided in me his fears of possible assassination but as he came from a rural area of County Tyrone he felt he was unlikely to be recognised on the Derry campus. I wasn't so sanguine, thinking of the many self-identified republicans and former prisoners on the course, and told him so. I didn't know the numbers then but we now know that more than forty-two *former* members of the UDR were put to death during the course of the Troubles.

18 As late as 2018 the assistant chief constable of the PSNI stated the force was reluctant to deploy Catholic officers in their home areas because of their vulnerability to assassination by IRA groupings. *Irish News*, 11 October 2018.

19 See, for instance, Ware, "The Spy in the IRA," BBC Panorama investigation, broadcast 11 April 2017.

20 McKittrick *et al.*, *Lost Lives*, 555–7

21 Ibid., 1479–84.

22 For an insider view by a former security officer of the effectiveness of the intelligence services see Matchett, *Secret Victory*. See also the views of Lord West, former chief of Defence Intelligence, speaking at the Policy Exchange think tank, Westminster, 9 May 2017: "Spies – Not Talks – Brought Peace to Northern Ireland" at http://www.thedailybeast.com/articles/2017/05/09/ex-intel-boss-blair-airbrushed-northern-ireland-peace-process?via=News Letter&source.

23 McGartland, *Fifty Dead Men Walking*.

24 Ibid.; O'Callaghan, *The Informer*. Alan McQuillan, a former deputy chief constable of the PSNI and former head of Special Branch went so far as to claim in the Panorama program mentioned above, "The bottom line is that there are thousands of people walking around our streets today – literally thousands – who if we hadn't had the intelligence services and we hadn't had the police running informants, they wouldn't be here today. Included in that are a number of senior members of Sinn Féin." See also his comments in the *Belfast News Letter*, 12 April 2017. It must be said though that it is impossible to quantify with any precision the number of lives saved.

25 The year 1972 was the worst year of the Troubles in terms of killings; the period of the hunger strikes at the beginning of the 1980s was fraught in the extreme; the year 1993 witnessed the Loughinisland pub massacre, perpetrated by loyalists, and the bombing of Frizzell's fish shop on the Shankill Road by republicans.

26 In 1974 the British Prime Minister Harold Wilson considered the possibility

of a "doomsday scenario" in which the UK would withdraw from Northern Ireland, presumably to let the Irish fight it out among themselves (as one commentator caustically added). The possibility of a withdrawal greatly alarmed political leaders in the Republic of Ireland. On Wilson's thinking see Morgan, *Harold Wilson*, 450.

27 Some would date Ulster unionist rule from June 1921 when the Government of Ireland Act brought a northern parliament into being for the first time.

28 Walker, *A Political History of the Two Irelands*, 3–4.

29 Walker, *A History of the Ulster Unionist Party*, 73–4.

30 Ibid., 75; Bew, Gibbon, and Patterson, *Northern Ireland: 1921–2001*, 48–9, 142–57; Patterson and Kaufman, *Unionism and Orangeism*, 12–21. On the extensive gerrymandering of district boundaries in the contemporary United States see National Democratic Redistricting Committee https://democratic redistricting.com/.

31 Mulholland, *The Longest War: Northern Ireland's Troubled History*.

32 Whyte, "How Much Discrimination was there under the Unionist regime, 1921–68?," 1–35; Patterson and Kaufmann, *Unionism and Orangeism*, 45–55.

33 Gudgin, "Discrimination in Housing and Employment under the Stormont Administration," 97–121.

34 Rose, *Governing Without Consensus*, 293.

35 Ibid., 237.

36 Cameron Report, 56. It elaborates on the same page, "In the past for example it was considered natural that a Protestant Council would employ Protestants in all senior posts, and conversely that a Catholic-controlled Council would employ only Catholics." However, it also made clear that since most councils were controlled by unionists, such practices advantaged Protestants.

37 Sacks, *The Donegal Mafia*.

38 Foster, *Luck and the Irish*, 85–95.

39 Bartholomew, *The Irish Judiciary*. This is still the case though attempts at reform are afoot.

40 Lee, *The Modernisation of Irish Society, 1848–1918*, 167–8; Hayes, *Minority Verdict*, 19–20. Canvassing could apply to university positions as well. I recall one of my professors at UCC telling me with a wry smile – this was around 1969 – that he had felt it necessary to talk to as many as possible of the academic decision makers before his formal interview took place.

41 The tussle between merit and family obligation is nicely explored in Leyton's Ulster study, *The One Blood*.

42 Martin, "Social Policy and Social Change Since 1914," 315–20.

43 Edwards, *A History of the Northern Ireland Labour Party*, 144–9; Arthur, *The People's Democracy, 1968–1973*, 101–9.

44 Many years ago W.G. Runciman drew attention to the importance of relative deprivation and of comparative reference groups in animating organised groups to demand social justice, *Relative Deprivation and Social Justice.*

45 Johnson, *The Interwar Economy in Ireland*, 31–5.

46 A graphic illustration springs to mind. Gerry Adams senior, from an older generation of the IRA that was active in the 1940s, seems small and stocky in photographs standing alongside his tall, well-built son Gerry Adams junior, president of Sinn Féin and beneficiary of the British welfare state.

47 Some regard these as largely symbolic and of little value. Strangely, in other contexts, some of the same critics suggest that symbols are of paramount importance.

48 Rose, *Governing Without Consensus*, 477.

49 Hayes, *Minority Report*, 318.

50 Ó Broin, *Sinn Féin and the Politics of Left Republicanism*, 211–16. For an earlier, more partisan critique of the "Orange State," see Farrell, *The Orange State.*

51 Patterson and Kaufman, *Unionism and Orangeism*, 44–57.

52 *Report of the Committee on the Constitution* (Dublin, December 1967).

53 A BBC Spotlight sample poll in 2013 showed that only 17 per cent of people in Northern Ireland favoured leaving the United Kingdom. Even within the nationalist population a majority favoured remaining within the United Kingdom. Responses vary from opinion poll to opinion poll but generally a substantial majority favour the "remain" option. More recently, the pendulum has swung partly in the other direction as the United Kingdom's decision to leave the European Union has increased the attraction of membership of an Irish state within the European Union.

54 *The Belfast Agreement.*

55 Colley, *Britons*, 46, 324–34.

56 Brewer and Higgins, *Anti-Catholicism in Northern Ireland.*

57 Some historical episodes of aggressive sectarianism may be found in Stewart, *The Narrow Ground*; Dunne, *Rebellions*; and Donnelly Jr, *Captain Rock.*

58 Patterson, *Ireland's Violent Frontier*, 3–6, 193–9.

59 Quoted in Smyth, *Paisley*, 17. However, McClean later denied he had made this statement.

60 Bruce, *God Save Ulster!*, 142. Those who like their Paisleys well roasted may prefer Moloney's, *Paisley: From Demagogue to Democrat?*.

61 For a fiercely critical, end-of-life assessment of Paisley's political career see Ruth Dudley Edwards' column in the *Belfast Telegraph*, 22 September 2014: "And the truth as I see it is that Ian Paisley's influence on the island of Ireland for almost all of his life was malign."

62 I am grateful to Professor Paul Bew for sharing with me his insights into

Paisley's career. No one individual, I would accept, did more in the 1960s to destabilise Northern Irish society and politics (though perversely this is a claim the Big Man might well have found complimentary).

63 Kennedy, *Unhappy the Land*, 127–45. My critique of Carson and the UVF drew an immediate and critical response from a unionist-oriented historian. The ensuing exchange of views with CDC Armstrong may be found in the *Belfast Telegraph*, December 2015.

64 In recent times there have been claims, admittedly uncorroborated, that Paisley provided finance for the UVF bombing of the Silent Valley reservoir in the Mourne Mountains in 1969. The aim was to undermine the unionist prime minister Captain Terence O'Neill who was held to be pursuing a policy of appeasement in relation to the civil rights movement and Irish nationalism.

65 Smyth, *Paisley*, 112–13. It is also claimed by Smyth, who was a former member of the DUP, that the UDA gave electoral support to the DUP in East Belfast at the general election of 1979. Peter Robinson, who had cultivated links with the UDA, was returned as MP for the area. Smyth, *Paisley*, 107.

66 Moloney, *Paisley*, 515.

67 Cameron Report, 40, 89.

68 Moloney, *Paisley*, 156–7.

69 Bruce, *God Save Ulster!*

70 For example, Sean O'Callaghan, then a young IRA man, relates that within hours of murdering Peter Flanagan, a Catholic policeman enjoying a quiet drink in a pub, he was blessed by a priest who was sympathetic to the IRA. O'Callaghan, *The Informer*, 111–12. The infamous Tipperary-born priest Fr Patrick Ryan, again an exception, was a key figure in arranging arms shipments from Libya to the IRA.

71 *Protestant Telegraph*, 10–23 August 1974.

72 Smyth, *Paisley*, 28–34.

73 In 1974 British miners went on strike and the Conservative Prime Minister Edward Heath called a snap general election on the issue of "Who governs Britain?" I was living in Yorkshire at the time, was caught up in the excitement of it all, and canvassed for Labour in the two general elections of that year. Only later, after some direct experience of life in Northern Ireland did I come to realise the hydra-headed nature of "political strikes."

74 Smyth, *Paisley*, 173–4.

75 *Belfast News Letter*, 13 June 2016.

76 Hadden and Boyle, *The Anglo-Irish Agreement*, 10, 14, 69–71.

77 *Belfast Telegraph*, 1 March 2011.

78 *News Letter*, 4 May 2018, 1 October 2018; *Belfast Telegraph*, 17 December 2007, 1 March 2011.

79 This remarkable encounter between a victim's son and a mass murderer is
    described by John McGurk himself in a soul-wrenching account in the
    Sunday Life, 4 February 2013. My summary of the atrocity is based on
    newspaper coverage, including John McGurk's writings, a conversation with
    Robert McClenaghan, 12 June 2017, and email correspondence with Robert
    dated 27 June 2017.

80 On the Drumcree confrontations see Ryder and Kearney, *Drumcree: The
    Orange Order's Last Stand* and Kennaway, *The Orange Order*, 98–150.

81 One serious but exceptional lapse was the acquiescence of SDLP councillors
    in a decision to name a children's playground in Newry after Raymond
    McCreesh, an IRA hunger striker and suspect in the Kingsmill massacre.
    The SDLP centrally, however, opposed this move and advised its councillors
    to revisit the issue. The politicisation of the children's playground was taken
    a stage further in May 2018 when dissident republicans held a rally in the
    park to commemorate the death of McCreesh. *Irish News*, 21 May 2018.

82 As is evident from the "War News" section in successive issues of the Provi-
    sional Sinn Féin periodical *An Phobhlacht*, which first appeared in February
    1970 after the split in Sinn Féin in the preceding month.

83 On the social etiquette of getting on with the "other sort," see Donnan and
    McFarlane, "Social Life in Rural Northern Ireland," 281–97.

84 *Belfast News Letter*, 31 March 2017.

85 Northern Ireland being the small place it is, I later chaired a cross-commu-
    nity group in Belfast on which one of his daughters was a member.

86 Hanley and Millar, *Lost Revolution*, 29–51; Daly and O'Callaghan, *1916
    in 1966*.

87 All figures relating to deaths during the current Troubles have been taken
    from McKittrick et al. There are alternative estimates from other sources
    for certain types of killings and fresh information trickles in from time
    to time, but the broad contours are not in doubt. See also the CAIN web
    service, Ulster University, at http://cain.ulst.ac.uk/search.htm, which is
    regularly updated.

88 Nelson, *Ulster's Uncertain Defenders*, 87–107, 117–27.

89 In the opening phase of the Troubles Catholic aggression tended to focus
    on police stations and factory buildings, usually Protestant owned. It may
    be recalled that during the so-called Battle of the Bogside in August 1969,
    which claimed no fatalities, the call went out to take the pressure off nation-
    alist Derry. Militant Catholics in west Belfast heeded the call and attacked
    RUC stations at Springfield Road and Hastings Street in Belfast. Protestant
    mobs then formed and invaded Catholic residential areas. Thus the chain
    reaction extended from Derry to Belfast, and from Catholic to Protestant
    areas in the city, with a speed that left the police hopelessly overstretched.

Fearing a total breakdown of public safety, the British government, with scant regard for Stormont, ordered in British troops. O'Doherty, *The Trouble with Guns*, 30–3.

90 Cusack and McDonald, UDA: *Inside the Heart of Loyalist Terror*. The claim about psychopaths, it is worth emphasising, refers to individual members of loyalist and republican paramilitary groups – a tiny minority who are perhaps better represented at more senior levels in these organisations – and not to the generality of these volunteers.

91 Bardon, *A History of Ulster 1992*, 664–6; Edwards, *Northern Ireland Labour Party*, 158–78.

92 McKittrick et al., *Lost Lives*, 1476.

93 See the earlier observation on Frank Wright's notion of "representative violence," Wright, *Northern Ireland*, 11.

94 Cameron Report, 15. See also Prince and Warner, *Belfast and Derry in Revolt*, 135–9 and Bew and Gillespie, *Northern Ireland: A Chronology of the Troubles*, 12.

95 Purdie, "Was the Civil Rights Movement a Republican/Communist Conspiracy?," 33–41; Prince, *Northern Ireland's '68*, 60.

96 Some see a private meeting in Maghera, County Londonderry, in the autumn of 1966 as the point of origin of the civil rights agitation. Those present included Roy Johnston, an influential voice in terms of political development within the IRA, the journalist Eoghan Harris, some IRA, and some socialists. (I might mention here I follow the naming conventions of the journal, *Irish Historical Studies*, which recommends the terms Derry for the city on the Foyle and Londonderry for the county.)

97 Prince, *Northern Ireland's '68*, 156–61.

98 Republicans within the organisation had not renounced physical force nationalism and their objective remained that of a united Ireland. In republican thinking at the time this would eventually require force of arms. The campaign for civil rights was an important element in broadening the struggle but not the ultimate destination.

99 The chairman of NICRA in 1969 Frank Gogarty was supportive of provoking the police through street violence. (This was the recollection of a member of his family who spoke to me about the late Frank Gogarty in February 2017.) When the split between Official and Provisional republicans took place in 1969–70, Mr Gogarty favoured the more right-wing Provisional movement.

100 I am grateful for the recollections of the writer Anne Devlin who in 1969 resigned from NICRA. Some other youthful socialists withdrew their support, including my Jewish colleague of many years standing Dr Max Goldstrom. What was happening was a filtering of the original membership and, in effect, the "greening" of NICRA.

101 Bardon, *History of Ulster*, 306–7, 349–52, 380–2.

102 Edwards, *Northern Ireland Labour Party*, 149.

103 The electoral data refer to the NILP's share of the vote at the Stormont elections of 1967 and 1969 and to the local elections in Northern Ireland in 1973. See Edwards, *Northern Ireland Labour Party*, 145, 199–200 and Elliott, *Northern Ireland Parliamentary Election Results, 1921–1972*, 116. There was temporary remission for the NILP in that in the UK general election of June 1970 its candidates secured 13 per cent of the vote. But with rising violence the point of no return – a vote share of less than 3 per cent – quickly followed. By way of a postscript and an epitaph for political labour, the only socialist and trade union candidate in the first elections to the European Parliament, which took place in 1979, was the staunchly antisectarian Paddy Devlin. As he ruefully recalls, "Most of the 572,239 votes cast were allotted on a tribal basis." He attracted a measly 1.1 per cent of the vote. Devlin, *Straight Left*, 283–4.

104 Purdie, "Civil Rights Movement," 40.

105 The judgement is mine but I would like to thank the writer Anne Devlin and the political scientist Henry Patterson for their recollections of the decision to march and the expectation that the march was likely to provoke violence. See also Arthur, *The People's Democracy*, 42–4.

106 Cameron Report, 84.

107 Deeply researched and compelling accounts of the civil rights movement and the conflicts it engendered may be found in Prince, *Northern Ireland's '68* and Prince and Warner, *Belfast and Derry in Revolt*.

108 Mac Stiofáin (1928–2001) was the first chief of staff of the Provisional IRA; the even older McKee (1921–2019) was the first Provisional IRA commander in Belfast and a daily communicant.

109 The full text of the declaration may be found on the CAIN website: Joint Declaration on Peace: The Downing Street Declaration, Wednesday 15 December 1993, http://cain.ulst.ac.uk/events/peace/docs/dsd151293.htm.

110 Miller, *Queen's Rebels*, 87–106; Boyce, *Nationalism in Ireland*.

111 The subvention is the difference between public spending in Northern Ireland and the revenue raised in Northern Ireland. The figures in the main text are taken from *Northern Ireland Net Fiscal Balance Report 2012–13 and 2013–14*, October 2015, produced by the Department of Finance and Personnel, Northern Ireland. The subvention in 2018–19 was £10–£11 billion, depending on the method of calculation.

112 Morgan, *Harold Wilson*, 407–11, 485–90.

113 FitzGerald, *All in a Life*, 244, 252–6, 268–73.

114 Lynch, *The Northern IRA and the Early Years of Partition*, 98–105.

115 Breen, *My Fight for Irish Freedom*, 240.

116 Phoenix, *Northern Nationalism*, 177–91; Buckland, *The Factory of Grievances*, 226–8, 249–50.

117 Sean Lemass was taoiseach or prime minister from 1959 to 1966; Jack Lynch, his successor, was taoiseach from 1966 to 1973. He headed another Fianna Fail administration in 1977 but resigned a few years later as the faction round Charles Haughey came to the fore. See Chambers, *T.K. Whitaker*, 305–18.

118 Hanley and Millar, *Lost Revolution*, 152.

119 There was always the risk of running into a Garda checkpoint. I may be mis-remembering this detail but I have a recollection that he used his credentials as a medical doctor on duty as a cover in making these journeys. He also re-lated how, by chance, he had attended to one of the cooks on the prison ship the *Maidstone* who happened to fall ill while on leave in Dublin. Dr Paddy extracted the vital piece of information that there were no antipersonnel de-vices in the water to prevent escape. Sometime later there was a mass escape by IRA detainees who dived overboard from the *Maidstone* into the waters of Belfast Lough.

120 We had many conversations during the 1990s and beyond. I was best man at his wedding when he was in the shadow of death due to terminal cancer. I have a copy of his unpublished memoir, which recounts his time in the IRA and his subsequent political development.

121 Some of his writings are contained in the (sometimes daily) Irish language paper, *Lá*, as well as in *Fortnight Magazine*. These are in the political collec-tion of the Linen Hall Library, Belfast.

122 O'Malley, *Conduct Unbecoming*, 53–61, 90–9; Chambers, *T.K. Whitaker*, 251–70.

123 Sean Lemass was taoiseach for the years 1959–66; T.K. Whitaker was the young, dynamic secretary of the Department of Finance and author of the hugely influential report *Economic Development* (1958).

124 In 2013 the Irish government apologised to the families of two RUC men who had been ambushed and killed close to the Irish border as a result of information supplied to the IRA from within the Dundalk Garda station. This followed the findings of the Smithwick Tribunal, which concluded there had been collusion. *Irish Times*, 4 December 2013. For other claims of collusion between the Garda and the IRA, see the recollections of a former IRA director of intelligence, Kieran Conway, in the *Irish Times*, 4 December 2014. Though some unionists made much of these deadly activities, it should be emphasised that such instances were the exception.

125 When tutoring one of my students in the Crumlin Road jail during the early 1980s – he was awaiting trial for the attempted murder of British soldiers – I was introduced to the star ratings for prison hospitality in Ireland. The

Crumlin Road jail was rated best, followed by the Maze prison, and at the
bottom of the hierarchy was Portlaoise jail. I cannot vouch personally for
these ratings.

126 On ambivalence see O'Brien, *Passion and Cunning and Other Essays*, 295–7
and *Neighbours*, 17–24. Adrian Guelke makes the important point in relation
to the Irish and British states that both shared "the same objective of quar-
antining the conflict and preventing its intrusion into their domestic
politics." Guelke, *Northern Ireland: The International Perspective*, 3.

127 On feuding within the INLA see Holland and McDonald, *INLA*. One of
those tortured, murdered and subsequently "disappeared" by his former
comrades was a teacher, Seamus Ruddy, whose remains were only recovered
in 2017 (*Guardian*, 6 May 2017). This was thirty-two years after his "disap-
pearance."

128 McKittrick et al., *Lost Lives*, 1475.

129 The interview with Vincent Browne, editor of the *Sunday Tribune* was published on 27 November 1983. For a discussion of this remarkably revealing
interview see Heskin, "The Terrorists' Terrorist," 97–108.

130 Coogan, *The Troubles*, 279.

131 Holland and McDonald, *INLA*, 226–7.

132 McKittrick et al., *Lost Lives*, 963–4. Holland and McDonald, *INLA*, 2.

133 *Irish News*, 31 January 2012.

134 *Irish News*, 14 February 1994; *Belfast News Letter*, 14 February 1994; *Independent*, 14 February 1994; *Herald Scotland*, 14 February 1994; *Irish Times*,
22 April 2014.

135 Liam McMillen, head of the Official IRA in Belfast, speaking at the annual
Wolfe Tone commemoration at Bodenstown, July 1973. The full text may
be found in *Liam McMillen, Separatist, Socialist, Republican*.

136 Johnston, *Century of Endeavour*, 185–205.

137 Hanley and Millar, *Lost Revolution*, 102–3.

138 Ibid, 109; Mac Stiofáin, *Memoirs of a Revolutionary*, 119–31.

139 Announcing the ceasefire, the northern republican clubs stated, "The over-
whelming desire of the great majority of all the people of the north is for
an end to military actions by all sides." See "Official IRA Declares Ceasefire,"
BBC News, 30 May 1972; *Irish News*, 21 February 2018; Hanley and Millar,
Lost Revolution, 180–2.

140 McMillen, *Liam McMillen, Separatist, Socialist, Republican*.

141 Hanley and Millar, *Lost Revolution*, 180.

142 Of course some rogue elements within the RUC and the UDR would have
maintained a sectarian mind-set but their role and influence would have
been limited in these circumstances. As argued later, other republican groups
offered virtually no protection to Catholic and nationalist communities.

143 In a later edition of McKittrick et al (2007) the total of deaths for the period
     1966–99 was revised upwards to the slightly higher level of 3,645. For the
     longer period 1966–2006 the total is reckoned to be 3,720, though inevitably
     there is some ambiguity at the edges as to what constitutes "Troubles" deaths.

144 Much the same point might be made had the Sunningdale Agreement of
     1973 been accepted by armed republicans.

145 Some 40,000 individuals were injured, some horribly so, during the course
     of the Troubles (up to the year 1998). See Fay, Morrisey, and Smyth, *North-
     ern Ireland's Troubles: The Human Costs*, 201.

146 Ruth Jamieson and Adrian Grounds found a majority of those in their small
     sample of former republican prisoners suffered from depression, while alco-
     hol abuse was also a problem. *No Sense of an Ending*, 51–3. Later work by
     Jamieson, Shirlow, and Grounds found that of a sample of 190 loyalist and
     republican former prisoners, almost half were not in paid employment,
     40 per cent had mental health problems, over half had "symptoms characte-
     ristic of post-traumatic stress disorder," and almost 70 per cent were drink-
     ing at levels deemed hazardous. The study is entitled *Ageing and
     Social Exclusion Among Former Politically Motivated Prisoners in Northern
     Ireland* (Belfast, 2010).

147 McWilliams, "Masculinity and Violence," 15–25.

148 As reported in the *Belfast News Letter*, 19 October 2018.

149 On the transgenerational legacy of the Troubles see O'Neill et al., *Towards
     a Better Future: The Trans-Generational Impact of the Troubles on Mental
     Health* and also Hanna et al., *Young People's Transgenerational Issues in
     Northern Ireland*.

CHAPTER TWO

1 The original Defenders were a secret Catholic society formed in late eight-
   eenth-century County Armagh to combat the Protestant Peep O'Day Boys.
   The brotherhood later spread to other parts of the north of Ireland and was
   animated by economic grievance, sectarian animosities, and some crude
   political aspirations. Connolly, *The Oxford Companion to Irish History*, 147–8.

2 Sharrock and Devenport, *Man of War, Man of Peace?*, 71–9.

3 The sectarianism of northern republicans is discussed in the writings of the
   Kerry-born IRA volunteer, Sean O'Callaghan. See in particular *The Informer*,
   80–3.

4 *Report of the Advisory Committee on Police in Northern Ireland*, chaired by
   Baron Hunt, Belfast: H.M.S.O., 1969, 25. "Our proposals offer a new image
   of the Royal Ulster Constabulary as a civil police force, which will be in
   principle and in normal practice an unarmed force" (page 9 of the report).

5 *Guardian*, 25 November 2014; *Belfast Telegraph*, 26 November 2014.

6 The so-called Battle of St Matthew's in the Short Strand, Belfast, in June
   1970 is the most frequently cited example. For an account see English,
   Armed Struggle, 134–5, 351.

7 English, *Does Terrorism Work?*, 110–12; Cunningham, "Repertoires of
   Violence."

8 Their names are John Patrick Scullion and Peter Ward, murdered in 1966 by
   the self-styled Ulster Volunteer Force, and Gerald McAuley shot by a loyalist
   gunman in 1969. All were from West Belfast. McKittrick et al., *Lost Lives*,
   25–8, 38–9. Other Catholic civilians, it should be noted, were killed by the
   police and British army in this period. To summarise, in the four-year
   period 1966–69 the security forces were responsible for ten deaths, republicans for five deaths, and loyalists for six deaths.

9 Calculated from McKittrick et al., *Lost Lives*, 1484. The 2007 edition gives
   a marginally different figure of thirty deaths.

10 The various causes of death may be traced in McKittrick et al., *Lost Lives*
   (1999 and 2007) and in Bew and Gillespie, *A Chronology of the Troubles,
   1968–1999*.

11 Calculated from McKittrick et al., *Lost Lives*. This helps explain the fear that
   haunted many mothers and fathers, that their children might be attracted
   into a paramilitary organisation.

12 *An Phobhlacht*, no. 1, February 1970.

13 Mac Stiofáin, *Memoirs of a Revolutionary*, 2. This is from a speech from the
   dock by Cathal Goulding who became chief-of-staff of the IRA and later
   chief-of-staff of the Official IRA. Standing beside him, Mac Stiofáin assented
   and there is nothing to suggest he ever changed his mind.

14 Ibid., 289.

15 Ibid., viii.

16 Sinn Féin, *Éire Nua: The Social and Economic Programme of Sinn Féin*, 8.

17 Bew and Gillespie, *Chronology of the Troubles*, 345.

18 *Belfast Telegraph*, 1 May 2017.

19 Ruedy, *Modern Algeria*, 190.

20 Horne, *A Savage War of Peace*, 25–8.

21 Taylor's fine books include *Loyalists* and *The Provos: The IRA and Sinn Féin*.

22 *Republican News*, 21 September 1974 and McKittrick et al., 474–5.

23 Durcan, *The Laughter of Mothers*, 46. Durcan's mother, Sheila McBride, was
   a niece of Major McBride and his estranged wife, Maud Gonne.

24 "War News," *An Phobhlacht*, 25 February 1982.

25 According to the author Martin Dillon an extraordinary conference between
   loyalists and republicans took place within Long Kesh prison in 1975. Both
   sides had become worried that sectarian killings were getting out of hand.

The loyalists proposed that in exchange for an end to the murder of Catholic civilians that republicans would cease killing off-duty RUC and UDR members. This was agreed though the Provisional IRA insisted on the "right to kill police and members of the UDR when they were on the streets wearing uniform." An interesting point here is the apparent acknowledgement by republicans that targeting members of the local security forces when out of uniform might be a debatable way of conducting an insurgency and perhaps there was also an implicit recognition that there was some asymmetry as to the visibility of targets on either side of the conflict. Dillon, *The Shankill Butchers*, 41–2.

26 Sean O'Callaghan, who was active with the Provisional IRA in the mid-1970s in rural west Ulster, came to a rueful conclusion: "I might want to attack a British army patrol or barracks, but the local IRA men would rather shoot a Protestant neighbour who was in the UDR or police reserve." See O'Callaghan, *The Informer*, 81. Even if one includes the UDR and the RIR – locally recruited and Protestant in the main – the share is still under 20 per cent.

27 For a definition of civil war see Prince and Warner, *Belfast and Derry in Revolt*, 2. We cannot be absolutely precise about the proportion of Ireland-born dead, though the broad magnitude is not in doubt. While most bombings and shootings took place in Ireland, a small proportion occurred in Britain and continental Europe. Of these killings, 124 took place in Britain and eighteen in continental Europe. The RUC contained small numbers of British-born officers while, on the other hand, the British army contained some Irish-born recruits. The conclusion stands: the proportion of fatal victims of the Troubles who were born in Ireland was in excess of 80 per cent. Calculated from McKittrick et al., *Lost Lives*, 1473–84 and bearing these qualifications in mind.

28 For a wider view of the politics of divided societies see Guelke, *Politics in Deeply-Divided Societies*. Terminology is a minefield in Northern Ireland. Many Protestants and unionists find the term "the north" demeaning. I use it for stylistic variety or when the geographical scope of an argument is blurred. I use Derry for the city of Derry/Londonderry and Londonderry for the county, in line with the conventions of the venerable *Irish Historical Studies*.

29 There were gun-wielding, macho-posturing groups associated with the cause of civil rights for African Americans, notably the Black Panthers, but such armed groups played only a peripheral role in the social ferment of the 1960s. They proved to be ineffective if not actually counterproductive.

30 *Civil Wrongs of Irishwomen*, as quoted in the *Irish Times*, 10 June 2013.

31 Borooah and Forsythe, *Gender and the Earnings Gap*, 1, 56–7. The pay gap

in the Republic of Ireland in the 1960s was much the same as in Northern Ireland. Commission on the Status of Women, *Report to the Minister for Finance*, 26.

32 Borooah and Forsythe, *Gender and the Earnings Gap*, 1. For further insights into women and the labour market see Trewsdale and Trainor, *A Statistical Survey of Women and Work in Northern Ireland*.

33 "A History of Women in the UK Civil Service," http://www.civilservant.org. uk/library/2015_history_of_women_in_the_civil_service.pdf. For an excellent survey of the position of women in Ireland, north and south, see Hill, *Women in Ireland* and for a stimulating Marxist variant see Horgan, "Changing Women's Lives in Ireland," 53–91.

34 McCormick, *Regulating Sexuality*, 180, 191–4.

35 For an insightful history of the Irish women's movement see Connolly, *The Irish Women's Movement*. With a more specifically Cork focus there is the manifesto produced by an organisation of women students at University College, Cork at the precociously early date of 1969. (UCC student magazines and pamphlets in the possession of the student activist, Judy Barry. I am grateful to Judy for photocopies of these rare, ephemeral publications.)

36 *Belfast Telegraphy*, 12 October 2015.

37 Prince, *Northern Ireland in '68*; Prince, *Belfast and Derry in Revolt*; Guelke, *Northern Ireland: The International Perspective*.

38 Dawe, *In Another World*, 7–15.

39 Ibid., 13.

40 *An Phobhlacht*, 28 July 2005.

41 Fay et al., *The Cost of the Troubles Study*.

42 Wright, *Northern Ireland*, 11–20.

43 English, *Does Terrorism Work?*, 107–11.

44 In July 1971, when debate on Ireland's entry into the then European Economic Community was reaching fever pitch, *An Phobhlacht* warned that the effects would be disastrous. "The potential for achieving national independence would be destroyed."

45 Kennedy, *The Modern Industrialisation of Ireland, 1940–1988*, 28.

46 McKittrick et al, *Lost Lives*, 769.

47 Communal pressure was not the only force at play. More conventional but surely subsidiary explanations include the drift to the suburbs of middle-class residents and greater economic opportunity elsewhere.

48 O'Malley, *On Another Man's Wound*, 370.

49 Bowman, *De Valera and the Ulster Question: 1917–1973*, 318.

50 Ibid., 318.

51 Miller, *Peep O'Day Boys and Defenders*, 9–37; Bardon, *A History of Ulster*, 471;

Patterson, *Class Conflict and Sectarianism*, 131–3. There were of course smaller-scale expulsions of Protestants from pieces of territory down the generations as well, including during the recent Troubles, most notably in Derry and New Barnsley and Ardoyne in Belfast.

52 In the early seventeenth century, at the very foundation of the Plantation, the gender imbalance among early colonists resulted in "mixed" marriages with "native" women, thereby spoiling notions of racial purity. Similarly with later "mixed marriages." See Kennedy, *Unhappy the Land*, 42–52.

53 The English language lacks a noun that sums up ethnic prejudice in the way that racism refers to racial prejudice. In Northern Ireland the intermingling of ethnic, communal, and sectarian hatreds seems to be akin to racism or at least bears a close relation.

54 The history and role of the GAA in Irish society cannot be summed up in these terms. I am an enthusiast for its purely sporting role rather than its "soft power" in relation to nationalism. As a boy, I thought of little else but hurling. On my mother's side of the family there was a string of All-Ireland hurling medals gained by members of the Tipperary hurling team. Tipperary was fine but translated into the context of a deeply divided society in Northern Ireland the cultural exclusiveness of the GAA had the latent effect of fostering sectarian division and ambivalence towards political violence.

55 Rouse, *Sport in Ireland: A History*, 302–8.

56 Bairner, "Sport in the Nineteenth and Twentieth Centuries," 268.

57 Akenson, *Education and Enmity*, 72–88; Fleming, "Education since the Late Eighteenth Century," 218–23.

58 On *Ne Temere* see Herbermann et al. eds., *The Catholic Encyclopaedia*, 699. For a representative, aggrieved reaction from the Church of Ireland there is the lecture by the archbishop of Armagh, J.A.F. Gregg, *The "Ne Temere" Decree: A Lecture*.

59 Ruane and Todd, *Dynamics of Conflict in Northern Ireland*, 290–5.

60 Samuel, a taxi driver in his early 40s, had been batoned in his own home by members of the RUC who had been pursuing rioters. The attack had taken place on the 19 April, some three months earlier. He never recovered from his injuries and died on 16 June 1969. Despite the tragic outcome, no policeman was charged with any offence.

61 Writers and journalists have proved to be more socially engaged as can be seen from the searing indictments handed down by Liam Clarke, Eoghan Harris, Kevin Myers, Eilis O'Hanlon, Lindy McDowell, and indeed many other of their colleagues, some of a younger generation.

62 There is a large and convoluted literature on structure–agency issues. A survey that ranges across many contributions and that also offers new

theoretical insights may be found in Emirbayer and Mische, "What is Agency?," 962–1023.

63 See the tables and figures in this volume and in particular table 2.1.

64 For an exposition of the Catholic doctrine on a just war see Edwards, *The Seven*.

65 Moloney, *A Secret History of the IRA*, 447–54.

66 This responsibility is clear-cut, irrespective of whether one considers the Provisional IRA a terrorist organisation or not, though there seems little doubt on that score. PIRA has the distinguishing marks of a terrorist organisation: it did not have a mandate from the Irish people to wage war; it sought to intimidate its opponents into submission and drive them into a state they had no wish to enter; it promoted itself through acts of violence designed to attract recruits and publicity for the "cause"; it sought to provoke its opponents, and particularly the British state into over reaction, so as to broaden and deepen support for its campaign of violence.

67 O'Keefe, "Suicide and Self-Starvation," 349–63. I am grateful to Onora O'Neill for this reference and for her discussion of "martyrs" in "Justice without Ethics: A Twentieth Century Innovation."

68 For an IRA insider's account, though one at variance with the standard Sinn Féin narrative, there is O'Rawe, *Afterlives*.

69 Conversations with Paddy Devlin whom I was fortunate enough to know in his later years. Paddy was particularly concerned about and naturally angered by abuse directed at one of his daughters who lived at home as part of the campaign to drive him out. For an account of his tumultuous political life, see Devlin, *Straight Left*.

70 Ibid., 285.

71 Electoral fraud was widely associated with Sinn Féin in the 1980s and the 1990s, so it is likely the practice artificially inflated its share of the vote. While this may have been important in some tightly contested constituencies, such as Fermanagh–South Tyrone and Belfast West, it is unlikely to have been on such a scale as to distort greatly the overall voting pattern. I might add, one old campaigner from the Official republican movement confided in me that he had voted sixteen times in an election in the 1970s, though to no avail in terms of the outcome.

72 The year 1992 was a low point for Sinn Féin. Opposition to the "Provisionals' war" was gathering support, north and south. I suspect the loss of the one parliamentary seat held by Sinn Féin, and the defeat of its leader, helped convince leading republicans that the militarist game was up and that a "peace strategy" was the only show in town.

73 Technically this was not a ceasefire, but this is the term that is usually used for this cessation of violence.

74 The SDLP secured 24 per cent of the total vote in Northern Ireland at the UK general election of 1997; Sinn Féin received 16 per cent. Thus the ratio between the two parties, in terms of voting support, was 1.5 as to 1, in favour of the SDLP. A decade later the ratio would be reversed, and by the Assembly elections of 2016 the decline of the SDLP had reached the point where Sinn Féin had double the number of votes of the SDLP.

75 The IRA resumed its armed campaign in February 1996 until a new ceasefire was arranged in July 1997. It is significant that loyalist paramilitaries, despite the resumption of violence by the IRA, did not go back on their 1994 cease-fire declaration.

76 The poignant story of the killing and the subsequent cover-up of the murder of Robert McCartney by republicans has been told by his sister Catherine McCartney. Her *Walls of Silence* is one of the outstanding studies of the Troubles. It is unusual in that it is written from inside the world of a tight nationalist community. In an example of political cleansing, the McCartneys were later driven out of the Short Strand, a small nationalist enclave in east Belfast that was the family's home area. I am grateful for conversations with Catherine and Paula McCartney at the time and subsequently.

77 If one treats the People Before Profit alliance as "nationalist," which is questionable, then the Sinn Féin share reduces to 67 per cent.

78 *Irish Times*, 24 September 2011.

79 Sandy Row Community Forum, *Shoulder to Shoulder: Moving Forward* (Belfast, 2013), 18.

80 Here as elsewhere, the election results are taken from Nicholas Whyte's data sets (though making one correction to the figures published for the West-minster election of October 1974). See Northern Ireland Elections: Who Won What When and Where? http://www.ark.ac.uk/elections.

81 *Irish Times*, 29 December 1997; *An Phoblhacht*, 5 February 2009.

82 As many as twenty-nine prison officers, virtually all from the Protestant community, had their lives cut short by the IRA: see McKittrick et al., *Lost Lives*, 1484. The authors do not classify prison officers as civilians.

83 Brett, *Long Shadows Cast Before*, 101.

84 Walker, *Two Irelands*, 23, 27, 110–12; Akenson, *Education and Enmity*, 177–9.

85 Patterson and Kaufmann, *Unionism and Orangeism*, 31–57.

86 The final chapter of Richard Rose's *Governing without Consent* draws some illuminating historical comparisons with other polities.

87 The seminal moment was the setting up of the Commission on the Status of

Women in March 1970. It issued its findings in 1972. See also the historically informed series of articles on women in Irish society during May 2010 in the *Irish Times*.

88 On the moral stance of one active IRA man who took responsibility for his actions, see Collins, *Killing Rage*. Two years after the book was published he was murdered by former comrades. By contrast, there is little sense of moral scruples apparent in the recollections of an IRA veteran such as Gerry Bradley. See Bradley, *Insider: Gerry Bradley's Life in the IRA*, 7–16.

89 The first republican to die in the Troubles was Gerald McAuley. He was a member of Na Fianna, the youth wing of the IRA. He was a schoolboy, fifteen years of age. Though the use of children in conflict zones is recognised internationally as a war crime, this did not attract that kind of attention at the time.

CHAPTER THREE

1 The ordeal of a Belfast Protestant, Andrew Peden. In writing this chapter and the following chapter I am grateful for the help and advice of various friends and colleagues over many years, some sadly now dead. These include Eileen Bell, Irene Boada Montagut, Lea Cramsie, Alun Davies, Paddy Devlin, Carmel Donnelly, Brice Dickson, Ruth Dudley Edwards, Patricia Mallon, Jeff Maxwell, Clare Murphy, Brian Garrett, Damien Gough, Anne Holliday, Hugh Lewsley, Jeff Maxwell, Jim McAllister, Sam McAughtry, Catherine McCartney, Michael Nugent, Seán Ó Cearnaigh, Sean O'Callaghan, Malachi O'Doherty, Bernadette O'Rawe, Katy Radford, Henry Robinson, Sean Reilly, as well as others (mainly victims and their relatives) who wish to remain anonymous. The statistics branch of the Police Service of Northern Ireland was both helpful and efficient. I am also grateful for discussions with several members and ex-members of Sinn Féin, as well as to a number of young loyalists from Tiger's Bay, Belfast. It seems appropriate to mention at this juncture that I was a member of various peace and human rights groups during the 1990s and beyond. Interviews from these engagements, personal diary entries, and other writings on paramilitary punishments have been collected by the writer. These are in the Northern Ireland Human Rights Archive (hereafter NIHR Archive), which will be lodged with the Public Record Office, Northern Ireland. I draw on this voluminous documentation (extending to more than a thousand pages) at various points in this and the following chapter.

2 The account of the torture and mutilation of Andrew Peden is taken from various media reports including a heartrending interview with John Mullin of the *Guardian*, 19 January 1999. See also Hodge, "No End to Violence: Each side now kills its own," *New York Times*, 5 March 1999, http://www.nytimes.

com/1999/03/05/world/no-end-to-violence-in-ulster-each-side-now-kills-its-own.html.

3 Rifles instead of handguns were used by the Provisional IRA in 1992 to shoot the legs and hands of members of the rival IPLO. The reason was "to cause greater injury to their victims' limbs," according to Holland and McDonald in *INLA*, 341–2.

4 An easily forgotten aspect of the Troubles, also contributing to the policing vacuum, was the deliberate targeting of Catholic members of the RUC by republican paramilitaries and the intimidation of Catholics who considered joining. The strategic aim was to make the police force as Protestant and hence as unacceptable as possible.

5 Adams, "But there was also, particularly in the first two decades of the conflict a more brutal form of rough justice." See his blog "How Republicans dealt with Allegations of Child Abuse," 19 October 2014: http://leargas.blog spot.ie/ and also the *Irish Examiner*, 20 October 2014. The implication that punishments were less brutal during the next two decades is taken up later in this chapter. Adams has also described the IRA as acting as a police force, *Irish Examiner*, 20 October 2014.

6 Other paramilitary organisations, such as the Red Hand Commandos, the Loyalist Volunteer Force, the Official IRA, the Irish National Liberation Army, the Irish People's Liberation Organisation, the self-styled Óglaigh na hÉireann, have also been responsible for beatings, shootings, and exiling, but to a lesser degree. The length of the title of some of these organisations was in inverse proportion to the size of the organisation.

7 Donnelly Jr, *Irish Agrarian Rebellion, 1760-1800*; Madden, *Forkhill Protestants and Forkhill Catholics, 1787-1858*; Mac Suibhne, *The End of Outrage*; Hughes and MacRaild eds., *Crime, Violence and the Irish in the Nineteenth Century*.

8 Donnelly Jr, *Captain Rock*, 342–5.

9 Murray, "Agrarian Violence and Nationalism in Nineteenth-Century Ireland," 56–73.

10 This is based on conversations during the early 1990s with the late Seán Ó Cearnaigh (NIHR Archive).

11 There is a suggestion of this in Monaghan, "The Return of 'Captain Moonlight,'" 41–4, 52. While her historical discussion is on the light side – Captain Moonlight did not return – there is valuable contemporary material in the article.

12 Morrisey and Pease, "The Black Criminal Justice System in West Belfast," 159–66.

13 Foucault, *Discipline and Punish*, 8.

14 Ibid., 14

15 I have talked to victims whose lesser complaints included the claim that they

had not been given a warning before they were assaulted or shot. On the trauma experienced by two young people who had been placed under threat, from the manifold examples, see the *Derry Journal*, 22 November 2007.

16 The republican papers *An Phobhlacht* and *Newry News* carried such threats as did some loyalist magazines. Catholic priests and other intermediaries were sometimes given a list of names to pass on to parents. *An Phobhlacht* sometimes carried news of these assaults, along with attacks on the army or police, under the heading "War News."

17 BBC Three documentary "Shot By My Neighbour" aired 18 September 2018.

18 My impression, and it is no more than that (as, to the best of my knowledge, paramilitary organisations do not publish financial accounts), is that this was not common practice, though I did speak to one mother from the New Lodge area of Belfast in the 1990s who said she had twice paid fines for her wayward son.

19 Silke, "The Lords of Discipline," 125–6. I am also grateful to the veteran republican Joe Austin for a number of frank conversations on "paramilitary policing."

20 "Punishment" by Seamus Heaney from his collection *North*, 37. Possibly also the poem relates to state violence against individuals as well as the more obvious paramilitary punishments.

21 *Irish Times*, 11 November 1971.

22 There are various contemporary newspaper accounts, including those of the *Belfast Telegraph*, *Londonderry Sentinel*, and the *Irish Times*. An insightful study, which heavily influenced the writing of this section, is by Roleke, *Mother Ireland and her Soldier Dolls*. A further overview is provided by a BBC Radio 4 program, broadcast on Sunday, 29 November 2009, entitled "Tarred and Feathered." A picture from 1971 of a Derry woman tied to a lamp post, with her hair cropped, and a black substance poured over her head may be found on the BBC website, "Has Northern Ireland left the Past behind?": http://news.bbc.co.uk/1/hi/northern_ireland/8381652.stm.

23 *Irish Times*, 11 November 1971. Tar was difficult to handle so thick diesel oil or paint was sometimes substituted.

24 Munck, "Repression, Insurgency, and Popular Justice", 86. Later, on page 92, he writes of an imperative: "In practical terms, traitors or informers must be eliminated if the movement is to survive."

25 *Irish News*, 20 March 2003.

26 Roleke, *Mother Ireland*, 40.

27 Nicholas, Barr, and Mollan, "Paramilitary Punishment in Northern Ireland," 90. A related article, one also not for the faint-hearted, is Barr and Mollan, "The Orthopaedic Consequences of Civil Disturbance in Northern Ireland," 739–44.

28 *First Report of the Independent Monitoring Commission*, 21.

29 BBC report, "A Punishment Second only to Death," http://news.bbc.co.uk/ 1/hi/northern_ireland/433580.stm.

30 Northern Ireland Affairs Committee, *Third Report: Relocation following Paramilitary Intimidation*, House of Commons, QQ 2–4, 20 (22 November 2001).

31 *Derry Journal*, 15 February 2002; Gary Kent, "Exile – A Terrible Price to Pay," *Irish Post*, 21 June 2001. Kent's article focused on the plight of one such exile, Joseph McCloskey, his wife, and their six children who were forced to move to England. According to Kent, Northern Ireland ministers admitted there were 3,000 or more exiles still unable to return home several years after the signing of the Good Friday Agreement. The annual reports of the Northern Ireland Association for the Care and Resettlement of Offenders (NIACRO) contain information on referrals from people who may have been "at risk of violence in the community." This category includes threats of expulsion. In the year 2013–14 there were 1,041 referrals to the agency, only some of which involved intimidation by paramilitary organisations. NIACRO, *Annual Report 2013–14* (Belfast, 2014), 10.

32 *Telegraph*, 27 August 2000.

33 *Irish Times*, 30 April 2012.

34 Based on conversations with victims of paramilitary attacks, as well as medical and care workers in Northern Ireland. I am particularly indebted to the Maranatha Christian church for discussions over many years on how they have given succour to people from Northern Ireland "exiled" by paramilitary bodies. This included arranging travel routes, material and psychological support, and temporary accommodation.

35 Silke's intensive study of paramilitary attacks for the subperiod 1994–96 (thirty months) found that 1 per cent of these attacks resulted in death. Silke, "War Without End," 249–66. He also found that IRA attacks resulted in more serious injuries to their victims and that loyalist vigilantes were four times more likely to be prosecuted than IRA vigilantes.

36 *Irish Times*, 15 November 2014. In the early 1990s a republican from the Newry area of Northern Ireland, Maurice Healy, claimed publicly that he had been sexually assaulted during the course of four days of interrogation and torture by the IRA: He was suspected of being an informer, a charge he rejected. I met him on two occasions in 1991 (NIHR Archive, 1991).

37 This was during the course of a heated Dáil debate on child sexual abuse and the Provisional republican movement. The full text is available at Dáil Éireann debates –Wednesday, 12 November 2014: http://oireachtasdebates. oireachtas.ie/debates%20authoring/debateswebpack.nsf/takes/dail2014111 200030.

38 Collins, *Killing Rage*; *Guardian*, 3 July 1999.

39 Silke, "The Lords of Discipline," 122.

40 *Irish Times*, 22 October 2007; *Belfast Telegraph*, 23 October 2007; *Times*, 23 October 2007.

41 *Sunday Tribune*, 28 October 2007; *Irish News*, 19 November 2007.

42 *Irish News*, 19 November 2007.

43 *Guardian*, 23 October 2005; *Newry Democrat*, 27 February 2008.

44 *Irish News*, 20 August 2008.

45 Silke, "The Lords of Discipline," 128. The mean length of stay in hospital for an uncomplicated punishment shooting was six days, but for an injury with complications it could be as long as seventy-six days. See Nicholas et al., "Paramilitary Punishment," 93–4.

46 Silke, "War Without End," 262.

47 This is from one of the best pieces of investigative journalism on paramilitary punishments. Written by John Conroy, a fellow of the American-based Alicia Patterson Foundation, the article is titled simply "Kneecapping." It was published in 1980. The text may be found at http://aliciapatterson.org/stories/kneecapping.

48 Ibid.

49 Ibid. "Kneecapping" was the popular or generic term used for shootings to the knee but often to another part of the leg as well, so the term should not be taken too literally. For a medical view see Barr and Mollan, "Kneecapping: A Misnomer."

50 Morrow, "Shared or Scared?," 4–6. The full survey results are available on line: see Northern Ireland Young Life & Times, http://www.ark.ac.uk/ylt/2004/Community_Relations/. The sample size was just over 800 young people.

51 Morrow, "Shared or Scared?," 5.

52 It is possible to use other sources as demonstrated by Silke to fill some gaps. For the period July 1994 to December 1996 Silke used media reports to count 277 punishment beatings, two-thirds of which were due to republican paramilitaries. See Silke, "War Without End," 255.

53 Comments made to me at a meeting of the RUC Historical Society in the early 2000s where a much earlier version of this chapter was presented. See also the introduction to the report by the Northern Ireland Affairs Committee, *Relocation following Paramilitary Intimidation*, which indicates that instances of "exiling" were also under reported.

54 Nicholas et al., "Paramilitary Punishment," 91–2.

55 This was impressed on me by former Sinn Féin councillor Jim McAllister. According to him, there were many beatings in the South Armagh region

that few people knew anything about. The families and the victims felt isolated, embarrassed, ashamed. And of course they were fearful of talking. See notes on a telephone conversation with Jim McAllister, 13 January 2008 (NIHR Archive). It may be that the under reporting was especially pronounced in rural areas.

56 See http://www.ark.ac.uk/ylt/2004/Community_Relations/.

57 Silke, "The Lords of Discipline," 128; Silke, "Rebel's Dilemma," 90.

58 Based on interviews with a number of those directly involved in this resistance episode (NIHR Archive, 1991–92).

59 See *Daily Mail*, 19 August 1991 and other daily newspapers that Monday. Cardinal Daly's statement was also carried by the Catholic periodical the *Tablet*, 24 August 1991; the article contains interesting material on the views of local priests.

60 Much of the detail for this episode is based on contemporary newspaper reports, conversations with the two families, and conversations also with members of Families Against Intimidation and Terror (FAIT), the main campaigning organisation at that time working on behalf of the families. I also draw on my own recollections as a member of one of the campaigning groups supporting the families.

61 At least half of those who believed or claimed they were under threat did not end up as cases of exiling. However, not all cases were processed through Base 2. Some individuals and families made their own private and hence unrecorded moves. Others dealt directly with other agencies or with the exemplary interdenominational Christian organisation Maranatha. The picture of the extent of exiling is a murky one. What we can be sure of from the fragmentary statistical sources is that the numbers affected during the Troubles ran into the thousands. The most comprehensive account may be found in the House of Commons paper *Relocation Following Paramilitary Intimidation* (2001).

62 Northern Ireland Young Life & Times.

63 Jarman, *Intimidation in Northern Ireland, 2010–2014*.

64 For an overview of continuing paramilitary criminality in Northern Ireland see the *First Report of the Independent Reporting Commission* (Belfast, October 2018). In 2018 there were sixty-eight paramilitary-style attacks – seventeen shootings and fifty-one assaults. PSNI, *Police Recorded Security Situation Statistics: Monthly Update, covering the 12 month period 1st January 2017–31 December, 2018* (Belfast, 2019).

65 In addition to the fact that many instances went unreported, the nonrecording of punishment beatings before 1982 means that the true figures are some multiple of the official totals. The very low figures for 1982 and 1983 might

suggest that the information-gathering machinery was not fully effective at first. The three years 1970–72 are a statistical blank also for shootings, beatings, and related forms of intimidation.

66 Roleke, *Mother Ireland and her Soldier Dolls*, 91–2.

67 *Relocation Following Paramilitary Intimidation* (2001).

68 My sense though is that beatings were less likely to be reported by victims of republican vigilante attacks, so the small differences may be very small indeed.

69 A more refined chronological treatment might separate out loyalist and republican attacks, though it is important also not to lose sight of the interactions between the activities of orange and green paramilitaries.

70 A balanced assessment of criticisms of the RUC from nationalist and republican viewpoints may be found in Doyle, "The Politics of the Transformation of Policing," 167–211.

71 As quoted on the BBC website, "Exile – a punishment second only to death," http://news.bbc.co.uk/1/hi/northern_ireland/433580.stm.

72 *First Report of the Independent Monitoring Commission*. The twenty-six reports of the IMC, published up until July 2011, provide much insight into organised crime linked to paramilitaries. These reports may be accessed at http://cain.ulst.ac.uk/issues/politics/docs/imc/imcreports.htm. The decade or so since the paramilitary ceasefires of 1994 may well have constituted the golden age of organised crime in Northern Ireland.

73 Interview with Patrick Doherty, 22 September 2014 (NIHR Archive).

74 In early 2017 UDA vigilantes were reported to have attacked and beaten two alleged paedophiles, which is one way of currying favour at a neighbourhood level. *Irish News*, 10 January 2017.

75 I have been told the choice depended on the availability of guns in a locality and the ease with which these might be carried safely to and from an arms dump. There may be something to this but this can only be part of the story (NIHR Archive). I have also been told that beatings were reserved for "serious cases" of (alleged) antisocial behaviour.

76 The NIHR Archive contains some 300 pages of observations and notes on the intimidation of a South Armagh farmer by local paramilitaries for the period 2010–17 for what was in effect a "land grab." There was little indication that the PSNI had been accepted by the ex-combatants and at least some local people.

77 Harris over many years has contributed some of the sharpest critiques of the Provisional IRA, writing particularly for audiences in the Republic of Ireland where ambivalence or ignorance was sometimes pronounced.

78 Lindsay, *No Dope Here?*, 221–2, and conversations with the author who lives in Derry.

79 The case of RAAD also illustrates the point that a small paramilitary group-
    ing can exercise a hugely disproportionate influence over a large population,
    if sufficiently ruthless, with families rather than individuals being a particu-
    lar point of vulnerability.

80 This was in no sense unique to Derry. The following week in Belfast dis-
    sident paramilitaries ordered a teenager to turn up by appointment. If he
    did not, they would in addition shoot his brother. He duly turned up under
    this pressure and was shot in both legs. He underwent four hours of surgery
    at Belfast's Royal Victoria Hospital. See the report in the *Guardian*, 4 May
    2012. Shooting by appointment was also a feature of Belfast life in earlier
    decades.

81 "Father saw gunmen shoot his son on Londonderry street," http://www.bbc.
    co.uk/news/uk-northern-ireland-17296109, 8 March 2012.

82 Stewart, *The Narrow Ground*, 179–82.

83 "A Mother's Love's A Blessing," http://www.youtube.com/watch?v=XDtBF
    ikqgBA.

84 *Belfast Telegraph*, 17 May 2012; *Irish Times*, 30 April 2012; BBC News "Mother
    says son shot in Derry because of drugs," http://www.bbc.co.uk/news/uk-
    northern-ireland-17867319, 27 April, 2012.

85 A correlation coefficient of one would indicate a perfect relationship or as-
    sociation between the two variables while a zero result would imply no rela-
    tionship. The correlation technique employed here uses first differences, so
    there are forty observations for the period 1973–2013. For the time span
    1973–2005, that is lopping off the more recent time period, the correlation
    coefficient is higher still at 0.69.

86 R = 0.59 with thirty-two observations for the period 1982–2013.

87 There is a weak suggestion of this for the period as a whole for republican
    paramilitaries but not for loyalists. Again using first differences, the correla-
    tion coefficient between republican shootings and beatings has the expected
    sign and the r value is -0.21.

88 *Relocation Following Paramilitary Intimidation* (2001).

89 On signs of change, usually temporary in nature, in paramilitary thinking,
    see Silke, "Rebel's Dilemma," 83–4 and Kennedy, "Nightmares within Night-
    mares," 78–9. Attacks could also be switched on or off as political circum-
    stances dictated, as for example in the run-up to President Clinton's first
    visit to Belfast in 1994: see *Relocation Following Paramilitary Intimidation*
    (2001).

90 There was an important one-off change in the recording system of the stat-
    istical division of the RUC in 1998. Reports were published in calendar years
    from 1968 until 1997. Since then reports were based on financial years (April
    to March). It may be noted also that the police sometime reclassify crimes

in later periods as new information becomes available, but this has only a
marginal effect on the data presented here.

91 Roleke, *Mother Ireland and her Soldier Dolls*, 34.

92 This continues to be the case. See *First Report of the Independent Reporting
Commission* (Belfast, October, 2018).

93 Kennedy, "Nightmares within Nightmares," 74, and Silke, "War Without
End," 249–66.

94 Data from the statistics branch of the Police Service of Northern Ireland.

95 A detailed study of vigilantism for the short time interval July 1994 to
December 1996 found that 8 per cent of loyalist victims were women while
5 per cent of republican victims were women, Silke, "War Without End," 255.

96 McKendry, *Disappeared*; McBride et al., *The Disappeared of Northern
Ireland's Troubles.*

97 One of the most powerful accounts of the McConville tragedy was a
documentary film shown by the BBC in 2013 entitled *The Disappeared:
The Hidden Story of the Troubles.*

98 Northern Ireland Young Life & Times.

99 Jarman and Tennant, *An Acceptable Prejudice?*, 65–6.

100 Duggan, *Queering Conflict*, 36.

101 *Belfast Telegraph*, 9 December 1992; *Irish News*, 14 December 1992; *Independent*, 20 December 1992.

102 Thompson and Mulholland, "Paramilitary Punishments and Young People,"
55. See also Duffy, Gillespie, and Clark, "Post-Traumatic Stress Disorder," 1–7.

103 Notes on a conversation, one of many extending over a period of years, 9
June 2004 (NIHR Archive). According to one of Brian's friends, the punishment squad had been seen drinking beforehand, presumably to fire themselves up for the task ahead. (I may add, at the time of writing, Brian still
suffers physical as well as psychological pain.)

104 Knox and Monaghan, *Informal Justice in Divided Societies*, 34; interview with
Patrick Doherty, 22 September 2014 (NIHR Archive).

105 There were instances, however, of more than one victim being attacked at
the same time, in public places rather than in homes.

106 One can only try to imagine the anguish of a father listening to his fifteen-
year-old son crying out, "help me, help me" as he was set upon by masked
men armed with hammers. The father in this case was held at gunpoint
during the beating, which took place in Derry city in April 2012 See "Father
says he was 'powerless' to stop son's attack," http://www.bbc.co.uk/news/uk-
northern-ireland-foyle-west-17655944.

107 Based on conversations with family members, community workers, and
local councillors during the 1990s and beyond (NIHR Archive).

108 Kennedy, "Northern Ireland." The *Belfast Telegraph* reported on its front

page as late as 2017 that the family of a farmer tortured and executed by the IRA in July 1991 was still afraid to speak openly of its desire for justice. This was twenty-six years after the murder. *Belfast Telegraph*, 5 September 2017.

109   *Guardian*, 9 August 2002.

110   These may be consulted at the Linen Hall Library, Belfast (Political Collection).

111   *Combat*, July 1989 (Political Collection, Linen Hall Library, Belfast). While the term "social unit" is used here, I am not aware that the UVF or the UDA had specialist punishment squads. As so often with paramilitary organisations, rhetoric and reality, never mind history, failed to rhyme.

112   Rolston, "Morality Play," 7. But crime surveys have shown that Northern Ireland actually had a lower incidence of "ordinary" crime than many regions of the United Kingdom. It is possible, indeed probable, that paramilitary control and the normalisation of violence associated with paramilitary activity had the effect of amplifying the degree of deviance and antisocial behaviour found in working-class areas.

113   On vigilante activity in South African townships following the end of the apartheid regime see Knox and Monaghan, *Informal Justice in Divided Societies*, 43–50.

114   Research by Nicholas et al., 93, for the years 1986–89, indicates that most shootings took place between October and May and most hospital admissions were between 9pm and 3am in the morning.

115   Munck, "Repression, Insurgency, and Popular Justice," 81, 90.

116   What follows is based on Paul Smyth's account, entitled "Harrowing Story of how One Young Victim Prepared for His 'Punishment' by Getting Tea Towels to Mop Up the Blood," *Belfast Telegraph*, 12 August 2017. I do accept that the Provisional IRA and Sinn Féin just might have handled things differently – this was one of the new IRAs in action – and the organisation might have been less untrustworthy. But the scenario, with some change of detail, is only too familiar from the days when the Provisionals administered their form of "popular justice."

117   Danny Morrison, "Myth of 'totalitarian militarism' in republican areas needs challenging," *Daily Ireland*, May 2005. For a similar view by the president of Sinn Féin, Mr Adams, see his Léargas blog "How Republicans dealt with Allegations of Child Abuse," 19 October 2014, http://léargas.blogspot.ie/.

118   A fascinating fictional account, based on the life story of Denis Donaldson, is Chalandon's *Return to Killybegs*.

119   A voluntary community worker in west Belfast spoke to me of his surprise on being shown such files at Connolly House. This was in 1997. He had been interceding on behalf of several youths who had been threatened (NIHR Archive). The victim-support group Families Against Intimidation and

Terror campaigned in the 1990s to have Connolly House closed down on the grounds that it was a centre for the administration of torture (NIHR Archive). Files relating to FAIT may be consulted at the Linen Hall Library, Belfast (Northern Ireland Political Collection).

120 On the operation of "civil administration" by the IRA see Bradley's *Insider*, 196–202.

121 For what it's worth, while canvassing in Belfast during the general election of 2005 I recall being told frankly by a young woman that she favoured punishment attacks – what alternative was there? – though she added that her husband, who was absent at the time and allied to the Workers Party, was opposed.

122 But see McEvoy, "Women Loyalist Paramilitaries in Northern Ireland," 262–86.

123 Ibid.

124 McDonald and Cusack, UDA, 57–8.

125 *Belfast Telegraph*, 13 December 2013. Three loyalist women served prison sentences arising out of the murder. A community worker from a loyalist background told me that he knew one of the assailants who became a well-known alcoholic in the Sandy Row, Belfast (NIHR Archive, 2014).

126 Based on her ethnographic work in Catholic working-class communities in Belfast Elena Bergia argues that the "empowerment thesis" oversimplifies the myriad roles and experiences of women during the Troubles. Bergia, "Women and War: A Complex Matter," 22–3.

127 The use of the term "the community" when discussing the Troubles can be almost cringe-making as it frequently means whatever the speaker wants it to mean. Typically it means the fraction of people within a roughly defined area who agree with the speaker, with the remainder dismissed or rendered invisible.

128 Vintage Everyday, "Pictures of Female IRA Fighters in the 1970s," https://www.vintag.es/2014/08/pictures-of-female-ira-fighters-in-1970s.html.

129 NIHR archive.

130 Heaney, "Punishment," 37.

131 Avila Kilmurray, who was also a trade union activist, later played a major role in community development at a Northern Ireland level. Her feminist commitment was further evidenced in the late 1990s when she was one of the negotiators with the Women's Coalition during the talks surrounding the Good Friday Agreement. It was my privilege to have known her as a colleague at Magee University College, Derry, at the end of the 1970s.

132 Once again, this needs more documentation but the claim has been made to me on a number of occasions, with individual women party members being singled out by name. Seán Ó Cearnaigh (see earlier) related to me the story

of a woman well known as a Sinn Féin councillor in Belfast who was allegedly complicit in the execution of a local Catholic man accused of being an
informer. She delivered the news to the parents that their young son had
been executed and later helped out in the family kitchen by making sand-
wiches for the wake. That's what neighbours do.

133 The journalist Eilis O'Hanlon wrote in the *Sunday Independent*, 19 October
2014, that her late sister Siobhan O'Hanlon, along with other Sinn Féin
women, was among those who participated in the interrogation of Mairia
Cahill by the IRA. See also the *Irish Times*, 20 and 21 October 2012, and subsequently for the course of this controversy. Heather Hamill has written of
the role of women from Cumann na mBan in a punishment attack on a
woman deemed deserving of a beating. Hamill, *The Hoods*, 43–64.

134 *Sunday Independent*, 19 October 2014.

135 Interview with Dolours Price in *The Telegraph*, 23 September 2012. See also
McKendry, *Disappeared*.

136 I've argued this in more detail in the *Belfast Telegraph*, 10 September 2019
and 16 September 2019.

137 Jamieson and Grounds, *No Sense of an Ending*, 38.

138 Drawing on United States military experience in recent wars Joshua Reynolds
in *Weekend America* observes, "There's not much research into the trauma
inflicted on torturers, but what little there is suggests that torture has two
victims." See http://weekendamerica.publicradio.org/display/web/2008/10/
18/torturers.

139 Conceivably psychopaths and sadists were overrepresented in the higher
echelons of paramilitary organisations, thereby exercising a disproportionate influence relative to their overall numbers within these organisations.

140 NIHR Archive (2010).

141 The program *Talkback*, presented by William Crawley, BBC Northern
Ireland, 10 November 2014.

142 Brian, for instance, whose experiences were recalled earlier, claims that of
the two IRA men who gave him his first of several IRA beatings, one died of
alcoholism and the other, also an alcoholic, is well down the road to following him. Gerry Bradley, who was involved in numerous IRA operations since
the early 1970s has spoken of "a big drink culture" in the IRA in *Insider:
Gerry Bradley's Life in the IRA*. Similar claims emanate from within the
loyalist community. See Sandy Row Community Forum, *Shoulder to
Shoulder*, passim.

143 Up to thirty masked loyalists invaded a pub in Belfast in 2018 to assault
their victim. This seems an untypically large number, suggestive perhaps of
underemployment in paramilitary ranks. *Irish News*, 23 February 2018. But
an average of five per incident seems on the low side.

144 Silke, "Rebel's Dilemma." See also Bradley, *Insider*, 196–7, 198–9.

145 O'Doherty, *The Trouble with Guns*, 107; conversation with O'Doherty, 5 June 2014.

146 McCartney, *Walls of Silence*, 5, 48. Newspaper reports, and other sources, claimed crimes of child sexual abuse, stabbings, and woman-beating on the part of some members of this battalion in the Markets area. See *Telegraph*, 1 March 2005; *Irish Independent*, 8 April 2005. On other allegations of child sexual abuse within the movement, there are the statements of Mairia Cahill who unusually and at great personal cost did go public. See the *Irish Times*, 18 October 2014, *Sunday Independent*, 19 October 2014. Child sexual abuse by loyalists, centring on the notorious boys' home at Kincora, Belfast, during the 1970s is well known and led to convictions for some but almost certainly not all of those involved.

147 This former IRA officer spoke to me in May 2005 and confirmed the details in an email dated 4 June 2014 (NIHR Archive). He also cautioned against believing too strongly in "grandiose titles and structures ... but of course things on the ground were not always like that."

148 NIHR Archive. Bill is now a prominent member of Sinn Féin. The party denies involvement in the punishment system.

149 In the early 1980s the Derry Brigade of the IRA claimed, "the IRA are under considerable pressure from the nationalist community to kneecap far more people that they actually do." It saw kneecapping as a last resort. It then outlined "a strict procedure" that governed the punishment system. *An Phobhlacht*, 25 February 1982.

150 Ibid.

151 A variation on this argument is the training benefits of being able to "blood" young volunteers, of practising how to carry out an operation – one that was virtually risk-free – and of promoting group solidarity. These points were impressed on me by a former Sinn Féin worker who may or may not have been in the IRA (NIHR Archive).

152 *Irish Times*, 10 July 1995.

153 NIHR Archive (2014).

154 Silke, "The Lords of Discipline," 125.

155 Republicans in south Armagh were major exceptions to this generalisation, being deeply immersed in conventional criminal activity. See Harnden, *Bandit Country*, 178–9.

156 Bradley, *Insider*, 13.

157 Ibid., 270.

158 Elena Bergia draws a distinction between "seductive capital" and what has come to be labelled as "erotic capital." On the former see Bergia, "Unex-

pected Rewards of Political Violence," 1–21. On the latter see Harkin, "Erotic Capital," 499–518.

159 NIHR Archive (2014).

160 Most were men and the inherited structures were patriarchal, but there were women in the ranks of both loyalist and republican organisations.

161 McDonald and Cusack, *UDA*, 57.

162 The circumstances of the murder and the family's quest for justice are recounted by his sister Catherine McCartney in *Walls of Silence*. In addition to talking to Catherine and Paula McCartney, I have also discussed that fatal night with Brendan Devine who received serious stab wounds but survived the attack.

163 McKittrick et al., *Lost Lives*, 1415–16.

164 Dillon, *The Shankill Butchers*.

165 Ryder, NIHR Archive.

166 Holland and McDonald, *INLA*, 41-8.

167 *Irish News*, 2 November 1992; Holland and McDonald, *INLA*, 341–2. This onslaught on rival republicans secured a monopoly of coercive power within the nationalist community and made it easier for the Provisionals to consider a ceasefire farther down the line. But of course many other factors went into the making of the embryonic peace process and this monopoly never went entirely uncontested.

168 *Relocation following Paramilitary Intimidation* (2001), Appendix 8.

169 NIHR Archive (conversation in the spring of 2004).

170 The Continuous Household Survey "consistently found that victimization for such offences as burglary, vehicle thefts, and vandalism was lower than that in England and Wales as measured by the British Crime Survey." It needs to be cautioned that comparisons of crime rates or of self-reported crimes across time and region are fraught with difficulties. See Brewer, Lockhart, and Rodger, *Crime in Ireland, 1945–95*, 82–3.

171 See *Belfast Telegraph*, 8 December 2014.

172 Kennedy, "We've Come for Your Boys," 14–15. The detailed results of the Ardowen survey are in this article. I participated with others in conducting the survey.

173 Gramsci, *Prison Notebooks: Volume 1*, 57.

174 Hayward et al., "Belonging and Alienation in the New Northern Ireland," 1–4.

175 As one Belfast community worker put it to me, the paramilitaries switched on young, unemployed males to riot, burn buses, and stone the security forces and then seemed surprised when these same youths stole and burned cars, thereby earning themselves the opprobrium of the local community and the paramilitaries.

176 NIHR Archive.

177 Conversations with Sean Reilly, Jasmine Walk, Belfast (NIHR Archive).

178 There were deviations from this ideal, it has to be said, most notably during the period of internment without trial in the early 1970s, but taking the period of the Troubles as a whole these were the exception.

179 Burgers and Danelius, *The United Nations Convention against Torture: A Handbook on the Convention Against Torture and Other Cruel, Inhuman, or Degrading Treatment or Punishment*, 177–90.

180 Young girls were also involved in joyriding, which seems to have had an addictive quality, but typically as passengers. This led to the killing in disputed circumstances of Karen Reilly of Twinbrook, Belfast, in 1990. A British army patrol opened fire on a stolen car. Her stepfather, with the help of the RUC, sought to have the soldiers, including Corporal Lee Clegg, convicted for unlawful killing. See *Guardian*, 13 March 1999 and NIHR Archive (conversations with Sean Reilly). Many felt that the soldiers lied about the circumstances of the shooting.

181 Thompson and Mulholland, "Young People in West Belfast," 60–1.

182 Ryder, NIHR Archive.

183 Ibid.

184 Hamill, *The Hoods*, 43–64.

185 *Sunday Independent*, 15 September 2002.

186 Burns, *Milkman*.

187 McCartney, *The Ghost Factory*.

188 Silke, "War Without End," table 11, 260.

189 Strictly speaking, the period 1973–1994 as we have no equivalent statistics for the years 1970–72, though of course paramilitary-style attacks were taking place then.

190 That is, taking into account the smaller share of Catholics in the overall population. Since the Good Friday Agreement the pendulum has swung in the other direction.

191 Kotsonouris, *Retreat from Revolution*. The reference to a polity within a polity is from the foreword by Brian Farrell on page 3. The "justice" system initiated by the Provisional IRA and also adopted by loyalists was less systematic, more militarist, and more brutal than the procedures and punishments adopted by the Dáil courts during the revolutionary years.

192 Here I must mention the outstanding and courageous investigative journalism of Malachi O'Doherty who explores these processes in detail. See also his *The Trouble with Guns*.

193 Collins, *Killing Rage*, 164–5.

194 Ulster Political Research Group, *Common Sense: An Agreed Process* (1987), available in the Northern Ireland Political Collection, Linen Hall Library,

Belfast. See also Gary McMichael (son of the assassinated loyalist leader, John McMichael), *An Ulster Voice.*

195 For a nuanced reading of loyalism in this period see Monaghan and Shirlow, "Forward to the Past?," 649–65.

196 Collins, *Killing Rage,* 350.

197 This was in response to a question by the writer at the launch of the Sinn Féin election manifesto in west Belfast at the general election of 1997. On the other hand, one of Adams's closest aides and a convicted IRA man, Terence "Cleeky" Clarke, now dead, was said to have driven and turned a screwdriver through the elbow joint of a young delinquent in a punishment attack, to make sure he could never drive a car again. In an ironic twist of fate, Clarke and the young man both ended up in the Crumlin Road jail around the same time in the 1980s. Clarke is said to have been embarrassed by the other's presence and in an awkward sort of way tried to befriend his young victim (NIHR Archive).

198 The case for this view is cogently presented in Silke, "The Lords of Discipline," 145–8.

199 See the earlier account of this attack in the section on "Forms of 'Punishment.'"

200 *Third Report of the Independent Monitoring Commission,* 7.

201 The following account is based on a recorded interview with Patrick Doherty, 22 September 2014.

202 On paramilitary activity in the new century see the many reports of the Independent Monitoring Commission.

203 For example in 1995 a loyalist paramilitary group, the Protestant Action Force, named five individuals in the Larne area as drug dealers and threatened to execute them (*Irish Times,* 22 May 1995). But loyalist paramilitaries were themselves major suppliers of drugs in Larne as elsewhere in urban areas of Northern Ireland.

204 Monaghan and Shirlow, "Loyalist Paramilitarism in Northern Ireland," 650.

205 McDonald and Cusack, *UDA,* 323–40.

206 On crime and loyalist paramilitarism see *Eight Report of the Independent Monitoring Commission,* 1 February 2006.

207 To use a Provisional IRA term (loyalist paramilitaries used different terms to define their activities).

208 Carson, *Belfast Confetti,* 71.

CHAPTER FOUR

1 "Sister's anguish over night the IRA 'beat up my little brother,'" *Times,* 15 September 1999.

2 *Times,* 18 September 1999.

3 A striking parallel with punishment attacks was the effort put into silencing victims. On the use of canon law and Vatican power structures to protect the abusers rather than the abused, see Robertson, *The Case of the Pope*.

4 *Irish News*, 12 March 2001. I spoke to the boy's mother in her home some weeks later. She seemed dazed, was possibly on tranquilisers, and worried not just about the physical injuries but also about his psychological state and the long-term disruption to her son's schooling.

5 *Observer*, 7 January 2001.

6 John Ware, "How, and Why, did Scappaticci Survive the IRA's Wrath?," *Irish Times*, 15 April 2017.

7 There is no suggestion that Gerry Adams favoured punishment attacks. On a number of occasions he has stated publicly that he is "totally opposed" to such measures.

8 Silke, "The Lords of Discipline," 127.

9 More detailed annual and monthly information is contained in the NIHR Archive.

10 For the full text of the convention see United Nations, *Legislative History of the Convention on the Rights of the Child*, 909–22.

11 This means that child victims accounted for 12 per cent of all attacks across the full age range.

12 *Los Angeles Times*, 19 February 1989; *Irish Independent*, 7 May 2015.

13 There was extensive newspaper coverage of the case of Jean McConville and her family down the years in national newspapers such as the *Irish Independent*, *Irish News*, *Irish Times*, and *Irish Examiner*. An important interview with Michael McConville may be found at "Michael McConville says the IRA will kill him if he names those involved in his mother's murder," http://www.thejournal.ie/michael-mcconville-jean-mcconville-murder-gerry-adams-ira-1442811-May2014/. See also McKendry, *Disappeared*. In 2018 I spoke to two of the sons, Thomas and Jim McConville, of the terrible night their mother was taken away (NIHR archive).

14 Bradley, *Insider*, 198.

15 Lindsay, *No Dope Here*.

16 Collins, *Killing Rage*, 296.

17 Some selection bias is possible, however, as loyalist women may have been more likely to report assaults to the RUC, later the PSNI. This might be the case also for male loyalist victims.

18 Morrow, "Shared or Scared?," 1–16; for the full survey results see Northern Ireland Young Life & Times.

19 I am particularly indebted to Bernadette O'Rawe and Angela (surname withheld), both from West Belfast, for insights into these issues (NIHR Archive).

20 A general practitioner in Poleglass in west Belfast told me in May 2005
that it was almost invariably women who came to surgery to voice their
worries about sons in trouble with the paramilitaries. What they sought
was a listening ear and tranquilisers, lots of tranquilisers. It was her impression that it was the women who also took responsibility for interceding
with the paramilitaries. "The men were useless," was her comment (NIHR
Archive, 2005).

21 *Observer*, 12 November 2000. The eventual outcome is not known to me.

22 Lindsay, *No Dope Here*, 308–9.

23 *Derry Journal*, 7 March and 16 March 2012.

24 *Guardian*, 6 November 2007.

25 I came to know both women through their activity in human rights groups,
and no doubt there are many others whose role may or may not become apparent in time. Their families bear silent witness to the devotion and cour-
age of such women. Nancy Gracey was a cofounder with Henry Robinson of
the victim-support group, Families Against Intimidation and Terror (FAIT).

26 *Irish Independent*, 9 February 2002; *Irish News*, 7 September 2002. The quote
is from "Ulster's Exiles of Terror," *Belfast Telegraph*, 19 March 2002, 11.

27 *Irish News*, 15 April 2003. Needless to add, the attack on the McCloskey
home with guns and sledgehammers was not consistent with Article 16 of
the Convention on Children which seeks to protect the child's privacy,
family, and home life.

28 *Belfast Telegraph*, 19 March 2002; *The Telegraph*, 2 October 2002.

29 The outcome was not so good for Danny McBrearty. For his defiance, and
while driving a bus ferrying old people, he was attacked by masked IRA
men. He was beaten with a hammer and shot in both legs as he grappled
with his assailants in what may have been an assassination attempt. See his
interview with Anthony McIntyre, "Bridie McCloskey's Story," *The Blanket:
A Journal of Protest and Dissent*, 24 November 2002.

30 Ibid.

31 As it happens, I was asked by a member of the family to make the contacts
and also asked by her to attend the meeting as a witness (possibly because
I had recently written a report on continuing paramilitary violence in the
aftermath of the Good Friday Agreement). I contacted the commissioner,
Professor Brice Dickson, who agreed at once to the family's request but
acting in a private capacity. Fr Reid was out of the country at the time and
a Redemptorist priest at Clonard Monastery offered some assistance after
initially berating me for naivety.

32 *Save the Children* leaflet (London, 2003).

33 A qualification is that some may have been acting reluctantly under group
pressure and military-style authority.

34 For an example see the article by William Scholes, *Irish News*, 22 February 2003.

35 *Telegraph*, 18 February 2004; *Guardian*, 17 February 2004.

36 *Guardian*, 17 February 2004.

37 *Telegraph*, 18 February 2004.

38 Ibid. 18 February 2004. In a comment on the Ardoyne suicides the writer Eamonn McCann railed against the "guttersnipes with guns who think they've done a great day's work for Ireland if they've managed to maim another working-class child." See McCann, "Ardoyne Suicides," *The Blanket: A Journal of Protest and Dissent*, 7 March, 2004.

39 *Guardian*, 17 February 2004.

40 Northern Ireland Affairs Committee, *Relocation following Paramilitary Intimidation*, 94.

41 NIHR Archive.

42 Knox and Monaghan, *Informal Justice in Divided Societies*, 172–5; also Kennedy, *They Shoot Children, Don't They?*

43 Under the decisive leadership of Les Allamby the Northern Ireland Human Rights Commission has taken a stand in recent times.

44 Cited in Feenan, "Justice in Conflict," 151–72.

45 A number of members, including the writer, resigned from the organisation because of its determined opposition to looking at the most common forms of human rights abuses in Northern Ireland.

46 Dickson, "The Problems with Human Rights," Annual Stephen Livingstone Lecture, Queen's University Belfast, 2019.

47 NIHR Archive.

48 Human Rights Watch Helsinki, *Northern Ireland, Human Rights Abuses by All Sides.*

49 Human Rights Watch Helsinki, *Human Rights in Northern Ireland*, 105.

50 See report by Shawn Pogatchnik, 14 November 1993 for Associated Press, "Plucky Belfast Cab Driver Defies the IRA and Pays a Brutal Price: Northern Ireland: 'Provos' shoot Catholic in both legs for refusing to surrender his taxi for a terrorist mission," http://articles.latimes.com/1993-11-14/news/mn-56631_1_northern-ireland.

51 After almost two years of one-sided correspondence, I finally extracted an anodyne reply from the Children's Law Centre on its attitude to paramilitary punishments of children (NIHR Archive).

52 "The Crisis in the Human Rights Commission," *Irish News*, 15 November 2003.

53 My contribution to the series was titled "The Paramilitary Abuse of Children in Northern Ireland," delivered on the 18 October 2004. The analysis was conducted within the framework of the UN Convention on the

Rights of the Child, with particular reference to Articles 9–11, 20, and 37.

54 This was all the more curious because Save the Children had taken a high-profile position on loyalist hate-protests directed against Catholic school-children attending Holy Cross Girls' School in north Belfast a few years earlier. For an outline of this attempted blockade of the school by loyalists, which involved loyalist paramilitary elements, see the CAIN website: http://cain.ulst.ac.uk/othelem/chron/cho2.htm.

55 NIHR Archive, discussions with former members of Save the Children in 2004 and again in 2014.

56 I spoke to three long-standing residents of the Markets some months after the murder of Mr Davison. Once his name was mentioned, they froze. One summed up the climate of fear that surrounded any talk either of the murdered man or his comrades: "No one can talk about Jock Davison, except his family." The code of silence ruled. NIHR Archive.

57 *Belfast Telegraph*, 7 May 2015. See also the extensive media attention that attended the killing.

58 *Belfast Telegraph*, 13 May 2015.

59 *Irish News*, 9 December 2016.

60 See "Dee Stitt row: MP says loyalist should not be in CEO post," http://www.bbc.co.uk/news/uk-northern-ireland-37750648.

61 *Irish News*, 9 December 2016. I might add a personal observation. In 2019 I attended a meeting convened by the Reverend Chris Hudson that included former paramilitaries from the UVF, Red Hand Commando, and the UDA. All were involved in community initiatives. At one point I asked, "As it is now a quarter century since the loyalist ceasefire of 1994, why is it that you have not disbanded?" The response was as clichéd as it was less than reassuring: "We are on a journey."

62 An example of the harnessing of human rights concerns to contemporary political concerns was the naming of a human rights organisation after an Irish republican lawyer. Pat Finucane was a defence lawyer (not a human rights lawyer, as was retrospectively claimed) who was murdered by loyalists in 1989. It was a horrific killing and involved collusion on the part of some members of the British security forces. It has been claimed publicly that Pat Finucane was a member of the IRA or an agent of the IRA. In view of the degree of doubt attaching to his relationship with the IRA – the organisation responsible for the most serious human rights abuses in Northern Ireland – linking his name to the cause of human rights seemed curiously partisan. One of Pat Finucane's brothers, a labourer, John James Finucane, was killed in 1972 while on active service with the IRA. Two other brothers, Dermot Finucane and Seamus Finucane, were imprisoned on terrorism charges. See McKittrick et al., *Lost Lives*, 209; *Observer*, 20 January 2002; *The Telegraph*,

18 April 2003; and the *Belfast Telegraph*, 23 February 2011 and 28 February 2014.

63 There must be exceptions to this generalisation but outside of those mentioned earlier it is not easy to find examples in the written record. The Greater West Belfast Community Association was one honourable exception. It was chaired in the 1990s by Margaret Walsh who came from a Catholic, nationalist, and working-class background and was one of the many unsung heroes of community action in Northern Ireland.

64 This paragraph is a distillation of dozens of conversations over many years with community activists on paramilitary involvement in community affairs. Note also the comment by Dr Katy Radford, "These violations of children's rights appear to be the elephant in the kitchen, often seen but rarely mentioned, for fear that breaking the silence will upset the fragile checks and balances regulating public discourse and disclosure in a highly politicised society." Radford, "'And Stay Out,'" 149.

65 That some Provisional republicans joined community associations for personal or largely idealistic reasons is readily acknowledged but control was a leadership objective from the mid-1970s following a template originally mapped out by the Official republican movement. As one former Official IRA man remarked bitterly to me in 1991, "We taught them everything they know." NIHR Archive, 1991 and 2014.

66 The British-subsidised and Belfast-based Irish language paper, *Lá*, was largely supportive of northern republicanism and the IRA.

67 More research is needed on the relationship between loyalist paramilitary organisations and the community sector in working-class Protestant areas. An interesting example of an organisation that promotes the Irish language and that eschews political associations is *Turas* ("Journey" in English) based in unionist east Belfast. For the background see the *Belfast Telegraph*, 9 March 2005.

68 The IMC published some two dozen reports into paramilitary and related activity between 2004 and 2011. These reports contain much more detail of the human suffering than is possible here.

69 *Diary entry written while making final revisions to this text, Saturday, 2 November 2019*: this morning watching the final of the rugby world cup between England and South Africa; lunchtime, my friend Máire (not her real name) and her partner called round for what I thought was a routine social visit. She broke down in tears as she poured out her story. She learned not long ago that her two grown-up daughters, children at the time, had each been shown pornographic images and had been sexually assaulted by an IRA man. The eleven-year-old had been raped. The band of brothers of the local IRA closed ranks to protect its comrade. The family felt helpless. This is not

easy to listen to. Máire believes there were other instances in the neighbourhood. The police have been made aware of the name of the alleged offender
who has a mark of honour, a conviction for a terror-related offence. Apart
from other feelings, I can't help reflecting that the sexual abuse of children
in both loyalist- and republican-controlled communities can only have
been facilitated, and the extent of abuse concealed by the omnipresence
of unaccountable paramilitary power.

70 Paramilitary organisations cast a long shadow. My attempt to interview two
victims of a paramilitary expulsion order in Newry, Co. Down, more than a
decade after the event had taken place, was rebuffed in a friendly but firm
manner: "You never know what the organisation might do." (NIHR Archive,
1991 and 2001).

71 Clapham, *Human Rights Obligations of Non-State Actors*, 561.

72 Ibid., 58.

73 See reference to Ardoyne and the dissident republican reign of terror in
the area.

74 UK-based and international groups ploughed much the same territory in
relation to women, ethnic and sexual minorities, so the positive point may
be overstated. To the extent that Northern Ireland was radically different it
was because of the existence of a paramilitary punishment system. This was
where these groups could have made a distinctive and important contribution, and this was precisely where these groups were found wanting.

75 The exceptions were Families Against Intimidation and Terror and the tiny
Northern Ireland Human Rights Alert, and later still the voluntary organisation Children of the Troubles.

76 The title of a poem written by Seamus Heaney during the 1970s. He was of
course invoking a colloquial phrase that is deeply embedded in the culture
of the north.

CHAPTER FIVE

1 On the seventy-fifth anniversary of the Nazi annexation of Austria the
Vienna-based newspaper *Der Standard* published the disturbing results of
an opinion poll it had commissioned. It found that 42 per cent of those
polled believed "life wasn't all bad under the Nazis"; 39 per cent thought a
resumption of anti-Semitic persecution was likely; 54 per cent thought it
would be highly likely that Nazis would win seats in a forthcoming election
if allowed to stand; and 61 per cent wanted to see a "strong man" in charge
of government. (London) *Independent*, Sunday, 10 March 2013. On the outcome of the Austrian general election of that year in which far-right parties
secured 30 per cent of the popular vote, see the *Economist*, 5 October 2013.

2 Honig and Both, *Srebrenica: Record of a War Crime*.

3 O'Callaghan, *The Informer*, 203–9. O'Callaghan died accidentally in 2017. At a commemorative service in the church of St Martin-in-the-Fields, Trafalgar Square, London, 21 March 2018, he was honoured by the public representatives of two countries, Ireland and the United Kingdom, as well as by a packed church of family members, politicians, peace campaigners, trade unionists, and friends from across the ethnoreligious divides.

4 The writer and historian Ruth Dudley Edwards is currently researching a biography of Sean O'Callaghan.

5 For examples of Shane Paul O'Doherty's pungent critiques from the world of blogging see, "The Irish Peace Process": https://irishpeaceprocess.blog/2018/04/17/relatives-for-justice-time-for-truth-or-time-for-really-big-lies/ and https://irishpeaceprocess.blog/2019/08/27/the-ira-the-catholic-church-big-lies/.

6 Dillon, *The Shankill Butchers*, 27.

7 Foreword by O'Brien to Dillon's impressive investigation of these serial loyalist killers.

8 One of those suspected of the Omagh bombing in 1998, in which thirty-one souls were lost, was Seamus McKenna. Now dead, his later years were lived out as a "lonely, chronic alcoholic who died penniless" and whose life, by his own admission, was "a largely unhappy existence." Profile by Sean O'Driscoll, *Belfast Telegraph*, 29 July 2013. On depression, excessive use of alcohol, suicidal tendencies, personality change, and relationship problems among former long-term republican prisoners see Jamieson and Grounds, *No Sense of an Ending*.

9 Combatants suffered subsequently in terms of mental health. Sample studies have suggested that many former paramilitaries experienced depression, and drugs and alcohol abuse. Whether this was due in part to individual feelings of guilt or recollections of violent acts, or a combination of causes and circumstances, is not clear. See, for example, Sandy Row Community Forum, *Shoulder to Shoulder* and the literature cited therein.

10 The question of land ownership in seventeenth-century Ireland is more complex than appears at first sight. As elsewhere in Europe it was the elites, in this case the Gaelic elites, who held ownership rights and not the mass of their followers and dependents. So the great likelihood, despite Gaelic surnames on both sides of my family, is that I (and most other Kennedys and Ryans) are not descended from dispossessed Gaelic nobility. Doubtful claimants we may be but my father, like many others it may be said, thought otherwise. We were descended, not merely from a chieftain but a high king no less (Brian Boru).

11 The figures which follow were provided by the South East Fermanagh Foundation (SEFF), an organisation that supports victims and survivors of the

Troubles. My thanks to its director, Kenny Donaldson. See also SEFF, *"I'll Never Forget,"* 12–130.

12 Or 102 if one excludes two civilians dying of heart attacks at the scene of IRA operations.

13 To take the watershed year of the hunger strikes, 1981, there were 117 Troubles-related deaths. McKittrick et al., *Lost Lives*, 847. Almost half of these were of civilians, such was the indiscriminate slaughter. Republicans were responsible for sixty-four deaths, not including the ten republicans who died on hunger strike. Loyalists accounted for fourteen of the dead.

14 *Belfast News Letter*, 10 February 2010.

15 This was under the auspices of the West Belfast Summer School. The conference included testimony by Sean Reilly, a friend from Twinbrook, Belfast, whose stepdaughter had been shot dead by a British Army patrol in heavily disputed circumstances. The poet Michael Longley, as I recall, also spoke movingly of the emotional cost of the Troubles.

16 Sullivan et al., "Competitive Victimhood as a Response to Accusations of Ingroup Harm Doing," 778–95.

17 Ibid., 778.

18 The killing was on Tuesday, 7 April 1981. McKittrick et al., *Lost Lives*, 854.

19 Michener and DeLamater, *Social Psychology*, 116.

20 While acknowledging organised criminality on the part of paramilitary organisations, the Independent Monitoring Commission (IMC) was unsure about paramilitary funding of political parties, though it did call for a tightening of controls on donations and election expenses. *Third Report of the Independent Monitoring Commission*, 41–2.

21 To give one small example. In the 1990s I sometimes read the Belfast-based Irish language newspaper *Lá*. It is now defunct. It was stridently supportive of the republican cause and of IRA violence.

22 For a more comprehensive inventory see the blog by the former IRA volunteer Shane Paul O'Doherty, "The Irish Peace Process": https://irishpeace process.blog/2018/01/31/the-iras-legacy-of-lies/.

23 *Belfast Telegraph*, 29 March 2010.

24 Interview in the *Belfast Telegraph*, 29 April 2019.

25 O'Rawe, *Blanketmen*; O'Rawe, *Afterlives*. His wife Bernadette related to me how he was ostracised by former comrades and Sinn Féin members following the belated publication of the book. These books raise the disturbing possibility that at least six hunger strikers were coldly and needlessly sacrificed by the Sinn Féin leadership in pursuit of its party political objectives.

26 McCartney, *Walls of Silence*; NIHRA files relating to Belfast and South Armagh.

27 McKendry, *Disappeared*.

28 Moloney, *Voices from the Grave*. 121–32.

29 This is a borrowing from middle-English and makes a reappearance in
    Joyce's comic masterpiece, *Ulysses*.

30 In late 2019 the long-time director of the Pat Finucane Centre was revealed
    to have been a former IRA volunteer. See "Campaigner O'Connor was in
    IRA," *Irish News*, 22 November 2019; "Director of the Pat Finucane Centre
    admits he was member of the IRA in the 1970s," *Irish Times*, 23 November
    2019.

31 Dudgeon ed., *Legacy*.

32 Trimble, *To Raise Up a New Northern Ireland*, 62.

33 For a long-range perspective on anti-Catholic prejudice, written with gener-
    osity of spirit from within the Protestant evangelical tradition, see Brewer
    and Higgins, *Anti-Catholicism in Northern Ireland*.

34 Drescher et al., "An Exploration," 8–13.

35 Freire in *Pedagogy of the Oppressed* uses the term conscientization, that is,
    developing consciousness in a way that has the power to transform reality.
    The emphasis in this essay is more on the activation of conscience, at the in-
    dividual and societal level, which is also of course a form of consciousness
    change but more than that.

36 The notion of multiple identities is now widely accepted. It is noteworthy
    that on the eve of the Troubles one in five Protestants in Northern Ireland
    defined themselves as Irish, while a further 6 per cent saw themselves as
    sometimes Irish, sometimes British. See Rose, *Governing without Consensus*,
    208. The impact of the Troubles led most of these to abandon identification
    with Ireland, though more complex political identities have emerged or are
    reemerging in recent years.

37 This is at a minimum. The mass mobilisation of Ulster Protestants against
    Daniel O'Connell's campaign for repeal of the union is an early expression
    of collective political difference. See O'Ferrall, *Daniel O'Connell*, 83–7.

38 Annual Meeting of the Society for Co-Operative Studies, Termonfeckin,
    Co. Louth, in the early 1990s.

39 We later met on more friendly terms. I've drawn benefit from his partly
    autobiographical work *Century of Endeavour*.

40 Various clips showing Bono's evident outrage may be found on YouTube.
    The unexceptional quote from Michelle O'Neill, leader of Sinn Féin in the
    north, is taken from an article by Jim Gibney in the *Irish News* (11 April
    2018): "Republicans proud of their freedom struggle."

41 "Charging to the Right," *Newsweek*, 4 October 2008; "The Far Right is on the
    March Again: The Rise of Fascism in Austria," *The Mail*, 18 March 2009.

42 "Austria in crisis as the Far Right win 29% of the vote," *Guardian*, 30 Sep-
    tember, 2008.

43 *Irish Times*, 4 December 2016. There is no suggestion here that there are any close parallels between the history of Austria and that of Northern Ireland. The point being suggested is the importance for contemporary politics of historical truth seeking and the necessity of bravely and fairly confronting the past, however painful recollection may be.

44 *Irish Times*, 4 December 2016. On Austrian complicity in the Nazi project see Bischof and Pelinka, *Austrian Historical Memory and National Identity.*

45 Kennedy, *Unhappy the Land*, 27–30, 185–6. I should clarify that Carson and Craig were not motivated by a desire to oppress Catholics. Like their contemporaries in the Easter Rising of 1916 their aims related to politics and constitutional matters, in their case maintaining the union.

46 The question is sometimes posed: if it was all right for the IRA, drawing on the inspiration of Easter 1916, to kill and bomb to achieve a united Ireland, why isn't it all right for other, younger republicans to do the same? If they are "traitors to Ireland," as Martin McGuinness once put it, where, by the same logic, does that leave McGuinness and the Provisional IRA?

47 Fay et al., *Northern Ireland's Troubles*, 46

48 I acknowledge that when loyalists announced their ceasefire in 1994 a partial apology was incorporated into their statement. It needs to go further and accept that loyalist paramilitarism was murderous and unjustified, and is a matter for communal regret.

49 Guelke, *Politics in Deeply Divided Societies*, 77.

50 *Toronto Star*, 12 June 2008; also *Globe and Mail*, 15 June 2019.

51 McEvoy, Bryson, and Placzek, *Apologies in Transitional Justice*, 1–21.

52 Rothschild and Keefer, "A Cleansing Fire," 209–29. My thanks to Ruth Dudley Edwards who drew my attention to this article. I have benefited from an exchange of correspondence with Dr Rothschild for which I am very grateful.

53 *Aristotle: Poetics*, 6–7, 96–8.

54 Wohl and Branscolme, "Remembering Historical Victimisation," 988–1006.

55 Rothschild and Keefer, "A Cleansing Fire," 210.

56 The late Troubles included the bombing of a crowded shop on the Shankill Road, Belfast, in the autumn of 1993 in which ten people died and the indiscriminate shootings inside a pub in Loughinisland (County Down) in June 1994 in which six people were murdered while watching a football match.

57 The production was by the Kabosh theatre company and the performance I attended was on Saturday, 28 March 2015. For a profile of Laurence McKeown, covering his journey from gunman to playwright, see the *Irish Times*, 13 August 2016.

58 Ex-prisoner is a term frequently used as a badge of honour by republicans and loyalists. For many, at least in their familiar social settings, there is no

shame involved in having a paramilitary past. Quite the reverse. The same is true of regular soldiers or police, I would imagine. But guilt is different from shame and belongs to the inner life of the person. Thus an apparent lack of shame does not preclude feelings of guilt.

Bibliography

NEWSPAPERS AND PERIODICALS
Selective use has been made of the following newspapers and periodicals:
An Phobhlacht (Dublin); *Combat* (Belfast); *Belfast Telegraph*; *Chartist* (London); *Daily Mail*; *Daily Ireland*; *Der Standard* (Vienna); *Derry Journal*; *Dublin Review of Books*; *Economist*; *Fortnight Magazine* (Belfast); *Globe & Mail*; *Guardian*; *Herald Scotland*; *Independent* (London); *Irish Examiner*; *Irish Independent*; *Irish News*; *Irish Post*; *Irish Press*; *Irish Times*; *Lá* (Belfast); *Londonderry Sentinel*; *Los Angeles Times*; *Daily Mail*; *New York Times*; *News Letter* (Belfast); *Newry Democrat*; *Newry News*; *Newsweek*; *Observer*; *Protestant Telegraph*; *Republican News*; *Toronto Star*; *Sunday Independent*; *Sunday Life*; *Sunday Tribune*; *Tablet* (London); *Telegraph*; *Times*.

PRINTED AND OTHER SOURCES
Akenson, D.H. *Education and Enmity: The Control of Schooling in Northern Ireland, 1920–50.* Newton Abbott: David & Charles, 1973.
Aristotle. *Aristotle: Poetics.* Translated by Gerald F. Else. Ann Arbor: University of Michigan Press, 1967.
Arthur, Paul. *The People's Democracy, 1968–1973.* Belfast: Blackstaff Press Ltd, 1974.
Bairner, Alan. "Sport in the Nineteenth and Twentieth Centuries." In *Ulster Since 1600: Politics, Economy, and Society,* edited by Liam Kennedy and Philip Ollerenshaw, 260–74. Oxford: Oxford University Press, 2013.
Bardon, Jonathan. *A History of Ulster.* Belfast: Blackstaff, 1992.
Barr, M.J. and R.A.B. Mollan. "The Orthopaedic Consequences of Civil Disturbance in Northern Ireland," *Journal of Bone and Joint Surgery* 71-B (1989): 739–44.
Barr, M.J. and R.A.B. Mollan. "Knee-Capping: A Misnomer." *Journal of Bone and Joint Surgery* 71-B (1989): 875-80.
Bartholomew, Paul. *The Irish Judiciary.* Dublin: Institute of Public Administration, 1971.

Bergia, Elena. "Women and War: A Complex Matter." *Political Insight* (December 2017): 22–3.

– "Unexpected Rewards of Political Violence: Republican Ex-Prisoners, Seductive Capital, and the Gendered Nature of Heroism." *Terrorism and Political Violence* (June 2019): 1–21.

Bew, Paul and Gordon Gillespie. *Northern Ireland: A Chronology of the Troubles, 1968–1999.* Dublin: Gill & Macmillan, 1999.

Bew, Paul, Peter Gibbon, and Henry Patterson. *Northern Ireland: 1921–2001: Political Forces and Social Classes.* London: Serif, 2002.

Bischof, Gunter and Anton Pelinka, eds. *Austrian Historical Memory and National Identity.* London: Transaction Publishers, 1997.

Bishop, Patrick and Eamonn Mallie. *The Provisional IRA.* London: Heinemann, 1987.

Borooah V.K. and F.P. Forsythe. *Gender and the Earnings Gap: Unequal Treatment or Unequal Workers?* Belfast: Equal Opportunities Commission for Northern Ireland, 1997.

Bowman, John. *De Valera and the Ulster Question: 1917–1973.* Oxford: Oxford University Press, 1989.

Boyce, D. George. *Nationalism in Ireland.* London: Routledge, 1995.

Bradley, Gerry and Brian Feeney. *Insider: Gerry Bradley's Life in the IRA.* Dublin: O'Brien, 2009.

Breen, Dan. *My Fight for Irish Freedom.* Dublin: Talbot Press, 1924.

Brett, Charles. *Long Shadows Cast Before: Nine Lives in Ulster, 1625–1977.* Edinburgh: J. Bartholomew, 1978.

Brewer, John D., Bill Lockhart, and Paula Rodger. *Crime in Ireland, 1945–95.* Oxford: Clarendon Press, 1997.

Brewer, John D. and Gareth I. Higgins. *Anti-Catholicism in Northern Ireland: The Mote and the Beam.* Basingstoke: Macmillan, 1998.

Bruce, Steve. *God Save Ulster! The Religion and Politics of Paisleyism.* Oxford: Oxford University Press, 1989.

Buckland, Patrick. *The Factory of Grievances: Devolved Government in Northern Ireland 1921–39.* Dublin: Gill and Macmillan, 1979.

Burgers, J. Herman and Hans Danelius. *The United Nations Convention Against Torture: A Handbook on the Convention against Torture and Other Cruel, Inhuman, or Degrading Treatment or Punishment.* London: Dordrecht, 1988.

Burns, Anna. *Milkman.* London: Faber & Faber, 2018.

CAIN Web Service. Conflict and Politics in Northern Ireland website. Ulster University. https://cain.ulster.ac.uk/index.html.

Carson, Ciaran. *Belfast Confetti.* Oldcastle: Gallery Books, 1989.

Chalandon, Sorj. *Return to Killybegs.* Dublin: Lilliput Press, 2013.

Chambers, Anne. *T.K. Whitaker: A Portrait of a Patriot.* Dublin: Doubleday Ireland, 2014.

Clapham, Andrew. *Human Rights Obligations of Non-State Actors*. Oxford: Oxford University Press, 2006.

Colley, Linda. *Britons: Forging the Nation, 1707–1837*. London: Yale University Press, 2009.

Collins, Eamon. *Killing Rage*. London: Granta, 1997.

Commission on the Status of Women. *Report to the Minister for Finance*. Dublin: Stationery Office, 1972.

Connolly, Linda. *The Irish Women's Movement: From Revolution to Devolution*. Dublin: Lilliput Press, 2003.

Connolly, S.J., ed. *The Oxford Companion to Irish History*. Oxford: Oxford University Press, 2002.

Conroy, John. "Kneecapping." The Alicia Patterson Foundation. 1980: http://alicia patterson.org/stories/kneecapping.

Coogan, Tim Pat. *The Troubles: Ireland's Ordeal 1966–1995 and the Search for Peace*. London: Hutchinson, 1995.

Cunningham, Niall. "Repertoires of Violence: The Geography of Political Conflict in Belfast in the Twentieth Century." PhD thesis, University of Lancaster, 2014.

Daly, Mary and Margaret O'Callaghan, eds. *1916 in 1966: Commemorating the Easter Rising*. Dublin: Royal Irish Academy, 2007.

Dawe, Gerald. *In Another World: Van Morrison and Belfast*. Kildare: Merrion Press, 2017.

Devlin, Paddy. *Straight Left: An Autobiography*. Belfast: Blackstaff Press, 1993.

Dickson, Brice. "The Problems with Human Rights." Annual Stephen Livingstone Lecture. Queen's University Belfast, 2019.

Dillon, Martin. *The Shankill Butchers: A Case Study of Mass Murder*. London: Arrow, 1990.

Disturbances in Northern Ireland: Report of the Commission Appointed by the Governor of Northern Ireland. Belfast, September 1969.

Donnan, Hastings and Graham McFarlane. "Informal Social Relations." In *Northern Ireland: The Background to the Conflict*, edited by John Darby, 110–33. Belfast: Appletree, 1983.

Donnelly Jr, James S. *Irish Agrarian Rebellion, 1760–1800*. Dublin: Irish Academic Press, 1997.

– *Captain Rock: The Irish Agrarian Rebellion of 1821–24*. Madison: University of Wisconsin Press, 2009.

Doyle, John. "The Politics of the Transformation of Policing." In *Policing the Narrow Ground*, edited by John Doyle, 167–211. Dublin: Royal Irish Academy, 2010.

Drescher, Kent D. et al. "An Exploration of the Viability and Usefulness of the Construct of Moral Injury in War Veterans." *Traumatology* 16 (2011): 8–13.

Dudgeon, Jeffrey, ed. *Legacy: What to do about the Past in Northern Ireland*. Belfast: Belfast Press, 2018.

Duffy, Michael, Kate Gillespie, and David Clark. "Post-traumatic Stress Disorder in the Context of Terrorism and Other Civil Conflict in Northern Ireland: Randomised Controlled Trial." *British Medical Journal* (31 May 2007): 1–7.

Duggan, Marian. *Queering Conflict: Examining Lesbian and Gay Experiences of Homophobia in Northern Ireland*. Farnham, Surrey: Ashgate, 2012.

Dunne, Tom. *Rebellions: Memoir, Memory and 1798*. Dublin: Lilliput, 2010.

Durcan, Paul. *The Laughter of Mothers*. London: Harvill Secker, 2012.

Edwards, Aaron. *A History of the Northern Ireland Labour Party: Democratic Socialism and Sectarianism*. Manchester: Manchester University Press, 2009.

Edwards, Owen Dudley. *The Sins of our Fathers: Roots of Conflict in Northern Ireland*. Dublin: Gill & Macmillan, 1970.

Edwards, Ruth Dudley. *The Seven: The Lives and Legacies of the Founding Fathers of the Irish Republic*. London: Oneworld Publications, 2016.

Elliott, Sydney. *Northern Ireland Parliamentary Election Results, 1921–1972*. Chichester: Political Reference Publications, 1973.

Emirbayer, Mustafa and Ann Mische. "What is Agency?" *American Journal of Sociology* 103 (January 1998): 962–1023.

English, Richard. *Armed Struggle: The History of the IRA*. London: Pan, 2012.

– *Does Terrorism Work? A History*. Oxford: Oxford University Press, 2016.

Farrell, Michael. *The Orange State*. London: Pluto Press, 1980.

Fay, Marie-Therese, Mike Morrisey, and Marie Smyth. *Northern Ireland's Troubles: The Human Costs*. London: Pluto, 1999.

Fay, Marie Therese et al. *The Cost of the Troubles Study: Report on the Northern Ireland Survey: The Experience and Impact of the Troubles*. Derry: INCORE, 2001.

FitzGerald, Garret. *All in a Life: An Autobiography*. Dublin: Gill and Macmillan, 1991.

Feenan, Dermot. "Justice in Conflict: Paramilitary Punishment in Ireland (North)." *International Journal of the Sociology of Law* 30 (June 2002): 151–72.

Fleming, N.C. "Education since the Late Eighteenth Century." In *Ulster Since 1600*, edited by Liam Kennedy and Philip Ollerenshaw, 218–23. Oxford: Oxford University Press, 2013.

Foster, R.F. *Modern Ireland, 1600–1972*. London: Penguin, 1990.

– *Luck and the Irish: A Brief History of Change*. Oxford: Oxford University Press, 2008.

Foucault, Michel. *Discipline and Punish: The Birth of the Prison*. London: Penguin, 1991.

Freire, Paulo. *Pedagogy of the Oppressed*. Translated by Myra Bergman Ramos. New York: Penguin Books, 1972.

Gorman, Jonathan. "Historians and their Duties." *History and Theory* 45 (December, 2004): 1–15.

Gramsci, Antonio. *Prison Notebooks: Volume 1*. New York: Columbia University Press, 1992.

Gregg, J.A.F. *The "Ne Temere" Decree: A Lecture.* 17 March 1911. Dublin: Association for Promoting Christian Knowledge: 1943. Revised edition.

Gudgin, Graham. "Discrimination in Housing and Employment under the Stormont Administration." In *The Northern Ireland Question: Nationalism, Unionism, and Partition,* edited by Patrick J. Roche and Brian Barton, 97–121. Aldershot: Ashgate Publishing, 1999.

Guelke, Adrian. *Northern Ireland: The International Perspective.* Dublin: Gill and Macmillan, 1988.

– *Politics in Deeply-Divided Societies.* Cambridge: Polity Press, 2012.

Hadden, Tom and Kevin Boyle. *The Anglo-Irish Agreement: Commentary, Text and Official Review.* London: Sweet & Maxwell, 1989.

Hamill, Heather. *The Hoods: Crime and Punishment in Belfast.* Woodstock: Princeton University Press, 2011.

Hammersley, Martyn. *What's Wrong with Ethnography?: Methodological Explorations.* London: Routledge, 1992.

Hanley, Brian and Scott Millar. *The Lost Revolution: The Story of the Official IRA and the Workers Party.* Dublin: Penguin Ireland, 2009.

Hanna, Donncha, Martin Dempster and Kevin Dyer. *Young People's Transgenerational Issues in Northern Ireland.* Belfast: Commission for Victims and Survivors, 2012.

Harkin, Catherine. "Erotic Capital." *European Sociological Review* 26 no. 5 (2010): 499–518.

Harnden, Toby. *Bandit Country.* London: Hodder & Stoughton, 1999.

Hayes, Maurice. *Minority Verdict: Experiences of a Catholic Public Servant.* Belfast: Blackstaff, 1995.

Hayward, Katy et al. "Belonging and Alienation in the New Northern Ireland." *Research Update* 93 (June 2014): 1–4.

Heaney, Seamus. *North.* London: Faber, 1992.

Herbermann, Charles G. et al., eds. *The Catholic Encyclopaedia: An International Work of Reference on the Constitution, Doctrine, Discipline, and History of the Catholic Church, No. 9.* New York: Encyclopedia Press, 1913–50.

Heskin, Ken. "The Terrorists' Terrorist: Vincent Browne's Interview with Dominic McGlinchey." In *The Irish Terrorism Experience,* edited by Yoga Alexander and Alan O'Day, 97–108. Aldershot: Dartmouth, 1991.

Hill, Myrtle. *Women in Ireland.* Belfast: Blackstaff Press, 2003.

Hogan, Liam et al. "Why We Need to Confront the 'Irish Slave Myth' and How Terminology is not Simply Semantics." *History Ireland* 24 (2016): 18–22.

Hogan, Liam. "How the Myth of the 'Irish Slaves' Became a Favourite Meme Online." Interview by Alex Almend. Southern Poverty Law Centre, 19 April 2016. https://www.splcenter.org/hatewatch/2016/04/19/how-myth-irish-slaves-became-favorite-meme-racists-online.

Holland, Jack and Henry McDonald. *INLA: Deadly Divisions*. Dublin: Torc Books, 1994.

Honig, Jan Willem and Norbert Both. *Srebrenica: Record of a War Crime*. New York: Penguin Books, 1997.

Horgan, Goretti. "Changing Women's Lives in Ireland." *International Socialism Journal* 91 (Summer 2001): 53–91.

Horne, Alistair. *A Savage War of Peace: Algeria, 1954–1962*. London: Macmillan, 1977.

Hughes, Kyle and Donald MacRaild, eds. *Crime, Violence and the Irish in the Nineteenth Century*. Liverpool: Liverpool University Press, 2017.

Human Rights Watch Helsinki. *Human Rights in Northern Ireland*. New York: Human Rights Watch Helsinki, 1991.

– *Northern Ireland, Human Rights Abuses by All Sides*. New York: Human Rights Watch Helsinki, 1993.

Jamieson, Ruth and Adrian Grounds. *No Sense of an Ending: The Effects of Long-Term Imprisonment amongst Republican Prisoners and their Families*. Monaghan: SEESYU Press, 2002.

Jamieson, Ruth, Peter Shirlow, and Adrian Grounds. *Ageing and Social Exclusion among Former Politically-Motivated Prisoners in Northern Ireland*. Belfast: Queen's University Belfast, 2010.

Jarman, Neil and Alex Tennant. *An Acceptable Prejudice? Homophobic Violence and Harassment in Northern Ireland*. Belfast: Institute for Conflict Research, 2003.

Jarman, Neil. *Intimidation in Northern Ireland, 2010–2014*. Belfast: Institute for the Study of Conflict Transformation and Social Justice, Queen's University Belfast, 2015.

Johnson, David S. *The Interwar Economy in Ireland*. Dundalk: Economic and Social History Society of Ireland, 1985.

Johnston, Roy H.W. *Century of Endeavour: A Biographical and Autobiographical View of the 20th Century in Ireland*. Dublin: Tyndall Publications, in association with the Lilliput Press, 2006.

Kennaway, Brian. *The Orange Order: A Tradition Betrayed*. London: Methuen, 2006.

Kennedy, Liam. *The Modern Industrialisation of Ireland, 1940–1988*. Dublin: Economic and Social History Society of Ireland, 1989.

– "Nightmares within Nightmares: Paramilitary Repression in Working-Class Communities." In *Crime and Punishment in West Belfast*, edited by Liam Kennedy, 67–80. Belfast: Summer School, West Belfast, 1995.

– "We've Come for Your Boys." *Fortnight Magazine* (January 2000): 14–15.

– "Northern Ireland: Times of Terror, Times of Silence." *The Commonwealth Lawyer: Journal of the Commonwealth Lawyers' Association* XI (2002).

– "*They Shoot Children, Don't They?*" Third Report. Belfast: Queen's University Belfast 2003.

– *Unhappy the Land: The Most Oppressed People Ever, the Irish?* Dublin: Merrion Press, 2016.

Knox, Colin and Rachel Monaghan. *Informal Justice in Divided Societies: Northern Ireland and South Africa*. Basingstoke: Palgrave, 2002.

Kotsonouris, Mary. *Retreat from Revolution: The Dáil Courts, 1920–1924*. Dublin: Irish Academic Press, 1994.

Lee, J.J. *The Modernisation of Irish Society, 1848–1918*. Dublin: Gill and Macmillan, 1989.

Leyton, Elliott. *The One Blood: Kinship and Class in an Irish Village*. St John's: Institute of Social and Economic Research, Memorial University of Newfoundland, 1975.

Lindsay, John. *No Dope Here? Anti-Drugs Vigilantism in Northern Ireland*. Derry: Yes! Publications, 2012.

Lynch, Robert. *The Northern IRA and the Early Years of Partition*. Dublin: Irish Academic Press, 2006.

Mac Stiofáin, Seán. *Memoirs of a Revolutionary*. London: Gordon & Cremonesi, 1975.

Mac Suibhne, Breandán. *The End of Outrage: Post-Famine Adjustment in Rural Ireland*. Oxford: Oxford University Press, 2017.

Madden, Kyla. *Forkhill Protestants and Forkhill Catholics, 1787–1858*. Montreal: McGill-Queen's University Press, 2005.

Martin, Peter. "Social Policy and Social Change since 1914." In *Ulster Since 1600: Politics, Economy and Society*, edited by Liam Kennedy and Philip Ollerenshaw, 315–20. Oxford: Oxford University Press, 2013.

Matchett, William. *Secret Victory: The Intelligence War that Beat the IRA*. Belfast: William Matchett, 2016.

McBride, Alan et al., eds. *The Disappeared of Northern Ireland's Troubles*. Belfast: WAVE Trauma Centre, 2012.

McCann, Eamonn. *War and an Irish Town*. London: Pluto, 1993.

– "Ardoyne Suicides." *The Blanket: A Journal of Protest and Dissent*, 12 March 2004. http://indiamond6.ulib.iupui.edu:81/ardoynesem.html.

McCartney, Catherine. *Walls of Silence*. Dublin: Gill & Macmillan, 2007.

– *The Ghost Factory*. London: 4th Estate, 2019.

McCloskey, Bridie. "Bridie McCloskey's Story." Interview with Anthony McIntyre. *The Blanket: A Journal of Protest and Dissent*, 24 November 2002. http://indiamond6.ulib.iupui.edu:81/mccloskey.html.

McConville, Michael. "Michael McConville says the IRA will kill him if he names those involved in his mother's murder." Interview with Sean O'Rourke. *The Journal.ie*, 1 May 2014. http://www.thejournal.ie/michael-mcconville-jean-mcconville-murder-gerry-adams-ira-1442811-May2014/.

McCormick, Leanne. *Regulating Sexuality: Women in Twentieth-Century Northern Ireland*. Manchester: Manchester University Press, 2009.

McDonald, Henry and Jim Cusack. UDA: *Inside the Heart of Loyalist Terror.* Dublin: Penguin Ireland, 2004.

McEvoy, K., A. Bryson, and C. Placzek. *Apologies in Transitional Justice: United Nations Special Rapporteur on the Promotion of Truth, Justice, Reparations and Guarantees of Non-recurrence.* Geneva: United Nations, 2019.

McEvoy, Sandra. "Women Loyalist Paramilitaries in Northern Ireland: Duty, Agency and Empowerment. A Report from the Field." Chicago: International Studies Association, 2007 (unpublished conference paper).

– "Loyalist Women Paramilitaries in Northern Ireland: Beginning a Feminist Conversation about Conflict Resolution." *Security Studies* 18 (2009): 262–86.

McGartland, Martin. *Fifty Dead Men Walking.* London: Blake, 1997.

McKendry, Seamus. *Disappeared: The Search for Jean McConville.* Dublin: Blackwater Press, 2000.

McKittrick, David et al. *Lost Lives: The Stories of the Men, Women and Children Who Died as a result of the Northern Ireland Troubles.* Edinburgh: Mainstream, 1999.

McMichael, Gary. *An Ulster Voice: In Search of Common Ground in Northern Ireland.* Niwot, Colorado: Roberts Rinehart Publishers, 1999.

McMillen, Liam. *Liam McMillen, Separatist, Socialist, Republican.* Repsol pamphlet 21 (Dublin, 1976).

McWilliams, Monica. "Masculinity and Violence: A Gender Perspective on Crime in Northern Ireland." In *Crime and Punishment in West Belfast,* edited by Liam Kennedy, 15–25. Belfast: Summer School, West Belfast, 1994.

Michener, H.A. and J.D. DeLamater. *Social Psychology.* London: Harcourt Brace College Publishers, 1994.

Miller, David W. *Queen's Rebels: Ulster Loyalism in Historical Perspective.* Dublin: Gill and Macmillan, 1978.

– *Peep O'Day Boys and Defenders: Selected Documents on the Disturbances in County Armagh, 1784–96.* Belfast: Public Record Office of Northern Ireland, 1990.

Moloney, Ed. *A Secret History of the IRA.* London: Allen Lane, 2002.

– *Paisley: From Demagogue to Democrat?* Dublin: Poolbeg, 2008.

– *Voices from the Grave: Two Men's War in Ireland.* London: Faber, 2010.

Monaghan, Rachel. "The Return of 'Captain Moonlight': Informal Justice in Northern Ireland." *Studies in Conflict and Terrorism* 25 (2002): 41–56.

Monaghan, Rachel and Peter Shirlow. "Forward to the Past? Loyalist Paramilitarism in Northern Ireland since 1994." *Studies in Conflict and Terrorism* 34 (2011): 649–65.

Morgan, Austen. *Harold Wilson.* London: Pluto Press, 1992.

Morrisey, Michael and Ken Pease. "The Black Criminal Justice System in West Belfast." *The Howard Journal of Criminal Justice* 21 (1982): 159–66.

Morrow, Duncan. "Shared or Scared?: Attitudes to Community Relations among

Young People, 2003–7." In *Young People in Post-Conflict Northern Ireland*, edited by Dirk Schubotz and Paula Devine, 1–16, Lyme Regis: Russell House, 2008.

Mulholland, Marc. *The Longest War: Northern Ireland's Troubled History*. Oxford: Oxford University Press, 2002.

Munck, Ronnie. "Repression, Insurgency, and Popular Justice: The Irish Case." *Crime and Social Justice* (1984): 81–94.

Murray, A.C. "Agrarian Violence and Nationalism in Nineteenth-Century Ireland: The Myth of Ribbonism." *Irish Economic & Social History* 13 (1986): 56–73.

Nelson, Sarah. *Ulster's Uncertain Defenders: Protestant Political, Paramilitary and Community Groups and the Northern Ireland Conflict*. Belfast: Appletree, 1984.

Nicholas, Richard M., John Barr, and Raymond Mollan. "Paramilitary Punishment in Northern Ireland: A Macabre Irony." *Journal of Trauma Injury Infection and Critical Care* 34, no. 1 (1993): 90–5.

Northern Ireland Affairs Committee. *Relocation following Paramilitary Intimidation*. London: House of Commons, 2001.

Northern Ireland Association for the Care and Rehabilitation of Offenders (NIACRO). *Annual Report 201–14* (Belfast, 2014).

Northern Ireland Department of Finance and Personnel. *Northern Ireland Net Fiscal Balance Report 2012–13 and 2013–14*. October 2015.

O'Brien, Conor Cruise. *Neighbours: Four Lectures*. London: Faber, 1980.

– *Passion and Cunning and Other Essays*. London: Weidenfeld & Nicolson, 1988.

Ó Broin, Eoin. *Sinn Féin and the Politics of Left Republicanism*. London: Pluto Press, 2009.

O'Callaghan, Sean. *The Informer*. London: Bantam, 1998.

O'Day, Alan, ed. *Dimensions of Irish Terrorism*. Aldershot: Dartmouth Publishing Company, 1993.

O'Doherty, Malachi. *The Trouble with Guns: Republican Strategy and the Provisional IRA*. Belfast: Blackstaff, 1998.

O'Ferrall, Fergus. *Daniel O'Connell*. Dublin: Gill & Macmillan, 1998.

Office of the United Nations High Commissioner for Human Rights. *Legislative History of the Convention on the Rights of the Child*. Vol. 2. New York: United Nations, 2007.

O'Keefe, Terence M. "Suicide and Self-Starvation." *Philosophy* 59 (July 1984): 349–63.

O'Leary, Brendan and John McGarry. *The Politics of Antagonism: Understanding Northern Ireland*. London: Athlone Press, 1996.

O'Malley, Desmond. *Conduct Unbecoming: A Memoir*. Dublin: Gill & Macmillan, 2016.

O'Malley, Ernie. *On Another Man's Wound*. Dublin: Anvil Books, 1979.

O'Neill, Onora. "Justice without Ethics: A Twentieth Century Innovation." In *The Cambridge Companion to the Philosophy of Law*, edited by John Tasioulas. Cambridge: Cambridge University Press, forthcoming 2020.

O'Neill, Siobhan et al. *Towards a Better Future: The Transgenerational Impact of the Troubles on Mental Health*. Belfast: Commission for Victims and Survivors, 2015

O'Rawe, Richard. *Blanketmen: An Untold Story of the H-Block Hunger Strike*. Dublin: New Island, 2005.

– *Afterlives: The Hunger Strike and the Secret Offer that Changed Irish History*. Dublin: Lilliput, 2010.

O'Shea, Sinéad, dir. *A Mother Brings Her Son to be Shot*. 2017; Dublin: Blinder Films, 2017.

Patterson, Henry. *Class Conflict and Sectarianism: The Protestant Working Class and the Belfast Labour Movement, 1868–1920*. Belfast: Blackstaff, 1980.

– *Ireland's Violent Frontier: The Border and Anglo-Irish Relations during the Troubles*. Basingstoke: Palgrave Macmillan, 2013.

Patterson, Henry and Eric Kaufman. *Unionism and Orangeism in Northern Ireland since 1945: The Decline of the Loyal Family*. Manchester: Manchester University Press, 2007.

Phoenix, Eamon. *Northern Nationalism: Nationalist Politics, Partition and the Catholic Minority in Northern Ireland, 1890–1940*. Belfast: Ulster Historical Foundation, 1994.

Pogatchnik, Shawn. "Plucky Belfast Cab Driver Defies the IRA and Pays a Brutal Price: Northern Ireland: 'Provos' shoot Catholic in both legs for refusing to surrender his taxi for a terrorist mission." *Los Angeles Times*, 14 November 1993. See http://articles.latimes.com/1993-11-14/news/mn-56631_1_northern-ireland.

Prince, Simon. *Northern Ireland's '68: Civil Rights, Global Revolt and the Origins of the Troubles*. Dublin: Irish Academic Press, 2007.

Prince, Simon and Geoffrey Warner. *Belfast and Derry in Revolt: A New History of the Start of the Troubles*. Dublin: Irish Academic Press, 2012.

Purdie, Bob. "Was the Civil Rights Movement a Republican/Communist Conspiracy?" *Irish Political Studies* 3, (1988): 33–41

Radford, Katy. "'And Stay Out': Hoods and Paramilitarised Youth: Exiling and Punishment Beatings." In *Fragmenting Family?*, edited by David Ford, 133–54. Chester: University of Chester, 2010.

Report of the Advisory Committee on Police in Northern Ireland. Chaired by Baron Hunt. Belfast: H.M.S.O., 1969.

Report of the Committee on the Constitution. Dublin, December 1967.

Robertson, Geoffrey. *The Case of the Pope: Vatican Accountability for Human Rights Abuse*. London: Penguin, 2010.

Roleke, Juliane. *Mother Ireland and her Soldier Dolls: Republican Paramilitary 'Punishment' Attacks on Women in Northern Ireland 1971–1979*. Unpublished dissertation, Humboldt-Universitat Zu Berlin, April 2016.

Rolston, Bill. "Morality Play." *The Chartist* 7 (1991): 7.

Rose, Richard. *Governing Without Consensus: An Irish Perspective*. London: Faber and Faber Ltd, 1971.

Rothschild, Zachary K. and Lucas A. Keefer. "A Cleansing Fire: Moral Outrage Alleviates Guilt and Buffers Threats to One's Moral Identity." *Motivation and Emotion* 41 no. 2 (2017): 209–29.

Rouse, Paul. *Sport in Ireland: A History*. Oxford: Oxford University Press, 2015.

Ruane, Joseph and Jennifer Todd. *The Dynamics of Conflict in Northern Ireland: Power, Conflict and Emancipation*. Cambridge: Cambridge University Press, 1996.

– *After the Good Friday Agreement: Analysing Political Change in Northern Ireland*. Dublin: University College Dublin Press, 1999.

Ruedy, John. *Modern Algeria: The Origins and Development of a Nation*. Indiana: Indiana University Press, 2005.

Runciman, W.G. *Relative Deprivation and Social Justice: A Study of Attitudes to Social Inequality in Twentieth-century England*. London: Routledge and Kegan Paul, 1966.

Ryder, Chris and Vincent Kearney. *Drumcree: The Orange Order's Last Stand*. London: Methuen, 2002.

Sacks, Paul Martin. *The Donegal Mafia: An Irish Political Machine*. New Haven; London: Yale University Press, 1976.

Sandy Row Community Forum. *Shoulder to Shoulder: Moving Forward*. Belfast, 2013.

Sharrock, David and Mark Devenport. *Man of War, Man of Peace?: The Unauthorised Biography of Gerry Adams*. London: Pan, 1998.

Silke, Andrew. "The Lords of Discipline: The Methods and Motives of Paramilitary Vigilantism in Northern Ireland." *Low Intensity Conflict and Law Enforcement* 7 (Autumn 1998): 121–56.

– "Rebel's Dilemma: The Changing Relationship between the IRA, Sinn Féin and Paramilitary Vigilantism in Northern Ireland." *Terrorism and Political Violence* 11 (1999): 55–93.

– "War Without End: Comparing IRA and Loyalist Vigilantism in Northern Ireland." *Howard Journal of Criminal Justice* 39/3 (2000): 249–66.

Sinn Féin. *Éire Nua: The Social and Economic Programme of Sinn Féin*. Dublin: Sinn Féin [Provisional], 1972.

Smyth, Clifford. *Ian Paisley: Voice of Protestant Ulster*. Edinburgh: Scottish Academic Press, 1987.

Smyth, Paul. *Stop Attacks: Beyond the Communal Shrug*. Belfast: Wisebap, 2017.

South East Fermanagh Foundation (SEFF). *"I'll Never Forget": Innocent Victims and Survivors of Terrorism Recall their Experiences*. Enniskillen: SEFF, 2011.

Stewart, A.T.Q. *The Narrow Ground: The Roots of Conflict in Ulster*. London: Faber, 1989.

Sullivan, Daniel et al. "Competitive Victimhood as a Response to Accusations of Ingroup Harm Doing," *Journal of Personality and Social Psychology* 102 (2012): 778–95.

Sweeney, Maurice, dir. *I Dolours* (a drama documentary based on an interview given by IRA bomber Dolours Price to journalist Ed Moloney two years before her death), 2018. Toronto: Kew Media Group.

Sweetman, Rosita. *On Our Knees: Ireland 1972*. London: Pan Books, 1972.

Taylor, Peter. *Provos: The IRA and Sinn Féin*. London: Bloomsbury, 1997.

– *Loyalists*. London: Bloomsbury, 1999.

The Belfast Agreement: An Agreement Reached at the Multi-Party Talks on Northern Ireland. London: Stationery Office, 1998.

The Downing Street Declaration, Wednesday 15 December 1993, http://cain.ulst. ac.uk/events/peace/docs/dsd151293.htm.

Thompson, William and Barry Mulholland. "Paramilitary Punishments and Young People in West Belfast: Psychological Effects and the Implications for Education." In *Crime and Punishment in West Belfast*, edited by Liam Kennedy, 51–66. Belfast: Summer School, West Belfast, 1995.

Trewsdale, Janet and Mary Trainor. *A Statistical Survey of Women and Work in Northern Ireland*. Belfast: Equal Opportunities Commission for Northern Ireland, 1979.

Trimble, David. *To Raise Up a New Northern Ireland: Articles and Speeches by the Rt. Hon. David Trimble MP MLA, 1998–2001*. Belfast: Belfast Press, 2001.

Ulster Political Research Group. *Common Sense: Northern Ireland – an agreed process*. Belfast, 1987.

Violence and Civil Disturbances in Northern Ireland: Report of Tribunal of Inquiry. London, 1972.

Walker, B.M. *A Political History of the Two Irelands: From Partition to Peace*. Basingstoke: Palgrave Macmillan, 2012.

Walker, Graham. *A History of the Ulster Unionist Party*. Manchester: Manchester University Press, 2004.

Whyte, John. "How Much Discrimination was there under the Unionist regime, 1921–68?" In *Contemporary Irish Studies*, edited by Tom Gallagher and James O' Connell, 1–35. Manchester: Manchester University Press, 1983.

Wilson, Tim. "Frank Wright Revisited." *Irish Political Studies* 26 (2011): 277–82.

Wright, Frank. *Northern Ireland: A Comparative Analysis*. Dublin: Gill and Macmillan, 1987.

TV, RADIO, FILM, WEBSITES

BBC News Report. "Dee Stitt Row: MP Says Loyalist should not be in CEO Post." http://www.bbc.co.uk/news/uk-northern-ireland-37750648.

– "Father saw gunmen shoot his son on Londonderry street," 8 March 2012: https://www.bbc.com/news/uk-northern-ireland-17296109.

BBC Northern Ireland and Radio Telefís Éireann. TV documentary. "The Disappeared: The Hidden Story of the Troubles," 2013.

BBC Northern Ireland, News Report. "A Punishment Second only to Death," 31 August 1999. http://news.bbc.co.uk/1/hi/northern_ireland/433580.stm.

BBC Northern Ireland. *Talkback*, a current affairs radio program presented by William Crawley, 10 November 2014.

BBC Radio 4. "Tarred and Feathered," radio documentary broadcast 29 November 2009.

BBC Radio 3. "Shot By My Neighbour," radio documentary broadcast 18 September 2018.

BBC TV. "The Spy in the IRA," BBC *Panorama* investigation presented by John Ware, broadcast 11 April 2017.

Dáil Éireann debate, Leinster House, Dublin, Wednesday, 12 November 2014. http://oireachtasdebates.oireachtas.ie/debates%20authoring/debateswebpack.nsf/takes/dail2014111200030.

Northern Ireland Young Life & Times Survey. http://www.ark.ac.uk/ylt/2004/Community_Relations/.

Ulster University and Queen's University Belfast, ARK ("Northern Ireland's Social Policy Hub"). http://www.ark.ac.uk/.

Ulster University, CAIN website. https://cain.ulster.ac.uk/issues/violence/docs/kennedy01.htm.

OTHER

Northern Ireland Human Rights Archive, in the possession of the author.

Index